THE REGENERATORS

Social Criticism in Late Victorian English Canada

A crisis of faith confronted many Canadian Protestants in the late nineteenth century. Their religious beliefs were challenged by the new biological sciences and by historical criticism of the Bible. Personal salvation, for centuries the central concern of Christianity, no longer seemed an adequate focus in an age that gave rise to industrial cities and grave social problems.

No single word, Cook claims, catches more correctly the spirit of the late Victorian reform movement than 'regeneration': a concept originally meaning rebirth and applied to individuals, now increasingly used to describe social salvation.

In exploring the nature of social criticism and its complex ties to the religious thinking of the day, Cook analyses the thought of an extraordinary cast of characters who presented a bewildering array of nostrums and beliefs, from evolutionists, rationalists, higher critics, and free thinkers, to feminists, spiritualists, theosophists, socialists, communists, single-taxers, and many more. There is Goldwin Smith, 'the sceptic who needed God,' spreading gloom and doom from the comfort of the Grange; W.D. LeSueur, the 'positivist in the Post Office'; the heresiarch Dr R.M. Bucke, overdosed on Whitman, with his message of 'cosmic consciousness'; and a free-thinking, high-rolling bee-keeper named Allen Pringle, whose perorations led to 'hot, exciting nights in Napanee.' It is a world of such diverse figures as Phillips Thompson, Flora MacDonald Denison, Agnes Machar, J.W. Bengough, and J.S. Woodsworth, a world that made Mackenzie King.

Cook concludes that the path blazed by nineteenth-century religious liberals led not to the Kingdom of God on earth, as many had hoped, but, ironically, to the secular city.

RAMSAY COOK is a professor in the Department of History at York University. He is one of Canada's most distinguished historians and the author of *The Politics of John W. Dafoe and the Free Press*, *Canada and the French-Canadian Question*, *The Maple Leaf Forever*, and, with R.C. Brown, *Canada: A Nation Transformed, 1896–1914*.

RAMSAY COOK

The Regenerators: Social Criticism in Late Victorian English Canada

UNIVERSITY OF TORONTO PRESS
Toronto   Buffalo   London

© University of Toronto Press 1985
Toronto   Buffalo   London
Printed in Canada

ISBN 0-8020-5670-9 (cloth)
ISBN 0-8020-6609-7 (paper)

Canadian Cataloguing in Publication Data

Cook, Ramsay, 1931–
The regenerators : social criticism in late
Victorian English Canada
Includes bibliographical references and index.
ISBN 0-8020-5670-9 (bound). – ISBN 0-8020-6609-7 (pbk.)
1. Christianity – Canada – 19th century.
2. Sociology, Christian – Canada – 19th century.
3. Social gospel.   I. Title.
HN106.C66 1985   261.8'0971   C85-099465-9

49,506

PICTURE CREDITS
Archives of the United Church of Canada, Victoria University, Toronto:
Workman (p 22), Austin family (72), All Peoples' Mission (217); McGill University
Archives, Montreal: Dawson (22); Thomas Fisher Rare Book Library, University
of Toronto: Denison (81); The Richard Maurice Bucke Collection, Department of
Rare Books and Special Collections, The D.B. Weldon Library, University of
Western Ontario, London: Bucke (96); Public Archives of Canada C38581:
Thompson (170); PG-K, 166-3 Kingston Picture Collection, Queen's University
Archives, Kingston: Machar (190)

FOR ELEANOR

Contents

Acknowledgments

Many debts have been incurred in the writing of this book. Librarians and archivists from Halifax to Ottawa and Vancouver demonstrated the unfailing co-operation that makes historical research such a pleasure in Canada. Since some of my sources were especially obscure (at one point I was referred to the David Dunlap Observatory for copies of a forgotten newspaper – it had been given away), I want especially to thank Grace Heggie of the Scott Library, York University, for finding me copies of *Secular Thought*, Ernest Ingles of the Canadian Institute for Historical Microreproductions for turning up important books and pamphlets, and the Reverend Glenn Lucas and his staff at the United Church Archives for leading me to several treasures.

In my search for illustrations and photographs that would be integral to my argument rather than just decorations, I had the assistance of the United Church Archives, the Public Archives of Canada, the Ontario Department of Natural Resources, McMaster University, the University of Western Ontario, York University, McGill University, and the University of Toronto.

Financial support for the all-too-many years of research and writing came from York University, the Social Sciences and Humanities Research Council of Canada, and the John Simon Guggenheim Foundation. This book has been published with the help of a grant from the Social Science Federation of Canada, using funds provided by the Social Sciences and Humanities Research Council of Canada; publication has also been assisted by the Canada Council and the Ontario Arts Council under their block grant programs. Canadian scholars are among the specially favoured in the matter of financial assistance for research. My gratitude to those people who administer research funds in both Canada and the United States is, I hope, best expressed in the results of my labour.

Parts of this study have been published in other places and in different form: *Historical Papers of the Canadian Historical Association*, the *Canadian Historical Review*, *Transactions of the Royal Society of Canada*, and *A Political Art*, edited by William New. I must also thank audiences who listened to lectures based on material in this book at the University of Victoria, where I was Lansdowne Lecturer for 1983; Presbyterian College, McGill University, where I was Anderson Lecturer for 1984; and the University of Winnipeg, where I was Chancellor's Lecturer for 1985. Students and colleagues at Concordia University, McGill University, Saint Francis Xavier University, and the University of British Columbia were also subjected to my views on religion and social criticism.

There are debts to friends who have saved me from errors of fact and interpretation but who bear no responsibility for any that remain. These include busy people who read all or parts of the manuscript or who suggested sources that might otherwise have been neglected. Gregory Kealey, Russell Hann, Carl Berger, Susan Houston, Sam Shortt, Brian McKillop, William Klempa, and Ms Jennie Pringle. My York colleagues, especially Christopher Armstrong and Vivian Nelles, provided loud argument and enough *moules* to ensure that I would not take myself too seriously. Then there were my editors: Gerald Hallowell, whose devotion to scholarly publishing attracted me to the University of Toronto Press, and Kathy Johnson, whose careful copy-editing made my manuscript ready for the printer. Finally, I wish to thank Geoff Ewen, who prepared the index.

Eleanor, Maggi, and Mark have put up with the writing of another book, and with me, with their accustomed affection, intelligence, patience, and laughter. In our 'New Jerusalem boarding house' there are, mercifully, no regenerators.

RAMSAY COOK

THE REGENERATORS

Social Criticism in Late Victorian English Canada

1

Introduction

'Could you please explain to me,' he asked, 'why belief in God is ridiculous and belief in humanity is not; why belief in the Kingdom of Heaven is silly, but belief in utopias on earth is clever?'

Alexander Hertzen *From the Other Shore* (1848)

In 1893 *The Canadian Magazine* published a gentle satire on social reform and social reformers. Signed 'Uncle Thomas,' its author probably was S.T. Wood, a Toronto journalist whose talents combined an ability to make economics simple with a genius for describing the natural beauty he observed on his many rambles through Toronto's ravines. Sam Wood, whose friends called him 'Single Tax,' selected the title for his humorous piece with unerring accuracy, for he too on occasion 'undertook to regenerate the universe and oil the wheels of the social structure.' He laboured long and hard promoting Henry George's patented social medicine. He had made common cause with the men and women who in the late Victorian age had concluded that 'if things were not as they are they might have been otherwise.' And like them he believed that more was needed to perfect society than a few practical measures – single tax, prohibition, direct legislation, tariff reform, votes for women, co-operatives, compulsory arbitration, public ownership. Important as those might be, they were only the prosaic means toward a change so complete that it could only be described by a word drawn from a common religious vocabulary: regeneration. Hence, 'Uncle Thomas' naturally called the members of his little reform and dining club 'the Regenerators.'[1]

I have taken his title and his characters (while freely adding some of my own), for his subject and mine are the same. What I have tried to understand and explain in this book seemed simple at first. I wanted to discover and describe the nature of social criticism and social reform thought in English-speaking Protestant Canada. It was plain that to do so some consideration of religious matters was necessary. But the more I worked at the subject, the more I became aware that the relationship between religion and social criticism was far more complex and interesting than I had been led to expect. It quickly became obvious, in the first place, that the nineteenth-century intellectual crisis of Christianity needed much closer examination in Canada than previous writers on the so-called social gospel had given to it. Much more was going on in the Canadian backwater than had previously been imagined. Second, I discovered how frequently the word 'regeneration' was used by reformers, not in the traditional Christian sense of individual rebirth, but rather as a call for social salvation. Third, I realized that the society which the regenerators looked forward to, a Christianized social order, was no nearer to realization at the end of the period I examined than it had been at the beginning. Indeed, I have tried to make the case that Canadian society, or at least English Canadian social thought, had for all its religious rhetoric become markedly more secular. And so I began to wonder if the project of 'regeneration' and the outcome of secularism were connected. With the help of such theological writers as Visser't Hooft, Schweitzer, and Hutchison,[2] I came to see the nature of the connection, one which marked a singularly important change in the way that many English Canadians, over a half a century, had come to view their world. And so my argument: the supreme irony of the regenerators was that the new birth to which they contributed was not, as they had hoped, the city of God on earth but rather the secular city.

In the pages which follow, I have attempted to understand both the rise of social criticism and the decay of traditional or orthodox religious belief. My account of these twin developments may be summarized by the assertion, to be demonstrated in the body of the book, that the religious crisis provoked by Darwinian science and historical criticism of the Bible led religious people to attempt to salvage Christianity by transforming it into an essentially social religion. The orthodox Christian preoccupation with man's salvation was gradually replaced by a concern with social salvation; the traditional Christian emphasis on man's relationship with God shifted to a focus on man's relationship with man. This union of the sacred and the secular was followed, in my view, by the substitution of theology, the science of religion, with sociology, the science of society. In theological terms the development I have analysed is the emergence of a modernist theology which insisted that Christianity was not separate from modern culture but rather should be adapted to it. That theology was founded upon a denial of God's transcendence and an insistence upon his immanence in the world. It followed that a society in which God was immanent was one that could eventually become the kingdom of God on earth.

This transformation may be seen as the decline of traditional orthodoxy, a mere change in religious thinking, or it may be seen as part of something more radical, namely, secularization. In my view the shift in beliefs and values that took place in English Canadian society, and in other related Protestant societies coincidentally, was so fundamental as to deserve to be called 'secularization.' That, of course, does not mean that religious belief and practice disappeared in a twinkling, for they obviously did not. My investigation is designed to show something much more modest, but still important: the way in which social reform thought moved from a religious to a social science perspective. That change, in my view, was an important part of the more general process of secularization.

There is a substantial literature dealing with the complicated issue of secularization from theological, sociological, and historical viewpoints. My own thinking on this topic has been influenced particularly by a historian who approaches the subject from a theological perspective. Owen Chadwick, in *The Secularization of the European Mind in the Nineteenth Century*, and less explicitly in his monumental study *The Victorian Church*, describes secularization as 'a growing tendency of mankind to do without religion, or to try to do without religion.'[3] It is not merely changes in theological doctrine or religious ideas that offer evidence of secularization, though the two are obviously connected. Rather, secularization is the shift from a religious explanation of man's behaviour and relationships to a non-religious one. Thomas Haskell's *The Emergence of Professional Social Science* demonstrates that development persuasively and connects it with the emergence of professionalism. The new social science, which gradually replaced the old religiously based moralism, overcame the nineteenth-century crisis of authority that accompanied the questioning of religious certitude.[4] And with the new social science came a new professional leadership, replacing the older religious leadership. It is that transformation which I have tried to illustrate in another context.

There is naturally more to secularization than changing belief systems. Sociologists and historians have advanced the argument that secularization is a natural, almost inevitable, result of urban-industrial growth where socio-economic cleavages make it plain that there can be no real consensus about social values that once claimed the sanction of religious authority.[5] Others have argued that the decline of religion in modern society is a consequence of religion's inability to compete effectively in the free market of ideas. In advancing this interpretation, Jeffrey Cox adds the contention that religious belief was always based on a combination of both doctrine and social utility. Once social utility was weakened as other institutions took over the church's social functions, the appeal of religion was fatally undermined. Religion became irrelevant.[6] What this interpretation ignores, it seems to me, is the extent to which liberal Christians promoted this very development. By urging Christians to emphasize social utility and to downplay or ignore doctrine, these advocates of the social gospel were in fact making the church irrelevant in a world where other institutions were better equipped to perform the socially useful roles once fulfilled by the church. In short, then – and this is the main argument of my book – the manner in which liberal Protestants responded to the socio-economic, scientific, and historical challenges of the nineteenth century resulted in Christianity becoming less rather than more relevant. That in essence is what I mean by secularization. It is the ironic outcome of the Regenerators' quest for the kingdom of God on earth.

Historians, of course, are never surprised when history fails to work out in the expected fashion. So my intention is to understand rather than to laugh at the failure of nineteenth-century men and women to foresee the unintended consequences of their actions. If in the process I have done nothing more than to restore to the Canadian historical record a few undeservedly forgotten non-conformists – journalists, cartoonists, novelists, bee-keepers, versifiers – as well as offering a slightly different perspective on some better-known figures – preachers, politicians, and professors – then I shall be well satisfied. Like 'Uncle Thomas' I have found it a pleasure 'to sit and contemplate the social regenerators ... socialists, anarchists, single taxers, Christian Scientists, and candidates for the Legislature ... They talk freely of all problems, from the cutting of bay ice to the passing of a resolution on the destiny of the North American continent.' And best of all, at least in my account, they almost never 'alluded to the cultivation of a national sentiment.'[7]

2

The Roots of Modernism:
Darwinism and the Higher Critics

Karl Marx, no mere dabbler in theological questions, concluded in 1844 that 'the criticism of religion is the presupposition of all criticism.' To make his meaning unmistakable, he continued: 'The abolition of the *illusory* happiness of the people is the demand for their *real* happiness. The demand to abandon the illusions about their condition is the *demand to give up a condition that* required illusions. Hence criticism of religion is in embryo a *criticism of this vale of tears* whose halo is religion.'[1] For Marx the only salvation was to be found in this world, and the road to that predestined classless society followed the path traced by historical materialism. All other religions preached illusory destinies.

That religious belief sanctioned the social order became something of a commonplace conviction in the nineteenth century, even among non-Marxists. Those who agreed with Marx in wanting to change society attacked religious belief, at least as traditionally taught, for that very reason. If it could be demonstrated that religion was false, or at least misinterpreted and misapplied, then the legitimacy of the established order that religion supported could also be brought into question. For Marx, religious belief, particularly the Christian claim that man's ultimate relief from his sufferings in 'this vale of tears' would come in the eternal life hereafter, was nothing more than an opiate, sure evidence of alienation. Only in a world unfettered by such illusions, a secular world, would men and women be free to concentrate on mundane conditions and eventually realize that those conditions could be changed. Secularism then would not only destroy the claims of religion, it would also challenge the legitimacy of the social order.[2]

Though Marx's teachings played only a marginal role in the rise of Canadian social criticism,[3] his point about the role of religion in society was widely accepted both by conservatives and social critics. Indeed, in Canada criticism of society was rooted in criticism of religion. Yet in contrast to Marx, Canadian critics of religious orthodoxy were rarely advocates of atheism, nor would many of them have admitted that their goal was a thoroughly secular society. Instead, their aim was almost invariably a reinterpretation of Christianity to make it more relevant to the supposed everyday world of Canadians. Virtually every social reformer in late Victorian Canada wanted to stand orthodox Christian teaching on its head. Rather than sanctioning the social order, social critics argued, Christianity properly interpreted should provide the standard against which society should be judged. Implicit, sometimes even explicit, in that contention was the conviction that society so judged would be found sadly wanting.

I

The critique of religious orthodoxy which eventually led to the 'social gospel' that formed the essence of social criticism in English Canada originated in the religious and theological turmoil of the last third of the nineteenth century. That there was such a turmoil, even what could be accurately called a 'crisis of belief,' in Protestant Canada that paralleled similar events in Great Britain and the United States, is readily demonstrated.[4] Virtually every issue of the *Canadian Monthly and National Review*, the leading intellectual quarterly of late Victorian Canada, provided illustrations of that crisis. That publication and others regularly carried contributions by Goldwin Smith, Professor John Watson, Agnes Machar, Principal G.M. Grant, Principal William Dawson, and W.D. LeSueur, to name only the most prominent, on topics of science and religion, biblical criticism, positivism, and philosophical idealism. What was true of secular magazines was even more evident in the religious publications – *The Christian Guardian, The Westminster, The Canadian Methodist Quarterly*, and others. Nor were these topics ignored by the popular press. Within the courts and colleges of the Protestant churches and in the minds and consciences of individual ministers and laymen, questions of fundamental religious importance were regularly debated. 'The struggle for physical well-being, with which we in this country have hitherto been mainly occupied,' Professor John Watson of Queen's University wrote in 1876, 'has served as a breakwater to the tide of scepticism which has already swept over Europe; but the roar of its waters is now in our ears and its spray on our faces, and we can only hope to keep all that we most highly value from being torn from the grasp of the more cultured among us by calmly and manfully facing the emergency.'[5]

Watson had only just arrived in Canada, bringing to the department of philosophy at Queen's University a Scottish interpretation of Hegelian idealism that would become a major influence in the development of theological liberalism in Canada. Though he personally laboured manfully in facing the emergency he identified, his influence in the long run probably contributed in a major way to the triumph of the secular forces he had warned against. But he was certainly not the first to realize that Canadians were far from immune to the currents of religious and philosophical dispute so prominent elsewhere. As early as 1860 the then principal of Queen's University had rung the alarm bells loudly at the opening of the new university term. 'The newspaper, the magazine, the novel, teem with theological speculation, put in the most attractive forms,' he worried out loud, '... One cannot mingle much in society without finding that a large proportion of the well-educated classes are conversant with the questions which arise from the apparent conflict of faith and reason, and the difficulties started by the progress of science.'[6]

From the viewpoint of the leading spokesmen for Protestantism in English Canada, the most dramatic challenge to the traditional Christian understanding of man came from science. 'Assaults have been made upon her from various positions and by different engines,' Professor Watson, remarking upon the embattled position of theology, wrote in 1876, 'but it is probably from the vantage point of science, and by scientific artillery, that she has been exposed to the fiercest and roughest kind of battery.'[7] Science in general seemed to raise questions about religious teaching, but what most late nineteenth-century writers meant by 'science' was the view put forward in 1859 by Charles Darwin in *On the Origin of Species*. The debate that revolutionary volume set off in Great Britain and the United States had its counterpart in Canada.[8] Most of that controversy, at least in the non-scientific intellectual world, turned less on the validity of the evolution-by-natural-selection hypothesis than on the theological implications which Darwinism appeared to bear for the biblical account of creation and man. It was more a debate about 'evolution' than about Darwinism, more about religion than about science.

Nevertheless, the most important contributor to the Darwinian controversy in Canada took serious issue with the new wisdom on both scientific and theological grounds. Sir William Dawson, principal of McGill University, was Canada's most eminent scientist in the nineteenth century. A geologist of international standing, Dawson was also an accomplished university administrator and, not least important, a Presbyterian of unshakeable conviction.[9] As a scientist and a Presbyterian, Dawson belonged to that dominant pre-Darwinian school of geological thought which insisted that 'natural history must devote itself to exhibiting evidence of divine design and of material Providence.'[10] For Dawson, religion could no more be banished from science than it could be separated from life. He recognized that Darwin's determination to separate science from religion would almost certainly lead to a separation of religion from life. And that separation had implications that went far beyond the scientific laboratory. He therefore took up the defence of natural theology against the claims of scientific naturalism.

Dawson read, reviewed, and rejected − at least in part − *On the Origin of Species* almost immediately after it came off the press. His first response was temperate but firm. He confessed admiration for the careful empirical work upon which the study was based, but he rejected the Darwinian procedure. Dawson insisted that the Baconian empirical method was the only truly scientific one and that Darwin, by setting out to test a hypothesis, had sinned against orthodox science. (He would later refer to Darwin's rejection of 'the Baconian mode' as a 'return to the mediaeval plan of setting up dogmas based on authority only.')[11] Nor did he find Darwin's evidence compelling; as Dawson correctly pointed out, the fossil record contained too many gaps to support Darwin's contention that evolution of species rather than fixity of species should be accepted by science.[12] Though Dawson's first response to Darwin was moderate and based mainly on scientific reservations, he nevertheless shared the conviction expressed by Professor E.J. Chapman, who taught geology and mineralogy at the University of Toronto, and whose review of *On the Origin of Species* concluded with a reaffirmation of the traditional Paleyite argument for nature's divine design. 'Certain facts are given,' he wrote, 'certain remarkable phenomena are witnessed everywhere around us. We are asked to explain them. We are forced to confess they transcend our explanation. We are asked to explain how the world comes to be peopled by so many very different plants and animals. We reply, by the act of the CREATOR; these plants and animals being essentially unchanged descendants of species created at the commencement of the existing state of things.'[13] Indeed, in the same year that Dawson reviewed *On the Origin of Species* (1860) he published a fat volume entitled *Archaia; or, Studies of the Cosmogony and Natural History of the Hebrew Scriptures*, in which he mounted what he insisted was a scientifically documented defence of the Old

Testament account of creation. Dawson was never to be swayed from his conviction that 'it can easily be shown that there are important points of agreement between the simple story of Eden, as we have it in Genesis, and scientific probabilities as to the origin of man.'[14]

Though the Canadian scientific community gradually and quietly came to terms with the Darwinian hypothesis,[15] Principal Dawson, who after the death of Louis Agassiz in 1873 became the leading scientific anti-Darwinian, grew increasingly hostile and shrill. As Darwin's influence spread, Dawson's pen poured forth millions of words designed to stem the tide of the new biological thinking. While his objections continued to be illustrated by geological evidence and interpretation, the essential assumption of his position was that science 'is the exponent of the plans and works of the great Creative Will ... Men must know God as the Creator, even before they seek him as a benefactor and redeemer.' By the 1870s he had become convinced that by expelling God from science, Darwin had opened the doors to the deluge which, unless diked, would swamp not only true science but also religion, society, and man himself. A profound conservatism animated his condemnation of the 'evolutionists': 'They seek to revolutionize the religious beliefs of the world,' he wrote in *The Story of Earth and Man*, 'and if accepted would destroy most of the existing theology and philosophy. They indicate tendencies among scientific thinkers which, though probably temporary, must before they disappear, descend to lower strata, and reproduce themselves in grosser forms, and with most serious effects on the whole structure of society. With one class of minds they constitute a sort of religion, which so far satisfied the craving for truths, higher than those that relate to immediate wants and pleasures. With another, and perhaps larger class, they are accepted as affording a welcome deliverance from all scruples of conscience and fears of a hereafter. In the domain of science evolution has like tendencies. It reduces the position of man, who becomes a descendant of inferior animals, and a mere term in a series whose end is unknown. It removes from the study of nature the ideas of final cause and purpose.'[16]

To deny knowledge of the chief end of man and reject the idea of final cause and purpose in nature was, in Dawson's view, subversive. The struggle against Darwin was more than a scientific combat. That was important, for Dawson loved science only slightly less than he loved God, his family, and perhaps McGill University. But Darwinism was more than bad science, for bad science also threatened religious and social certainties. 'The mind of our time,' he wrote in 1890, 'is unsettled and restless. It has the vague impression that science has given it power to solve all mysteries. It is intoxicated with its physical success, and has no proper measure of its own powers.' Here was the making of an undisciplined and therefore dangerous intelligence, one that threatened to break the bounds of that moral authority founded on religion. The social consequences were ominous. 'At a lower level,' the McGill principal warned, 'it is evident that the ideas of struggle for existence, and survival of the fittest, introduced by the new philosophy, and its resolution of man himself into a mere spontaneous improvement of brute ancestors, have stimulated to an intense degree that popular unrest so natural to an age discontented with its lot, because it has learned what it might do and have, without being able to realize its expectations, and which threatens to overthrow the whole fabric of society as at present constituted.'[17] These dark forebodings were hardly surprising in a man of Dawson's religious persuasion. A God banished from Nature could hardly expect to remain a bulwark of the social order. Since Dawson believed in the 'fundamental unity and harmony of all truth, whether natural or spiritual, whether discovered by man or revealed by God,' the denial of God's place in the natural order undermined his role in the social order and promised social chaos. Social conservatism went hand in hand with scientific conservatism, and both were founded on religious conservatism.[18]

Though many late Victorian Canadians joined Dawson in the struggle against godless Darwinism,[19] few were as total in their rejection as the McGill geologist. Outside the scientific world the chief concern was not so much with Darwin's *On the Origin of Species* as with Darwin's *The Descent of Man*, published in 1871. The contention that man was an animal, perhaps just a little above the ape, rather than God's special creation was an 'unspeakably momentous' idea which many found too unsettling or too ludicrous to accept.[20] The Toronto magazine *Grip*, whose satire always had a serious Christian purpose, thought the whole idea could be reduced to ridicule. In an 1880 issue J.W. Bengough, the editor of *Grip*, published a poem entitled 'Evolution Made Plain.'

> Once upon a time
> There was a little bit of slime
>   In the deep, deep bottom of the sea;
> And it commenced to breathe,
> Without anybody's leave,
>   And that was the beginning of you and me.

It sucked the green sea water, –
It was neither son nor daughter,
  But a little bit of both done up in one,
And from it soon evolved,
While the old world still revolv'd,
  A being which we'll nominate its son.

The son the father hated,
And so 'differentiated';
  Its son in course of time just followed suit, –
So it grew by many stages,
Through fifty million ages,
  Till in the course of time it reached the newt.

The newt was awful gritty,
And *knew't* would be a pity,
  To leave the world no better than his *pater*
So he turned him inside out,
Knowing what he was about,
  And, lo! became an animal much greater.

He, too, went on evolving,
The riddle ever solving
  Of his destiny, and bound to solve it soon;
So he taller grew and fatter,
And one day commenced to chatter,
  And found himself a bouncing big baboon.

While his tail was long and growing,
He wore it quite off rowing
  A la HANLAN on a patent sliding seat;
Then he went and killed his brothers,
Made soup of some, and others
  Served up with roast potatoes and some beet.

The 'survival of the fittest,'
See! reader, as thou sittest,
  Is the proper and most scientific plan –
This ape surprised the others,
Both his sisters and his brothers,
  And in course of time became a gentleman.[21]

Even some prominent scientists found Darwin's conclusions unacceptable when applied to man. Alfred Russel Wallace, the co-discover of
evolution by natural selection, rejected the materialistic implications of
The Descent of Man and turned to spiritualism as a method of demon-
strating man's spiritual distinctiveness.[22] One of Dawson's fellow Canadian academics, Daniel Wilson, found an equally ingenious method of
escape. Wilson, who had scientific training, taught history and literature
at the University of Toronto. As befitted a nineteenth-century scholar, his
interests ranged widely and included ethnology and anthropology. In
1873 he offered his contribution to the growing list of speculations about
man's origins.[23] He turned to Shakespeare's *The Tempest*, arguing that
Caliban was the missing link, neither man nor animal, separating man,
with his mind, intelligence, morality, and spirituality, from even the
higher animals. 'In so far as it is a strictly physiological and anatomical
question, let physical science have untrammelled scope in deciding it,'
Wilson argued, 'but when it becomes a psychical question, it is not a mere
matter of sentiment that the mind revolts at a theory of evolution which
professes to recognize its own emanation as no more than the accumulation of impressions and sensations of the nervous organization gathered
in the slow lapse of ages, until at last it has culminated in a moral sense.
Our belief in a First Cause is inextricably bound up with our belief in the
human soul.' Wilson was willing to accept almost the whole of evolutionary theory, but he insisted on keeping man distinct. And nothing more
convincingly demonstrated that distinctiveness than man's capacity for
religious belief, 'especially the immortality of the soul and Christian
morality.'[24]

Wilson's rejection of scientific naturalism, his determination to save
religion and morality from the grasp of materialism, was an understandable and not illegitimate strategy.[25] In adopting it he was joined by John
Watson, who argued that 'the attempt being made to explain moral and
social phenomena by the doctrine of Evolution is an instance of the effort
to apply a hypothesis to a totally new class of cats.' Neither Darwinian
nor Spencerian evolutionary theory appealed to the Queen's philosopher
when applied outside science's legitimate realm. He was here pointing to
the way that modern biological theory and Christian teachings might both
be preserved, even made to work advantageously together, in a system of
philosophical idealism.[26]

A similar approach was adopted by the conservative editor of *The
Christian Guardian*, the Reverend E.H. Dewart. For him some formula-
tions of evolutionary thought were acceptable, provided they were

restricted to natural phenomena and made no pretence to reveal the 'mystery of mysteries.' Dewart adopted much of Dawson's outlook, relying especially on the Presbyterian scientist's geological evidence and his insistence that no provable links existed between inorganic and organic life.[27] But gradually he focused his attention on ways of combining evolution and Christianity. He summarized his conclusions in an editorial marking Darwin's death in 1882. 'The utmost that evolution can be said to do,' he argued, 'is to carry the design a little further back and make it a little more comprehensive. The teleological value of each particular adaptation in nature is not destroyed but magnified when it is referred to a universal law, working out a universal harmony and adaptation. It is a short-sighted philosophy, indeed, which in the presence of the far-reaching law, forgets the law-giver.'[28] In this fashion the essence of the Paleyite argument could apparently be preserved from Darwin's purposeless evolutionary scheme. Dr Dewart also took comfort from Alfred Russel Wallace, whom he heard speak at the University of Toronto in 1887. 'In these statements Dr. Wallace maintains that there is nothing in evolution inconsistent with man's spiritual nature and immortal destiny. Many on the contrary think that Darwin's theory of evolution lands in sheer materialism. Our own idea has always been that there is nothing inconsistent with Christianity in admitting natural development as one of God's methods of working out his plans.'[29] For Dewart, unlike Dawson, Darwinism and Christianity were quite compatible. But then Dawson actually understood Darwinism, while Dewart defined it to meet his needs.

E.H. Dewart, like many other Canadians – Goldwin Smith, Salem Bland, Mackenzie King, and W.C. Good, for example – had found great assistance in his effort to adapt evolution to Christianity in the works of the Scottish theologian and naturalist Dr Henry Drummond. His *Natural Law in the Spiritual World* (1888) and other works harmonized Christianity and evolution in a general doctrine of progress.[30] Yet Dewart was not unaware that such a mixture had its dangers. When the American liberal preacher, Henry Ward Beecher, author of *Evolution and Religion*, appeared in Toronto, *The Christian Guardian* contended that his message had its greatest appeal among 'the unbelieving and anti-Christian part of the audience.' The American had reconciled evolution and Christianity only by making the latter 'thin and vapory.' 'The Christianity he portrayed,' the paper remarked, 'was largely a sentimental humanitarianism without doctrinal background or definite scriptural form.'[31]

Implicit in this defence of traditional Christianity was Dewart's belief that if too much ground was conceded to the new science, the door would be opened to materialism and secularism; each denied God and insisted that only the affairs of this life mattered. 'Secularism is practical agnosticism,' *The Guardian* maintained in a warning against the dangers of secular influences among the working classes, 'as its professors hold that whatever religious and moral principles men have should be restricted to this present world without regard to future judgment and the life to come.' But what sanction would be left to morality if the existence of a transcendent and judging God was denied? In Dewart's view there could be no other effective sanction. 'Men live best in this world who live most for the world to come,'[32] he wrote in a summation that would have delighted, or infuriated, Karl Marx.

In his criticism of Henry Ward Beecher and in his insistence that morality was dependent upon religious belief Dewart was defending Christianity against the inroads of a modernism that insisted upon the immanence of God in the world and the primary ethical and social meaning of Christianity.[33] This was certainly the route that John Watson hoped his combination of idealism and evolution would follow. For that was the road 'of progress towards higher forms of individual, social and political life.'[34] A young Presbyterian graduate student, Mackenzie King, drew a similarly optimistic conclusion. 'The doctrine of evolution,' he recorded in his diary after reading one of Herbert Spencer's works, 'makes man one with the universe, he glories in all because he is greater than all, he finds himself the supreme product of creation ... all evolution points to immortality, creation alone finds completion only in immortal life and perfection.'[35]

This 'new theology,' as Dr William McLaren of Knox College pointed out to the readers of *Canadian Presbyterian* in 1886, taught 'the immanence of God in the Universe and united it with the doctrine of evolution.'[36] But he and others anxious to defend traditional Christian teaching realized that the 'new theology' – which they suspected of being old Unitarianism – drew its inspiration from other sources, too.

II

Professor McLaren, in his temperate and scholarly analysis of the sources of the 'new theology,' naturally had quite a lot to say about biblical criticism. Principal Dawson had also, less temperately, fixed upon this enemy. 'It is plainly shown by recent controversies,' he wrote in his *Modern Ideas of Evolution*, '... that the agnostic evolution and the acceptance of the results of German criticism in disintegrating the earlier books of the Bible, are at the moment combining their forces in the attack on Evangelical Christianity.'[37] Certainly by 1890, when Dawson published that warning, the debate over the higher criticism had reached a crescendo in Canadian Protestant circles. Higher, or historical, criticism, which had originated in Germany early in the century, raised questions about the authorship and even the authenticity of certain books of the Bible and particularly about the relationship of the synoptic Gospels to the Gospel of John. By insisting that biblical texts had to be understood in their historical context, that archeological and linguistic analysis had to be taken into account when interpreting biblical writing, these scholars were 'conducting a revolution in thought comparable to the Reformation itself,' for 'the dogma of the inerrancy of scripture' was being destroyed. To some, the higher critics were laying secular hands on a sacred book, 'reducing the Bible to the level of a mere product of natural law.'[38] That the higher criticism was often connected with the names of such writers as D.F. Strauss and Ernest Renan, who were openly sceptical about Christian teachings, led some to condemn it as nothing but 'the new Negation School.' J.W. Bengough used the term in a poem satirizing the higher critics as purveyors of 'modern doubts and theories' who told believing Christians:

> In short, my simple brother, you *must* not feel so sure;
> The Book you think inspired is only Jewish literature.
> Its authorships, chronologies and dates are quite astray;
> You must wait and hear what future excavations have to say.[39]

Like evolution, the higher criticism, or a somewhat popularized version of it, was a topic of fairly widespread discussion in Canada at least by the 1870s. It probably first made itself felt by the arrival from overseas of men like George Paxton Young, who already in the 1850s was introducing the new scholarship into his sermons.[40] His subsequent career, first as a professor of theology at Knox College in Toronto and, following his resignation from the Presbyterian ministry, as a professor of philosophy at the University of Toronto, may have confirmed the suspicions of conservatives about the inevitable drift of 'scientific' biblical scholarship.[41] The case of the Reverend D.J. Macdonnell, a Canadian educated at Queen's University and later in Scotland and Germany, added further to this suspicion. In 1875 his expressed doubts about the meaning of predestination led to heresy charges, several years of controversy and investigation, and finally to acquittal. That angry debate made a wider

Grip, 17 June 1876

public aware of the theological controversies that were disturbing the church; the acquittal only made conservatives more anxious.[42]

In fact, historical criticism appears to have been absorbed by Canadian Presbyterians, or at least a section of them who took their educational direction from Queen's University, with relative ease. The Reverend G.M. Grant, who became principal in 1877 and held the post until the end of the century, was already a 'modernist' when he arrived from the Maritimes. Indeed, one of his close Nova Scotia friends, himself under the influence of liberalism, felt constrained to rebuke Grant mildly for the sentiments expressed in his inaugural address. 'I infer that your theology is somewhat halting and uncertain,' he observed. 'I think that if you concede so much to the critics as to reduce to unauthenticated myths any portion of the Bible it will be of little use to cry out "Believe! Believe the spiritual truth the myth contains!" But this spiritual truth must be authenticated by something. If you allow the outward authority to go by the board, there is nothing but an inward something to appeal to; and this may vary from man to man ... I am not inclined to concede as much to German and other criticism as you.'[43]

Grant, deeply influenced by romantic idealists like Coleridge and Carlyle,[44] warmly welcomed most modern intellectual developments. He was convinced that the discoveries of modern science and the scientific method worked to the benefit of mankind and presented no unanswerable threat to religious belief.[45] Certainly the higher criticism caused him no unease. 'Just because Christianity is emphatically a historical as well as an ideal religion,' he wrote in answer to an opponent of the new biblical scholarship, 'it welcomes the new science of history which has given us new methods. In applying these methods to the early history of all nations, we discover that the legends or myths, once accepted literally, cover events, thoughts, and periods grander than the story; but in giving them a new interpretation we do not destroy but fulfill.'[46] If that comment was complacent, it was more often a spirit of optimism that infused Grant's writing. Certainly his study *The Religions of the World* (1895) not only revealed a remarkably tolerant attitude to non-Christian beliefs, but also underlined the extent to which Grant identified Christianity with contemporary liberal civilization. His message was that the Christian church should 'rise above that sectarianism which exhausts its strength, and go forward as one body to make the kingdoms of the world the Kingdom of God and His Christ.'[47] He knew that his liberalism might raise some eyebrows, but, he told a friend, 'everything depends on the spirit in which a book is written that deals with other religions. It must aim at getting a view of them from within and not from the outside; and such a point of view we are now somewhat prepared for, though to the theologians of the eighteenth century it would seem unChristian.'[48]

Grant was a popularizer, not a profound or even a systematic thinker. He spoke persuasively, wrote with clarity and directness, and, perhaps most important, never gave the slightest hint that he doubted anything he said. In 1879 a New Brunswick minister wrote him a long, anxious letter about the intellectual doubts which the higher criticism and liberal theology were causing him. 'Is it not obvious that the Churches are walking in the dark of night, and disputing about ways they cannot see but only guess?' he asked plaintively.[49] Grant's reply, unfortunately, is lost, but its contents can be imagined. Optimist and activist that he was, he almost certainly told his correspondent to quell his doubts and offer a straightforward, practical message. As he told a similar correspondent a few years later, 'The people will take anything from a Minister they trust, and who deserves to be trusted.'[50] Character rather than doctrine was what counted.

Certainly there were Presbyterians who had to struggle harder than the principal of Queen's before accepting the new theology. But on the whole the transition was made without any profound public crisis. In 1894 Professor John Campbell of Presbyterian College, Montreal, was accused of heresy as a 'higher critic,' but the charges were never heard. There could hardly have been much evidence against a man who had already dismissed German biblical scholarship with a quip: 'Get a man behind a Meerschaum pipe and a flagon of Piltzener,' he wrote, 'and he can think himself right, and all the prophets and apostles wrong.' In 1898 Knox College appointed to a professorship John McFadyen, whose German education and commitment to historical methodology were well known. His careful scholarship, undoubted piety, and attractive personality helped to ensure that modern biblical scholarship was accepted quietly. By the turn of the century John Scrimger, professor of exegesis at Presbyterian College, reflected the new outlook when he argued for a revision of the creed endorsing the fundamentals of liberalism. 'The new creed,' he predicted, 'will recognize that Christianity is more a life than a creed, and will acknowledge the real presence of the Spirit of God in the hearts of many who are not disposed to trouble themselves much with creeds of any kind, but who are following in the footsteps of Christ, trying to do good as they have opportunity.'[51]

The Methodists found the transition more difficult, noisier, and of longer duration. Doubtless that partly reflected a difference in personality. If there was a Methodist with the power and influence of G.M. Grant, he was the Reverend Dr Albert Carman, the Methodist general superintendent. But in contrast to the Kingston liberal, Carman was a conservative in matters of biblical interpretation, though not on social questions. Carman, ably seconded by the Reverend E.H. Dewart, editor of *The Christian Guardian*, was determined to scotch the serpent of liberalism at every opportunity – and there were several. But there was more to it than mere personality. For Canadian Methodists the doctrines of biblical inspiration and inerrancy were crucial, for their church had never developed a theology as systematic as that of Calvinism. Some Methodists appeared to fear that if the Bible was questioned there would be little to fall back on.[52]

The first round in the battle over the higher criticism in the Methodist church ended when the German-trained Professor George C. Workman was relieved of his post in the theology faculty of Victoria College in 1892. Workman's views, the result of five years of Old Testament study at Leipzig, appeared first in the form of a lecture on 'Messianic prophecy,' which was subsequently published in *The Canadian Methodist Quarterly*.

The reaction was immediate and hostile. As Workman admitted ruefully, 'Neither the country nor the church seems to have been so well prepared for scientific investigation of Prophetic scriptures as I had naturally supposed.'[53]

The essence of Workman's contention in 1890 (presented in fuller detail in two subsequent books) was simply that the Old Testament should be read in its historical context. Once that approach was accepted, it could no longer be argued that the Old Testament was full of predictions that would later be fulfilled in the New Testament. The Bible, in brief, should not be read literally. 'While ... the Scripture writers acted under a Divine impulse in apprehending and communicating their religious ideas,' he explained, 'we must not assume that every part of the Bible contains a divinely inspired statement or expresses a divinely inspired sentiment ... It is only the moral truths and spiritual principles of the Bible that are divinely inspired; and it is only these truths and principles taken together that constitute a trustworthy guide to life, and form a sufficient rule of practice.' Naturally, Workman was convinced that he was defending Christianity, for he was satisfied that any attempt to retain the literal account of the Bible's contents brought Christianity into an unequal conflict with modern scientific and historical knowledge.[54]

Carman and Dewart, however, believed that Workman's defence of Christianity amounted almost to unconditional surrender. In the columns of The Christian Guardian and The Canadian Methodist Quarterly, in books and pamphlets and in the church courts, the traditionalists counter-attacked and finally, though only temporarily, won. In Dewart's view the higher criticism could be valuable, but it too often led to extreme and unacceptable conclusions. For him, Old Testament prophecy was exactly what Workman denied: a foretelling of the Messiah's advent. To accept any other conclusion was to contribute further to an already threatening climate of intellectual doubt which, Dewart believed, had been sapping the vigour of Christian belief for several decades. 'We live in times of great mental unrest,' he wrote, introducing his detailed attack on Workman in 1891. 'The spirit of enquiry which has distinguished modern research in physical science, has made itself felt in all departments of thought. This is notably the case in regard to Biblical and theological subjects ... A spirit of doubt and questioning seems to pervade the intellectual atmosphere.' Dewart and his allies were unwilling to exchange certainty for what they saw as their opponents' offer of a better method of searching for the truth.[55]

To conservatives like Dewart and Carman, a full-scale defence of the

Principal J.W. Dawson   Rev. George C. Workman

dikes was called for. The seepage of modernism, whether carried by science or the new biblical criticism, could only dilute the full meaning of what they called 'evangelical Christianity.' There could be no retreat from the traditional teaching: God's transcendence, Christ's divinity, man's sinfulness, faith as the sole means of salvation, the life of holiness. These doctrines, Carman insisted, 'derived from a Bible whose divine inspiration must be unquestioned.'[56] To doubt these verities meant the deluge. 'The natural effect of these teachings [the higher criticism and liberal theology] with the ordinary man in the long run,' a Methodist writer contended, 'would be stealthily to unsettle his faith, produce disrelish and consequent disregard for the Word of God, engender want of confidence in the authority of Christ and his apostles, arouse doubt, if not denial of the inspiration of sacred writers, cause neglect of public worship, cut the nerve of evangelistic effort and, in short, promote the general lowering of the religious life of the people.'[57]

These apprehensions, though exaggerated, were not without foundation. Certainly the conservatives were correct in fearing that their version of orthodoxy was losing its appeal. By 1910, when the tumult over the higher criticism erupted again because of the teachings of the Reverend

George Jackson, Dewart was gone, his *Christian Guardian* fallen into liberal hands. Carman, still filled with righteous wrath, stood defiant but nevertheless defeated. Nathanael Burwash, natural scientist turned theologian and chancellor of Victoria College, shared the hope that the old man 'would refrain from attacking the millionaires [sic]' at the General Conference in Victoria, where the Jackson case was finally settled in the liberal professor's favour. Burwash and other leading Toronto Methodists apparently agreed, as Chester Massey put it, that up-to-date businessmen 'are not going to give liberally to a church whose institutions are not up-to-date, and who do not turn out up-to-date men ...' But Carman was not silenced, convinced as he was that in conceding the field to the theological modernists Methodism surrendered its soul to the monied middle classes – the Rowells, Masseys, Flavelles, Fudgers, and Eatons – who he believed found comfort in the attenuated doctrines of modern theology. 'Here is possibly our greatest danger,' he told an uncomfortable General Conference. 'We are becoming wealthy and may easily lose the vigour and tension of spiritual life and voice and tone of aggressive evangelism ... At such times and under such conditions novelties are preached for the well-proven doctrines of converting grace and sanctifying power ... Even good men are dazzled by the glitter of theories, and befooled with empty speculations.'[58] The aging general superintendent would soon be replaced by the energetic Dr Dwight Chown, for whom sociology took precedence over theology. Carman's worst fears were being realized.

III

The experience of the Reverend W.S. Rainsford perhaps epitomizes the transformation of Canadian protestantism in the late Victorian age. Rainsford, who served Toronto's fashionable St James's Cathedral in the late 1870s and early 1880s, was born in Great Britain. He had been caught up in the so-called evangelical revival of the mid-century. In 1876 he travelled to North America to conduct a mission first in New York and Boston and later in Toronto and London, Ontario. His mission, according to his own account, was a huge success and resulted in a call to St James's. It was during his Toronto pastorate that he absorbed 'the cataclysmic change ... the evolutionary hypothesis has effected in religious belief.' His newly adopted liberalism at first brought him into sharp conflict with the congregation that had earlier responded so warmly to his evangelical message, but he gradually won most of them over. Even

Goldwin Smith, Rainsford remembered with pride, joined his congregation. William Hume Blake, a leading evangelical, moved out. By the mid-1880s, having built up a 'great free and open liberal church for the people,' Rainsford accepted a call to St George's in New York, where he ministered to J.P. Morgan and others of economic power and social prominence. His 1913 book, *The Reasonableness of the Religion of Jesus*, displayed all of the fatal flaws that an Albert Carman (had he been willing to read a book by an Anglican), or a William Hume Blake would have expected from a theological liberal. 'By so much as Jesus is pronounced as supernatural by His birth, or death or rising from the dead,' he wrote soothingly, 'by so much are we robbed of our elder Brother, robbed of a real son of man who is a real practical guide and example; one we can follow and imitate down here on earth.'[59]

What Rainsford was saying – and in this he spoke for many of his and a later generation – was that the practical application of Christ's teachings was more important than theological controversy. Indeed, the new science and the new scholarship had left doctrine in the midst of shifting sands that might best be avoided. That was certainly the conclusion of the regular religious columnist of *The Toronto Mail* when in 1885 he asked the central question: 'Now what we demand is the authority by which these iron bound creeds and confessions are imposed?' He responded immediately: 'It certainly was not the Saviour, whose teaching was utterly free from even the suspicion of theology.'[60] Professor John Watson, whose Christian Hegelianism reduced the church to an organization for social betterment (he wrote a troubled Presbyterian minister in 1914: 'No creed or any Church can be accepted, and I don't think a church can be based on any belief except that it is an organization for making men better'[61]), explained the meaning of modernism to the readers of the *Knox College Monthly* in 1891: 'Christianity does not conceive of the future world as different from this, but as the present world in its ideal aspect; what a man is then, he is now, and what he is now is determined by the degree in which his life breathes the spirit of love. Christianity is above all things a religion of this world ... It is nothing if it is not social.'[62]

The young W.C. Good, the future intellectual leader of a succession of agricultural reform movements in Ontario, spent a good many of his spare hours as a science student at the University of Toronto in the 1890s listening to sermons and struggling with religious questions. He concluded that the conservative stand of the Dawsons and Carmans was indefensible and a waste of time. Instead he arrived, without the aid of Hegel, at a conclusion close to that of Professor Watson: 'the sooner people learn,' he wrote his sister in the self-confident tone that would characterize his whole career, 'that religion has a foundation quite apart from the Bible – though the Bible is a *means of grace* – the sooner will they quit worrying about comparatively trivial matters. The new historical criticism of the o.t. writings has made them once more a living book, when they were becoming dead to many people on account of foolish and unreal distinctions between secular and sacred etc. It is a transition period just now, and some friction is inevitable.'[63]

Good proved an astute observer. By the end of the Victorian age the foundations of religious orthodoxy had been shaken. And if the 'sacred' and the 'secular' were no longer distinct, then perhaps religion, rather than being the opiate of the masses, would become a recipe for social regeneration. The criticism of religion led, sometimes by sinuous routes, to the criticism of society.

3

The Anxieties of a Moral Interregnum

The great debate over God's place in the universe and man's place in nature that consumed so much energy in the post-Darwinian intellectual world was also, necessarily, a debate about God's and man's place in the social order. Sir William Dawson had recognized that, though it was not his major preoccupation. Others with much less scientific training became almost exclusively concerned with the social implications of the new biological hypothesis. Religious uncertainty might cause some to fret about immortality; for others the most immediate anxiety was about life here and now.

In 1886 a critique of socialism in *The Week* admitted that the 'opium of the people' was losing its potency. 'Among the principal causes of the political socialism which is now disquieting the world and disturbing industry may certainly be reckoned the decay of religious belief,' the editor observed. 'Looking forward no longer to compensation in a future state of existence for privations endured here, the working classes pant at once to realize their natural ideal; and they are no longer restrained by the conviction, which was perhaps even stronger than a belief in a future life, that the structure of society with its gradations of wealth and poverty are a divine ordinance in which all men must acquiesce.'[1] Just as Paley's God had created immutable species and supported an immutable and hierarchical social order, so Darwinian evolution challenged one and undermined the other.

I

No Canadian writer was more obsessed with the equation between religious uncertainty and social discontent than Goldwin Smith. 'God and future retribution being out of the question,' he wrote in a worried comment on *The Descent of Man*, 'it is difficult to see what can restrain the selfishness of the ordinary man, and induce him, in the absence of actual coercion, to sacrifice his personal desire to the public good.' A fundamental intellectual transformation was taking place; moral authority founded upon religious belief was shaken, and the questioning of political institutions and social unrest was merely the material manifestation. 'A crisis has been brought on, the gravity of which nobody can fail to see, and nobody but a fanatic Materialist can see without the most serious misgivings.'[2] Misgivings and anxieties were certainly characteristic of Smith's response. If the typical Victorian was uneasy about the implications of religious doubt, then no Victorian was more typical than Goldwin Smith.[3] Concern about religious doubt underlay many of the literally millions of words of social and political commentary that flowed from his ever-moving pen during the four decades he spent in Canada. And since Smith's writings provoked so many other Canadians to engage in the great intellectual questions of the day, it is important to focus clearly upon what the increasingly gloomy sage of the Grange guessed about the riddle of existence.

In 1871, at the age of forty-seven, Goldwin Smith decided to make Toronto his home. Having established a modest reputation as a historian and an essayist, he had left Britain in 1869 to take up a teaching post at Cornell University in New York state. But despite his enthusiasm for the idea of the United States, he found the reality of the post-Civil War republic less to his taste. In Canada, despite its deplorable colonial status, he felt more at home, especially after his marriage in 1875 to the wealthy widow of William Henry Boulton. For the remainder of his long life – he lived until 1910 – the Grange was his home. From there he launched his many projects, all designed to make Canada over in the image of his mid-Victorian liberal mind: Canada First, continentalism, voluntary relief of poverty, Sunday streetcars, and, above all, an improved intellectual life. There too he entertained and talked with visiting intellectuals and dignitaries, local professors and personalities, farm leaders and students. His guests were not always familiar with the standards of the Oxford common room. On one occasion Edward Farrer brought Joe Haycock, the leader of the Patrons of Industry in the Ontario legislature, to have a talk with 'the Professor.' Hospitality in the form of a bottle of whisky was produced and set on the table. 'Joe took the bottle and shook it vigorously before pouring out the whiskey into his glass. Afterward the Professor asked Farrer how it was that Haycock shook the bottle so. Farrer told him that in the country hotels the whiskey was often adulterated and that the water rose to the top and it was customary for farmers, when getting a drink at the bar, to shake the bottle before pouring out the whiskey into their glass and that Joe had acquired the habit ...'[4]

Meeting the farmers' leader was just one of Smith's many efforts to enlighten Canadian public opinion – in this case, Smith had acquired control of the Patrons' newspaper, *The Canada Farmers' Sun*. This was one of his final attempts to find a publication that would allow him to express freely and fully his ideas, opinions, and prejudices on almost every imaginable topic. The importance of Goldwin Smith to late nineteenth-century Canada was not the originality of his ideas, for there was little enough of that, or his capacity for controversy and his elegant writing style, valuable as they were. Rather, it was his somewhat paternalistic determination single-handedly to keep Canadians abreast of the main intellectual developments of the day. Though his most frequently remembered work is *Canada and the Canadian Question* (1891), which tenaciously argued the case for Canadian union with the United States, his contemporaries knew him as a man for whom history, literature, science, philosophy, and theology were at least as engrossing as Canada's political destiny. Indeed, in both his earliest and his last published writings, Smith made it plain that religion (and what he feared was happening to it) was his major preoccupation. Like Carlyle, Mill, Marx, the early Fabians, and a host of other Victorians, Goldwin Smith was convinced that no understanding of man and society could be arrived at without fully accounting for religious thought and conviction. He would certainly have agreed with his friend Matthew Arnold – perhaps they discussed the elegant paradox when the Arnolds came to the Grange in 1884 – that 'at the present moment two things about the Christian religion must surely be clear to anybody with eyes in his head. One is, that men cannot do without it; the other, that they cannot do with it as it is.'[5]

Smith's concern about the erosion of religious belief was apparent in one of his earliest ventures into public controversy, a decade before his arrival in Toronto. At that time he attempted to defend, against an Oxford philosopher's scepticism, a fairly orthodox argument for Christian belief. But the important point that Smith insisted upon and would continue to insist upon for the next half-century was that morality depended on religious belief. Religion, then, was the only sure basis for society, 'the only lasting spring of the unselfish affections and actions which bind men into a community and save that community from dissolution.'[6]

The defence of religion was thus, for Smith, a defence of social order. And that defence had somehow to take account of the two principal sources of difficulty: higher criticism and the new science. His knowledge of the discussions taking place in these fields was, as in most things, broad and somewhat superficial. (It is not without irony that the Reverend George Workman's book, *The Old Testament Vindicated* (1897), which got him in serious trouble with the Methodist authorities, was a defence of the Old Testament against what he convincingly demonstrated was Smith's misleading interpretation of modern biblical scholarship.) Smith himself was satisfied that historical criticism left little if any ground for the traditional claim that the Old Testament was divinely inspired. 'Human testimony, no doubt, may sometimes fail in minor particulars, while in the main account of matters it is true. But,' he asked rhetorically, 'is it conceivable that the Holy Spirit, in dictating the record of God's dealings with mankind for our instruction in the way of life, should simulate the defects of human evidence?' Since the answer was patently in the negative, there was no possibility of retaining the Old Testament as a foundation-stone of Christian belief. 'As a manifestation of the Divine the Hebrew books teaching righteousness and purity, may keep their place in our love and admiration forever; while of their tribalism, their intolerance, their religious cruelty, we forever take our leave.' Free, rational enquiry, Smith insisted, left no room for the mystification of 'supernatural revelation.'[7]

With the same ease as he accepted and even exaggerated the contentions of the higher criticism, Smith also absorbed what he took to be the meaning of Darwinism. He accepted evolution by natural selection as a scientific hypothesis. But he was not willing to adopt the materialistic implications of the new scientific teaching, and wholly rejected the idea that man was a mere beast. Though man could no longer be viewed as a separate, special creation of God, his distinctiveness nevertheless remained. 'A being apart from the other animals man remains in virtue of his reason, of which, other animals have at most, only the rudiments, and yet more perhaps in virtue of his aspirations and capacity for improvement, of which even the most intelligent of the other animals, so far as we can see, have no share. He alone pursues moral good; he alone is religious; he alone is speculative, looking before and after; he alone feels the influence of beauty and expresses his sense of it in poetry and art; what is lust in brutes in him alone is love; he alone thinks or dreams that there is in him anything that ought not to die.'[8] Man remained man, a creature apart.

That lengthy catalogue of man's distinctive characteristics depended, of course, on the further conviction that, as Darwin himself admitted, natural selection was an explanation at the level of secondary causes, leaving room for a belief in God as a first cause. 'Some power there must have been,' Smith wrote, 'if we can trust the indications of our intelligence on such a subject, to set evolution on foot and to direct it in its course.' Smith seemed to be saying – and he was not alone in taking this refuge – that though the Paleyite argument for the existence of God from the evidence of design in nature was destroyed, it was still possible to assume the existence of a Designer. But it was a diluted theism that remained, for the essentials of Christianity could hardly be defended in that manner. 'Darwin has proved that there was no fall of man,' Smith told Lord Mount Stephen. 'If there was no fall, how can there have been an incarnation or a redemption, and what becomes of the whole edifice of orthodox Christianity?'[9]

Smith's religious beliefs had been whittled down to the barest minimum. Almost nothing stood between him and atheism except the 'unpenetrable mystery of existence,' and the example of what he frequently called 'the great Teacher of Humanity.' That left the residue of a thin, liberal, rational faith. 'If we must resign miracles, the Messianic prophecies and their supposed fulfilment in Christ, and the Trinitarian creed, what remains to us of the Gospel? There remains to us the Character, the sayings, and the parables, which made and have sustained moral, though not ritualistic, dogmatic or persecuting Christendom ... If there is a Supreme Being, and if he is anywhere manifested in human history, it is here.'[10] Hardly the faith of an Apostle!

Smith's *Guesses at the Riddle of Existence* produced remarkably few firm answers to the religious anxieties that increasingly marked his later life.[11] Indeed, it is difficult – as secularists sarcastically pointed out[12] – to understand why he continued to cling to such an attenuated set of beliefs and even to attend church with some regularity. The explanation is that he feared profoundly not only the personal but perhaps even more the social consequences of the disappearance of religion. He might have had himself in mind when he wrote that 'it is probably the apprehension ... of the social and political consequences of atheism, not less than the influence of habit or fashion, that leads some, who themselves believe no longer, to support the church.' Though he could not 'profess belief in creeds,' he remained unable to break completely with 'the spiritual life embodied in the Christian communion.' He chose to attend a 'little Baptist church' because the members of that denomination, unlike others, had remained cool, 'comparatively true to what I regard as the principles of Christianity' during the Boer War agitation.[13]

His Opinion of Hereditary Aristocracy. 'If we were asked to say whose name among all our politicians has been most associated with the practice of corruption, are we sure that a baronet would not be the man?' – GOLDWIN SMITH'S LECTURE. *Grip*, 23 May 1891

That essentially political judgment of the value of the 'Christian communion' was perfectly in keeping with Smith's well-known anti-imperialism. But the significant point is that the choice was made for political and not theological reasons. For Smith the value of religion – other than personal consolation – was its social utility. Nothing reveals this view more explicitly than an article published in 1879 entitled 'The Prospect of a Moral Interregnum,' which stirred up widespread controversy both in Canada and abroad. The central problem posed by the article was simple: in the face of declining religious belief, what was the future of the ethical system that held society and civilization together? Could a new sanction for the social order be devised and win acceptance quickly enough to prevent the deluge? That question, Smith argued, was not treated with sufficient seriousness by the new breed of agnostics, who appeared to assume that 'under the reign of evolution, natural selection and the struggle for existence, the Sermon on the Mount will still be accepted as perfectly true; that the Christian beatitudes will still retain their place; and that meekness, humility, poverty of spirit, forgiveness, unworldliness, will continue to be regarded as virtues.'[14] Such complacency would not bear examination.

Smith maintained that his reading of history demonstrated that in the absence of religious belief ethical systems were built on sand. The collapse of the Roman republic, the chaos of Renaissance Europe, and the authoritarianism of Napoleon all showed to Smith's satisfaction the dangers inherent in religious scepticism. 'To me it seems that, historically, I will not say essentially, high and progressive morality is always connected, not with any particular form of belief in a future life, but with the belief that there is something beyond this life and this world,' he told the materialist John Tyndall.[15] If God was dead the world would be returned to a Hobbesian state of nature where the war of all against all raged. That surely was the social teaching of modern science, for the Huxleyite interpretation of the 'survival of the fittest' gave new emphasis to the doctrine that might alone is right. 'Evolution is force, the struggle for existence is force, natural selection is force,' Smith observed lugubriously. That meant that the Christian precepts of co-operation and human brotherhood would vanish. The new ethic of force was already evident in British imperial policy which no longer accepted that 'all men, and all races of men, however weak or inferior were equally entitled to justice and mercy.'[16] None of the efforts to 'Christianize' Darwin satisfied Smith. W.H. Drummond, Smith told Matthew Arnold, was 'most ingenious, but too good to be true.'[17] The threat of a moral 'social Darwinism' depressed him deeply.

II

Smith had always believed that the nineteenth-century capitalist order was founded upon the Christian virtues he so cherished. Once those virtues were threatened by creeping secularism, social upheaval would not be far behind. 'That which prevails as Agnosticism among philosophers and the highly educated prevails as secularism among mechanics, and in that form is likely soon to breed mutinous questionings about the present social order among those who get the poorer share, and who can no longer be appeased by promises of compensation in another world.' Here, then, was the nub of the matter: religious crisis was social crisis. Smith saw much evidence to substantiate his unease. First, perhaps, was the emergence of what he thought were bogus forms of religious belief. 'In each eclipse of religious faith,' he wrote, 'there has prevailed at once as a nemesis and as a spiritual makeshift, a charlatan superstition. In the case of Hellas, it was soothsaying; in that of Rome astrology and the thaumaturgic mysteries of Isis; at the present day it is spiritualism, while even astrology has, or recently had, its votaries in England.' While he could not countenance such 'irrational' religious manifestations, he saw that at least some of them, notably spiritualism, represented evidence that despite the growth of materialism men still craved some spiritual meaning and solace.[18]

Unorthodox religious belief was a sure sign of the intellectual anarchy resulting from the gradual disintegration of traditional theology. That, in turn, meant that the clergy, 'an order of men specially set apart as Ministers of Truth,' could no longer perform their intellectual and moral role effectively, since the ground of their authority had been cut out from under them. This was a situation that would allow 'a rather undue prominence to the man of science untrammelled by the shackles of the past.'[19] Worse, the clergy might be tempted along new and dangerous paths. Smith knew of the historic role of the clergyman as troublemaker, disturber of the social peace, *prophetae*. Could this role not be repeated in an age of religious and social uncertainty? 'Here is a great body of the very flower of our morality, as well as of our culture, committed to a calling the existence of which is bound up, so far as we can see, certainly with theism, if not supernatural religion. Supposing religion fails, what would the clergy do? Would they transform themselves into teachers of ethics and social guides? Would they starve? Would some of them be drawn into revolution and thus add to the seething elements of disturbances? A celibate priest is well prepared for adventure, and he may hope, however vainly, by throwing himself into a social revolution to find his authority anew. Clergymen read and think. Must not the mental state of some of them already be uneasy?'[20]

This, as events would at least partly substantiate, was a clear-eyed prophecy, for the role of 'teachers of ethics and social guides' would attract many liberal clergymen whose doubts about traditional Christianity threatened to leave them adrift in a secular sea. In fact, Smith had his eye fixed on a development already under way. To him the emerging 'social gospel' was both a sign of the religious malaise of the time and an example of the clergy's search for a new justification. 'Almost all the churches are troubled with heterodoxy,' he noted, 'and are trying clergymen for heresy. Quite as significant is the growing tendency of the pulpit to concern itself less with religious dogma and more with the estate of man in his present world.'[21] That coincidence was left without further comment, but Smith's perception was remarkably shrewd.

Yet Goldwin Smith could hardly object to the efforts being made by late nineteenth-century Protestant ministers to bring religion to bear upon social questions. Or at least he could hardly object and remain consistent. After all, he too judged religion by its social utility. Indeed, he had long held, and taught, that the nineteenth-century liberal capitalist order was itself part of God's grand design. 'The laws of production and distribution of wealth,' Professor Smith had declared during his inaugural lecture at Oxford in 1859, '... are the most beautiful and wonderful of the natural laws of God. To buy in the cheapest and sell in the dearest market, the supposed concentration of economic selfishness, is simply to fulfil the command of the Creator.'[22] Protestant Christianity was closely allied with the spirit of commerce and competitive enterprise. 'Capital and credit are the life of commercial enterprise,' he wrote in 1889. 'The Gospel inculcates the self-denial which is necessary to the accumulation of capital; and to say the least, it does not discourage the honesty which is the foundation of credit.'[23] The Nazarene carpenter's son may have thought he was building a church, but evidently it turned out to be a bank!

Given such faith in the divine origins of the nineteenth-century laissez-faire economic order, it is little wonder that Smith distrusted and denounced those Christians who tried to suggest alternative interpretations of the social teachings of their religion. Attempts to 'merge the theological and the social question,' he insisted, would only contribute to the victory of the secular over the sacred and the further decline of religion. Nor could he countenance any suggestion that Christ had been to any school of political economy other than the one directed by Adam Smith. It was true, he admitted, that Christ had sometimes used the rhetoric of social radicalism, but that had to be understood within the context of the small peasant society of Galilee. (This was an adept application of the methods taught by the higher critics.) The essential Christian message could not be confused with modern political ideology. 'Nor is Jesus, as some have called him, a socialist or a leveller. He preaches no social revolution. It is with the Kingdom of God that he deals throughout, not in any sense the Kingdom of this world.'[24]

Such a contention was, of course, quite inconsistent with Smith's repeated claim that God's worldly scheme was revealed in the political economy of Manchester. But perhaps he thought he had escaped the contradiction by insisting on what might be called a pre-Darwinian view of the laws of political economy as 'natural laws' fixed forever at the time of creation. They were scientific precepts, not ethical teachings or mere products of historical conditioning. 'Political economy,' Smith proclaimed in 1884, 'is not social morality: it simply teaches the laws which govern the production, accumulation, and distribution of wealth.'[25] But just as natural selection had stopped Paley's divine clock, so too the 'hidden hand' of Smith's natural economic universe was gradually being revealed. The historical methods of the higher critics, which introduced relativism into the discussion of biblical teachings, were being turned with similar results on the supposedly immutable laws of political economy. As W.J. Ashley, the newly appointed professor of political economy at the University of Toronto, contended in 1888, classical political economy could claim 'only a relative truth.'[26]

Such heresy was no real surprise to Goldwin Smith. Religious scepticism, he had repeated almost ad nauseam, would naturally be followed by the questioning of social verities, though oddly enough his own religious doubts never shook his faith in the economic convictions he had acquired in his youth. Consequently, where his religious doubts made him sympathetic to troubled clergymen, he had nothing but scorn for those who deviated from the paths of economic righteousness. Henry George's single tax, Edward Bellamy's 'Nationalism,' socialism, and feminism were all among the newly spawned social doctrines that Smith found propounded by those 'Prophets of Unrest' who polluted a world where religious faith was in decay. Few passages reveal as much about Smith's own social philosophy, a Manchester liberalism hardened into reaction, as one drawn from his review of Edward Bellamy's *Looking Backward* (published, like so much of Smith's writing, in both the United States and Canada). 'There is a general feeling abroad that the stream is drawing near a cataract now, and there are apparent grounds for the surmise,' the Cassandra of the Grange warned. 'There is everywhere in the social frame an outward unrest, which as usual is the sign of fundamental change within. Old creeds have given way ... Social science, if it is to take the place of religion as a conservative force, has not yet developed itself or taken firm hold on the popular mind. The rivalries of factions and demagogues have almost everywhere introduced universal suffrage. The poorer classes are freshly possessed of political power, and have conceived boundless notions of the changes which, by exercising it, they may make in their own favour. They are just in that twilight of education in which chimeras stalk.'[27]

By the 1880s, wherever he looked he thought he saw the bonds of intellectual, moral, and social constraint bursting. Anarchy seemed just around the corner. The view from the Grange suggested circumstances similar to those which had preceded the French Revolution, an event as worthy of celebration as 'the Earthquake at Lisbon or the Black Plague.' The signs of incipient nihilism were many, including those 'female votaries and coadjutors in the unsexed female students who go about with their hair cut short, smoking in the streets.' The Darwins, Spencers, and Comtes had taught that this world was man's only existence, and consequently 'social chimeras' that promised immediate material satisfaction won increasing popularity. 'Prophets have arisen,' he wrote, 'the St. Simons, the Proudhons, the Karl Marxes, the Lassalles, modern counterparts of John Ball, Muntzer and John of Leyden, with materialistic science in the place of Millenarian religion.'[28]

These ruminations on the decline and fall of just about everything and everybody that Goldwin Smith identified with civilization were the advanced symptoms of a severe case of 'cultural despair.'[29] His anxieties about the bleak future arose from a sense of loneliness and alienation in a world that seemed increasingly oblivious to the religious and social values that had once been all but taken for granted. Yet he had nothing substantial to offer as a panacea for the crisis he detected. Certainly the only 'social science' he had to offer as a substitute for religion as a 'conservative force' was a repetition of the well-worn clichés of mid-Victorian liberalism. To those who, like Henry George, proposed a new version of political economy, Smith's response was two parts complacency and one part denunciation. The result was brilliant, bitter, and ultimately barren rhetoric. 'Human society,' he wrote in *The Week* in 1884, 'like everything else in the universe science reveals, is imperfect in structure, though, as we hope or believe, as religious men at all events hope and believe, it advances through cycles of gradual improvement towards ultimate perfection. The accumulation of wealth brings with it undeni-able evils, overgrown fortunes, idleness, waste, luxury, frivolous display. Yet, on the whole, it has not only been manifestly helpful but indispen-sable to progress. Without it we could have had no great undertakings of any kind, no commerce but the pettiest barter; no science nor anything which science has brought; we would still be dwelling in caves and chumping acorns.' All was evidently for the best in the best of all improving worlds. Nor would it do to try to hurry on the process of perfection. 'Nor would the distribution of places in the cave and of acorns be more equal than the distribution of wealth in a civilized country: the stronger man should always take more than his share.' Smith himself was evidently capable of a little social Darwinism when the occasion demanded. And he was also capable of preaching the gospel of wealth: the rich man would surely always regard his economic success as a trust to be fulfilled in rendering service to humanity. Only the 'sybarite' would live only for the pleasures of luxury, a 'vile and miserable existence.' There were those who were worse. 'But the lowest of sybarites is nothing like so noxious to the community or practically so great an enemy to its progress as is the preacher of plunder, class emnity and social war.' Here were the confessions of a 'Liberal of the old school' whose jeremiads demonstrated the accuracy of his own dictum that 'there is no reactionary like the exhausted Reformer.'[30]

Certainly his deep depression was out of step with hopeful spirit of the age. Neither a 'secularist' like W.D. LeSueur nor a liberal protestant like Principal Grant could abide Smith's persistent predictions of moral chaos and doomsday. Responding to Smith's warnings about the dire prospects of a moral interregnum, LeSueur, the resident positivist, argued that the separation of religion and morality was both necessary and beneficial. A new morality based on natural laws, freed from the Christian preoccupa-tion with the sin of man and the corruption of society, would allow men to fulfil their human potential. 'The future of morality,' he argued, 'depends upon the extent to which men shall in the future be delivered from beliefs and conceptions that cramp and pervert their minds, and prevent them from realizing their capacities for good, and acting upon the promptings of their better natures.'[31]

For LeSueur religious systems served their purpose in the evolutionary process; but that process had reached a new level in which morality would rest upon 'such truth as [men] can discover in nature and in human relations.' Nothing that Herbert Spencer's enthusiastic Ottawa disciple wrote would have convinced Smith in the slightest. Indeed, his worst fears were documented by LeSueur's almost jubilant description of what he believed, and hoped, to be the true spirit of the age. 'Let anyone think but of the change that has come over society in the last generation in the matter of belief in the miraculous,' LeSueur wrote in 1880; 'let any man of mature years compare the intellectual atmosphere of today with that which surrounded him as a youth; let him but glance at our literature, and see how it has thrown off the fetters of theology; let him but think of our science and its fundamental assumption of unvarying law and if he does not conclude that the faith which found other faiths "hollow and worm eaten" is itself yielding to decay, he will be blind, indeed, to the signs of the times. True the land is dotted everywhere with churches, and more are rising; but are these churches, or those who minister in them, grappling with the real problems of the age, are they helping to clarify human thought, or to simplify human conduct, or are they, mainly, distracting and enfeebling the minds of their followers by impossible blendings of mundane and ultramundane morality, and of a natural and non-natural order of things?' The whole idea of a religion of humanity, which LeSueur proposed, was for Goldwin Smith a contradiction. The brotherhood of man without the fatherhood of God was an illusion.[32]

If Smith was sceptical about the validity of the Canadian Comte's proposed substitute for religion, he found Principal Grant's efforts to combine Christianity and modern thought equally unsatisfactory. Grant and Smith disagreed about virtually every important subject except, perhaps, Henry George, whom they both denounced as a rabble-rouser. On both the destiny of Canada and the destiny of man, they occupied opposite barricades. This well-known conflict, on the surface, appears to be a clash of liberal and conservative philosophies.[33] Yet the question of which one was the liberal seems more complex when fundamental assumptions about man and religion are examined. From this perspective Grant is the liberal anxious to bring theology into tune with modern thought. His muscular optimism was rooted in a belief that modern thought strengthened Christianity; Smith's pervasive angst was founded on the conviction that modern thought destroyed Christianity.

The contrast was evident in many of the Smith–Grant duels. In *Canada and the Canadian Question* Smith expressed real as well as rehearsed pessimism. Grant's spirited refutation exuded optimism about Canada's prospects. Where Smith saw religious unrest everywhere, Grant pronounced the religious condition of Canada excellent and improving. ('There is faith in the heart of young Canada,' he wrote in 1893.) In 1894 the editor of *The Week* invited Grant to comment on Smith's newly published collection, *Essays on Questions of the Day*. While none of the essays touched directly on theological problems, Grant recognized that a mood of pessimism informed the entire book, whether it discussed economics, prohibition, woman suffrage, or the empire. Together the essays were nothing less than an unrelieved lamentation for the unreasoning and hopeless state of mankind. Smith was too negative for Grant, too narrow-minded, too much the controversialist to allow any ray of light to break through the gloom. That certainly was not Grant's mood. Even more strongly than the agnostic LeSueur, the Presbyterian Grant contended that the best was yet to be. Smith's forebodings about the decline of religion, Grant retorted, were nothing more than a confession of his own loss of faith.[34] After all, the Victorian age had recorded triumph after triumph for the human spirit and social betterment, and still 'the dawn of a still better day may be discerned.' Any fair-minded observer would have to admit that 'wherever there are human beings, they are living now under more benign heavens than any previous age, and, better still, there is a striving upward to the light everywhere. All the influences and inventions of modern times tend to multiply opportunities for men and women to live a higher life, and just as sure as day follows night, there is a good time coming ...' Grant could find no argument or evidence in Smith's philosophy to shake his own conviction that reasonable men could conquer passion, for God himself was on the side of the reasonable. 'Why should any man despair,' Grant wrote in a mood of Hegelian idealism, 'who knows that reason is the organ of the Holy Spirit, and His office is to reveal the Son of Man to man?'[35] The power of positive Presbyterian thinking gave no ground to the dilettantish doubts of a transplanted English don.

III

If Smith observed the irony of the alliance between the agnostic and the Presbyterian, he appears, uncharacteristically, to have allowed it to pass. Yet that alliance, informal and undeclared as it was, was an extremely significant one: it revealed a growing liberal, modernist consensus among Canadian intellectuals. The old moral consensus, founded on religion, was breaking up gradually, to be superseded by a new secular order founded on science and materialism. For Smith that meant the fearful prospect of 'the idea of existence without God.' For LeSueur it meant a welcome liberation from superstition and the development of a naturalistic ethic of human brotherhood freed from the false hopes and fears of the hereafter. 'A true morality,' he claimed, 'it will be seen more and more as time advances, requires the acceptance of this life, not as something provisional merely, but as the appointed, and so far as we know, the only theatre of man's activities.' In short, the banishment of the sacred and the triumph of the secular. A liberal Presbyterian like George Grant was also ready to face a future defined by science and a new philosophy, but not in any expectation that religion would disappear. Christianity buttressed by idealism was vital enough to encompass modern thought. For Grant that meant erasing the boundary between the sacred and the secular by emphasizing the application of Christian teaching to society.[36]

Goldwin Smith, the sceptic who needed God, found neither the positivist nor the Presbyterian convincing. He was left with despair – in the comfort of the Grange. He may have been wrong in believing that the death of God would lead to moral chaos and social upheaval. The deterioration of Christian morality and the emergence of secularism was perhaps only part of a broader socio-economic change that caused the fragmentation of the old moral consensus and in turn led to the decline of religious belief.[37] But he was correct in his assertion that he lived in a time when the meaning and purpose of religion, especially the Christian religion, was experiencing a fundamental metamorphosis. The final outcome would take time to emerge, for religious rhetoric and sentiment remained powerful even as religious belief dissipated. 'You must wash the vessel more thoroughly,' Smith told Professor John Tyndall, 'before your experiment can be fully tried.'[38]

4

Positivism, Secular Thought, and the Religion of Humanity

'Scepticism is becoming more general and is protean in its adaptability to circumstance,' a worried Protestant clergyman wrote in 1880. 'There is philosophical scepticism for the cultured and popular scepticism for the masses, the Reviews for the select, Colonel Ingersoll for the people.' That was a neat summary of the religious atmosphere of 'the times,' when 'the work of a conscientious minister is becoming increasing difficult.'[1] Indeed, the very publication in which the Reverend Hugh Pedley expressed his uneasiness, the *Canadian Monthly and National Review*, frequently carried expressions of philosophical scepticism, mainly from the Ottawa savant and civil servant W.D. LeSueur. Moreover, not long before Pedley's lament Toronto had been the scene of a vigorous controversy surrounding a visit by Colonel Robert Ingersoll, the popular American sceptic and iconoclast. The theatrical colonel's disciples were numerous enough, well enough organized, and certainly aggressive enough to make the local clergy nervous. And Toronto was not the only source of concern: there were aggressive free thinkers and associations sprinkled at least from Montreal to western Ontario by the 1880s. Both the 'cultured' and the 'masses' were being served a fairly frequent diet of free thought.

I

'Men do not believe what they once did,' William Dawson LeSueur wrote in 1884; 'they cannot believe as they once did; though they may religiously utter the old formulas, and close their eyes harder and harder against the growing light.'[2] Such sentiments expressed by a positivist in the Post Office – even as sophisticated a one as W.D. LeSueur –can hardly be taken as conclusive evidence that religious belief in Canada was in imminent danger of disappearing. Indeed, LeSueur's successful career in the public service, his election to the Royal Society of Canada – delayed though it was – and his acceptance by the most respectable literary and historical organizations of his time, suggests that his views were not perceived as seriously subversive. Only that most cautious of Liberals, W.L.M. King, found LeSueur's writings threatening, and that was because the Ottawa writer was not sufficiently reverential toward King's grandfather.[3]

Nevertheless, the importance of LeSueur, or rather of what he represented, should not be underestimated. He was certainly taken seriously during his lifetime when he engaged in lengthy debates about religious, philosophical, and ethical questions. At a somewhat elevated, gentlemanly level, LeSueur exemplified exactly that which made Goldwin Smith and others uneasy: the serious questioning of religious belief by some Canadians. Yet that questioning took place within terms that were not so far beyond the limits of orthodoxy as to prevent LeSueur from retaining a secure place in the small intellectual establishment of late nineteenth-century Canada.

That W.D. LeSueur was a defender of Auguste Comte's positivism, Charles Darwin's theory of natural selection, and Herbert Spencer's naturalistic ethics and that he was also an admirer of Saint-Beuve, Matthew Arnold, Thomas Carlyle ('with all his faults one of the noblest of human souls'), and Ralph Waldo Emerson ('a pure soul if ever there was one'), might suggest nothing more than a confused eclecticism. But in fact this 'critical spirit' developed a fairly consistent philosophy of progressivism and humanism over his lengthy career as a literary man.[4] Despite his commitment to a naturalistic philosophy which insisted that man and society had to be understood in secular rather than theological terms and that natural, not divine, laws were the key to man's behaviour, he was above all a man of the golden mean. LeSueur insistently rejected all forms of dogmatism, religious or scientific, as 'nothing but the temper of command unreasonably exercised.'[5] Yet behind this apparent open-mindedness lay a firmly held set of convictions. 'My position,' he wrote in response to an attack which *The Toronto Mail* had launched against his scepticism in 1880, '... was – to put it briefly – that morality is a thing of natural growth, that it consists essentially of certain just and benevolent feelings – with their appropriate outcome in action – towards our fellow beings, and that no system of religion, past or present, can claim to have invented it, or to be alone capable of maintaining it in vigour.'[6]

One of LeSueur's principal concerns was to free moral teaching from religious belief; he considered this as urgent as Goldwin Smith considered it dangerous. Where Smith thought that religious sanction assured moral conduct, LeSueur argued exactly the opposite position. Defending Herbert Spencer against Goldwin Smith (Spencer himself had called Smith 'the bitterest bigot among those classed as orthodox'7), LeSueur wrote that 'it is the weakness not the strength of the theological and ultramundane doctrines that they lead, and have led, men to regard with more-or-less acquiescence the sufferings of this evil time.'8 And he was equally convinced of the error of those liberal Christians who argued that Darwinian evolution could be readily integrated into traditional religious belief, and those conservative Christians who rejected evolution completely. To the first group – to writers like John Fiske and Lyman Abbott – he replied that nothing could be 'gained by trying to read old theology into new science.' To the latter, the conservatives, he pointed out that evolution was a scientific hypothesis which did not claim to explain final causes. And for both camps he had a single message: 'The only escape from a situation that really threatens moral anarchy lies in the recognition of the fact that the universe, as related to man, has lessons to teach; and that these, as revealed as truths of reason to the mind and conscience, are not less authoritative than if thundered on affrighted ears from the cloud-capped summit of Sinai.'9

Despite his insistence on the autonomy of the natural world, a point he made repeatedly in his frequent exchanges with the Kingston feminist and theological liberal Agnes Maule Machar, LeSueur was far from rejecting theism. Modern science might impinge upon religious belief bringing into doubt certain traditional dogmas – special creation and providential design being examples – but that merely meant that some religious positions required rethinking to strengthen and clarify them. There was no necessary conflict between science and religion, 'between the scientific impulse to know that which can be known, and the religious impulse to worship a Power that cannot be known, and to frame higher sanctions for life than those of the market place and the law courts.' But where would a Comtean theist turn for guidance in formulating a modern ethical system? The answer, surprising as it may seem, was to Jesus Christ. As depicted in the New Testament, Christ was a man who 'dealt with life in the light of eternal principles ... raised the hearts and roused the consciences of men ... made truth and duty supreme over all lower motives, and pronounced a condemnation that has rung and shall ring, through the ages against every unworthy form of compromise, against every bartering of gold for dross, against every act that could dim the light of truth in the human soul. He was the highest type of "idealist" ... one who presented life in its highest conceivable aspect, as a struggle towards perfection.'[10]

LeSueur obviously fulfilled to near perfection Goldwin Smith's description of the modern thinker who believed himself emancipated from orthodoxy in religion, but who in reality still operated within its confines. The vessel had not been thoroughly cleansed. Yet there is something even more significant to be discovered in LeSueur's Comtean, Christian humanism than merely an example of the persistence of Christian rhetoric. Like many others of his generation, LeSueur lived in a twilight region between science and religion, convinced that the traditional claims of Christianity could no longer be defended, but unwilling to accept the total claims of scientific naturalism and materialism.[11] 'Materialism,' he wrote in rejecting it, 'is the refuge of minds that have been immaturely freed of spiritualism, or perhaps we may more fitly say, spiritism.'[12] The problem, as he saw it, was that the late nineteenth century was 'an age of intellectual terrorism when men are afraid and ashamed of being unscientific.' He defined his own position very well in replying to the charge made by the lord bishop of Ontario, the Reverend J.T. Lewis, that modern thought was just a polite name for agnosticism. LeSueur defended himself by arguing that modern intellectuals faced two essential problems: 'One is how to *put back* the thoughts of men so that all that was credible to their forefathers may be credible to them. The other is how to *put forward* men's thoughts so that they may harmonize with the new knowledge the world has acquired – so that a new intellectual and moral equilibrium may be established.'[13] Caught as he himself was between these supposed poles, LeSueur offered a humanistic ethic of Christianity without theology. This Christian liberalism, far from representing an unpopular or radical position, held much in common with a wide range of efforts to reformulate religious and ethnical teaching in late nineteenth-century Canada. 'The atheism which is wanted today,' LeSueur wrote, as he proceeded to demolish the lord bishop of Ontario a second time, 'is that which will strike from the Christian conception of God all – and there is much – that is oppressive to the heart, the conscience and the intellect. But the more strictly and courageously this duty is performed, the more devoutly shall we cherish whatever in that connection can nourish our moral life and build us up to the full stature of perfect men.'[14] As a definition of the Christian liberalism that was to become increasingly dominant in Canadian Protestantism by the end of the nineteenth century, LeSueur's statement could not be greatly improved upon.[15]

People who agreed with LeSueur concluded that science and the higher criticism had not only shaken the foundations of traditional belief. The advances of science demonstrated the heights to which the human intellect could reach. 'The prodigious development of natural science' was 'the cardinal fact of the nineteenth century.' Was it surprising then, LeSueur asked, that men waited upon science 'to heal their diseases, and even cleanse their iniquities?'[16] If the achievements of science were so impressive, who could doubt that a new ethical code could be evolved? That was certainly the conclusion of one aggressive defender of 'modern thought' against what he viewed as the outworn creed of men like the evangelists Moody and Sankey and even of so modern a theologian as G.M. Grant. 'Science is crowding new ideas upon us with wonderful rapidity,' LeSueur wrote under his pseudonym 'Laon,' 'but science does not speak to the heart, for a man may understand all mysteries yet be lacking that which alone makes him, in the highest sense, a man – Charity. What the world wants now is a union of the scientific spirit with the profoundly ethical and human spirit of the Gospel; and then, perhaps – certainly not until then – will humanity have entered upon the last and happiest phase of its career.'[17]

Once again, what is of peculiar interest here, apart from the naïve optimism of the writer, is the concern to retain the superstructure of Christian ethical teaching stripped of its theological underpinning. It is apparent, therefore, that what was unacceptable to progressive proponents of modern culture was not the whole of the Christian belief system, but rather its supernatural sanction and the traditional theological system that gave Christianity its meaning. Religion and culture, the sacred and the secular, were thus identified as one. Christian ethical belief could not only survive its liberation from orthodox theological claims, it would become even more widely accepted and practised as a code of individual and social conduct. Such free thinkers had no wish to relinquish the whole of their religious inheritance. And unlike Goldwin Smith, to say nothing of more orthodox Christians, these intellectuals believed that ethics could be preserved without the support of outworn creeds. 'The teaching that cannot rouse the conscience without insulting the intellect is not adapted to the nineteenth century.'[18] That sentence might have served as the touchstone for a growing number of English Canadian critics of traditional Christianity. But the limits of that criticism were accurately measured by the *Toronto Evening Mail*'s religious editorialist, who noted in 1881 that 'the age in which we live, in spite of all assertions to the contrary is eminently religious ... Even the scepticism of the day is, in a sense, religious. Agnosticism differs from all other passing fashions of doubt in this, that it proclaims the sacredness of duty, laying stress upon the sacred obligations of the golden rule.'[19] Yet the *Mail*'s definition of religion – essentially ethical conduct – was as revealing of the general atmosphere of the times as it was accurate as a description of the humanistic religion of a W.D. LeSueur.

II

The polite debate over scepticism and religious belief carried on among the intellectuals – the LeSueurs, Dawsons, Watsons, and Machars – in the reviews was only one sign of the growth of religious doubt in late Victorian Canada. There were many others. One was the attention the daily press gave to religious questions. The *Toronto Evening Mail*, for example, regularly carried sophisticated Saturday editorials on current religious controversies, and most other newspapers made sure that their readers' religious interests were catered to. So too there was a large amount of news about religious matters, especially if it contained any hint of scandal. In the 1870s the case of *Tilton* v *Beecher* in the United States was widely publicized: had the famous preacher Henry Ward Beecher seduced Elizabeth Tilton, a parishioner's wife?[20] The radical Toronto weekly *The National* reproduced almost verbatim reports of the trial in 1875, and many other newspapers provided regular summaries. In the 1880s the efforts of the militant agnostic Charles Bradlaugh to claim his seat in the British Parliament without taking a religious oath was followed in detail by both the *Mail* and the *Globe* in Toronto. Nor was the spice of Bradlaugh's association with the flamboyant Annie Besant missed.[21] And, of course, local heresy trials and troubles, such as those of the Reverend D.J. Macdonnell, Professor George Workman and, later, the Reverend George Jackson, were given special attention in the daily press.

A prurient interest in ecclesiastical scandal and theological quarrelling was hardly a sign of spreading religious doubt. But any evidence of clerical imperfection was speedily gathered up by the critics of Christianity to advance the cause of free thought. 'Mr. Macdonnell,' one secularist wrote,' has simply caught the spirit of the age and proposes to open the Westminster Confession of Faith and apply his intellectual scalpel to it.' Any church that tried to suppress the liberal dissenters could be charged with authoritarianism, even popery. But one that admitted that some of its traditional doctrines were no longer demonstrable left itself open to another accusation. 'The decadence of doctrinal Christianity is thus placed beyond doubt,' the same writer insisted. 'In England, Germany, the United States, and even to some extent in Conservative Canada, Rationalism is permeating all classes, especially the educated classes.'[22] *Secular Thought*, commenting on the struggle between the Reverend Albert Carman and the Reverend George Jackson over the higher criticism struck a telling blow in a different direction. 'The most comical part of Mr. Jackson's position,' the editor concluded, after first expressing his disdain for Carman's obscurantism, 'is the fact that he thinks it is possible to reject the Biblical myths and traditions because they are contradicted by science and philosophy, and yet to retain them as revelations of God's will in spiritual matters. As if it were possible to erect any substantially true and useful ethics upon a false and absurd foundation.'[23]

Protestant ministers frequently expressed deep concern and growing anxiety about the threat of advancing infidelity and open criticism of Christianity and the church. The Anglican bishop of Ontario at least twice publicly preached against LeSueur's opinions.[24] Archbishop Lynch of the Roman Catholic church forbade, with threat of punishment, his parishioners from attending free-thought meetings, causing one anti-clerical wag to observe that though 'the Bulls of Rome were long ago emasculated, yet, strangely enough, they still keep *multiplying!*'[25] Fulminations against atheism, agnosticism, and materialism were regular fare for the readers of the Methodist *Christian Guardian*.[26] By the late 1870's many orthodox Protestants probably would have agreed with the editor of the *Canadian Methodist Review* when he asserted that 'never were the attacks upon revealed religion more vehement and virulent than at the present time.'[27]

By that date free thought and anticlerical attitudes certainly had reached beyond the intellectual quarterlies and reviews. Nathanael Burwash recalled that as a young clergyman he had discovered that 'many of our most gifted and intelligent young men were drifting away from the evangelical faith under the influence of the modern scientific spirit.'[28] He was not alone in making this observation. One anonymous writer in 1877 expressed the conviction that, with the spread of popular education, the clergy were having an increasingly difficult time defending those portions of the Scriptures that were 'hopelessly at variance with common sense.'[29] And the young Reverend Hugh Pedley, of Cobourg, Ontario, who a few years later found consolation in Edward Bellamy's writings and became a Christian socialist, complained in 1880 of the inadequacy of theological education. A clergyman, he wrote, 'should not commence building his theology till he has struck down through the sand of traditional belief to the solid rock of ascertained fact. He should be able to deal bravely and skillfully with the actual world of today. He should be qualified to master the great flood of free thinking.'[30]

'Flood' may have been an exaggeration, but there was certainly more than a trickle of free thought in late nineteenth-century Canada. The activities and associations of free thinkers and secularists began to make their appearance in the 1870s, sometimes in the most improbable places. In the autumn of 1874 a heated controversy broke out in the small eastern Ontario town of Napanee. The trouble started when the town council withdrew from an agreement to rent the town hall for a series of free-thought lectures. The organizer of the meeting was a thirty four-year-old farmer – his specialty was bee-keeping – from nearby Selby named Allen Pringle. The son of a well-known Loyalist family in the area,[31] Pringle had briefly studied medicine and taught school before returning to farm in his native area. Though his family was strongly religious, Allen apparently lost his faith at an early age – perhaps at medical school. His first wife, who died shortly after their marriage at twenty-two years of age, apparently shared his dissenting views, for her gravestone epitaph read:

> Born to no sect and had no private road
> But looked from nature up to nature's God

and concluded:

> Her life, tho' short was pure and good
> Her mind was stored with choicest food
> From creeds and faiths and forms apart
> Her religion was works, her grace of the heart.[32]

Having quietly spread the secularist word for a few years in the Napanee area, Pringle and some friends decided the time had come for a more public airing of the free-thought doctrine. In the fall of 1874 they invited Benjamin Franklin Underwood, a prominent American free-thought lecturer,[33] to deliver a series of three lectures. The mayor of Napanee agreed to rent the town hall to Pringle, but when the lecture topics were advertised a storm of opposition erupted. The titles of the proposed lectures explain the uproar: 'Evolution vs. Creation,' 'What Liberalism Offers as a Substitute for Christianity,' and 'Fallacies and Assumptions of Theologians Regarding the Bible and Christianity.' The council, under strong pressure from some of the citizenry, tried to force the mayor to revoke the contract for the hall rental. The mayor, in turn, urged Pringle to find another hall. But when that failed – and one suspects that Pringle did not try very hard – Pringle and Underwood and their supporters attempted to break through a hostile crowd, and the local constabulary, to gain entrance to the town hall. But they were forced to beat a hasty retreat to the local hotel. The following day Pringle convinced a performing group that it should give up the local music hall, for a substantial price, to allow Underwood to deliver his lectures. For three nights he entertained and instructed a large and apparently even sympathetic audience.[34]

Pringle was not a man to let the issue of his right to rent the town hall drop. He believed that free speech was at stake, and he therefore sued the town for breach of contract. The case took nearly four years to work its way through the courts of Ontario. In 1878 the Court of Queen's Bench ruled against Pringle. The decision must have confirmed the worst fears of the secularists, for it was based on the argument that Christianity was part of the law of Canada and that therefore any attack on that religion was unlawful. The learned judges concluded that it was perfectly proper for the Napanee town council to break a contract with a group intending to use the hall for an unlawful purpose. 'The guardians of the town hall in Napanee,' Chief Justice Harrison wrote, 'simply refused, when they learned his [Underwood's] peculiar views, to permit him to express them in that hall. This was not more than the exercise of the legal right which they possess of refusing to allow their property to be used for what the law holds to be an illegal purpose.'[35]

The legal costs were heavy, and Pringle decided that an appeal to the Supreme Court would be useless.[36] But his disappointment at the legal ruling was counterbalanced by his conviction that the fight had to continue in the public arena. In July 1875, less than a year after the first controversy, McNeill's Music Hall, 'the best and most commodious hall in Napanee,' provided the setting for a return engagement for Underwood; this time he was to debate on four consecutive nights with the Reverend John Marples, a Presbyterian minister from Bracebridge, Ontario. More than three hundred people gathered each night to watch these gladiators joust. For two nights they disputed the resolution 'That Atheism, Materialism and Modern Scepticism are Illogical and Contrary to Reason.' The two final rounds were devoted to the proposition 'That the Bible, consisting of the Old and the New Testaments, contains evidence beyond all Books of Divine Origin.'

According to Phillips Thompson, who covered the event in great detail for *The National*, the event evoked widespread interest well beyond the Napanee town limits. ('We shall print a large extra number of papers to supply the anticipated demand,' *The National* reassured its readers.[37]) Those in attendance, according to Thompson's estimate, were divided almost equally between the two camps, as was the case with the organizing committee, which included, on the orthodox side, the two local members of the provincial parliament.[38] The first encounter, in which the debaters sharpened their wits on definitions of atheism, God, and materialism, appeared to have been carried by Underwood. In the final night's debate much was said about Paley, Darwin, and biblical prophecy. Perhaps because local clergymen overcame their initial prejudice against the outsider Marples and turned out for the final debates in large numbers, the tide was turned in favour of the religionists. The calm atmosphere that had prevailed at the earlier stages vanished on the final evening. Underwood declared that 'there were so many admirable elements in the character of Christ that all must admire. So were there in that of Buddha. Max Muller said his teachings and parables were equal to those of the New Testament. No precept of the Book could be proved original.' At that point 'hisses, yells and interruptions rose from all parts of the hall.' Marples, always a Christian gentleman, had to quiet the crowd, which began to threaten the American visitor. In the end, Thompson reported, the majority appeared to side with orthodoxy, 'but this, of course, was anticipated from the outset.'

These had been hot, exciting nights in Napanee. The debate was a serious one. The townspeople greatly impressed the somewhat radical and vaguely bohemian newspaperman from Toronto. 'The descendants of the U.E. Loyalists form a large element of the population and Napanee is probably one of the most thoroughly Canadian towns in the province. Many of the citizens display an intelligence, culture and liberality, in the best and broadest sense of that term, that a stranger would seek in vain in much more pretentious places.'[39] Some of them continued, no doubt, at least for the remainder of the summer, to mull over the momentous questions which the great debate had raised.

Certainly the debate's main sponsor, Allen Pringle, must have been satisfied with his success in bringing the light of rationalism to rural Ontario. Whatever Pringle's agricultural achievements – in 1893 he represented the Canadian Beekeepers' Association at the Chicago World's Fair – he was widely read in religious and scientific literature. A Darwinist and a materialist, this Canadian Ingersoll devoted much of his intellectual energy and erudition to clergy-baiting.[40] For example, when the *Napanee Express*, in 1877, published a burlesque on Darwinism, Pringle responsed belligerently. 'Regarding the vexed question of the origin of man upon this earth,' he wrote, 'there is the scientific solution of the matter, and the theological account, two theories as wide apart as possible. But before bestowing too much shallow ridicule upon the scientific presentment of the question, religionists would do well to clear away some of the many absurdities which cluster around their own theory. They ought to tell us for instance, if the "first man" was "made" less than 6000 years ago, when, how, and by whom, were the people made that Geology and Archeology demonstrate to have existed on this earth long ages before Adam's time?'[41] So much for Bishop Ussher!

Pringle was a prolific writer of letters to the editor and the author of some of the most polemical pamphlets published in late nineteenth-century English Canada. Phillips Thompson described the Selby secularist as 'a farmer by vocation who has rather the appearance of a professional or a businessman. He is a tall, straight, handsome man approaching middle age, of fine presence and intellectual aspect ... His manner is frank and open, and the leading part he has taken in Free Thought discussions has shown him to possess great activity and independence of character.'[42] But Pringle did not relish platform debate. So, having challenged Marples to debate, he invited Underwood to defend the free-thought position.

The Reverend Marples too was elated by the Napanee debate. So much so, in fact, that he decided to resign his regular pulpit to become a full-time 'opponent of infidel teaching ... confronting in public those who attack the truths of the Gospel.'[43] Underwood evidently also was satisfied with his Canadian excursion. He agreed to a rematch in Toronto in October 1875, when four more nights of debate were sponsored by the Toronto Liberal Association – a free-thought club, not a political party. Once again the air was filled with quotations from Darwin, Huxley, Haeckel, Paley, Agassiz, and the Scriptures. Several hundred listeners turned out each night to sessions presided over by such liberal clergymen as D.J. Macdonnell, T.J. Robb, and T.W. Jeffrey. *The National* reported that Underwood evoked the loudest applause when he praised 'Christ as a reformer and iconoclast who, were he to re-appear on earth today, would affiliate as of old with the abused, the downtrodden and the outcasts, and would find a readier acceptance in the halls of the Infidels than beneath the glided steeples of a formal Christianity.'[44] The Reverend Marples was vanquished.

The threads of free-thought activities are difficult to pull together, for much of the documentation has disappeared. By the 1880s the focus of activity was the Canadian Secular Union, successor to the Freethinkers' Association founded in Toronto in 1877. In 1884 an Englishman named Charles Watts settled in Toronto, having been invited by local free thinkers. He had previously been closely associated with Charles Bradlaugh and the free-thought *National Reformer*, but had broken with Bradlaugh and Annie Besant in 1877 over the publication of birth-control literature.[45] In Canada he assumed the editorship of *Secular Thought*, the principal organ of free-thought news and discussion in Canada from the 1880s to the end of the Laurier era.[46] Watts combined free-thought advocacy with radical activities and membership in the Knights of Labor, suggesting, not surprisingly, association with Phillips Thompson. One speech, delivered under the auspices of the Bellamyite Nationalist Club of Toronto, was entitled 'The Land, the People and the Coming Struggle,' exactly the title of one of Bradlaugh's frequently delivered lectures.[47]

After Watts returned to England, on Bradlaugh's death in 1891, *Secular Thought* was taken over by a Toronto printer named J. Spencer Ellis. *Secular Thought* published a large amount of material drawn from Great Britain and the United States in addition to comment on Canadian affairs. It took special pleasure in twitting Goldwin Smith for his refusal to adopt free thought; it sneered at spiritualist claims, defended free speech, and denounced every sign of what it considered superstition, whether in the form of orthodoxy, liberal deism, Christian Science, or theosophy. In politics it showed some sympathy for socialism, or at least co-operation, but its chief focus remained religion and science.[48] Its bedrock position was that 'Religion is the very foundation of political and social tyranny; and it is the bogey that frightens the masses into subjection; and today it is the chief agent in perpetuating the ignorance and credulity that make that subjection possible.'[49]

In the 1880s especially, the free-thought movement, led by Charles Watts, William Algie, Phillips Thompson, Allen Pringle, and, in Montreal, where the Pioneer Free Thought Club was established by a transplanted American, Robert Chambliss Adams, gained a certain momentum. Local societies were organized in Welland, St Thomas, Aylmer, Gananoque, Napanee, Belleville, Ottawa, and perhaps elsewhere.[50] For each of these groups the international connection was of great importance. No Canadian could draw an audience like the ones that flocked to hear such stars of the free-thought stage as Colonel Robert G. Ingersoll, who was viewed by Canadian secularists 'as one of the greatest men of the past century.'[51]

The Toronto Free Thought Association, whose president was Phillips Thompson, sponsored Colonel Ingersoll's visit to Canada in the spring of 1880. The colonel, a Civil War veteran and successful lawyer, was the most notorious of American free-thought missionaries. His lectures on such subjects as 'The Gods,' 'The Mistakes of Moses,' and 'Why I Am an Agnostic,' were delivered in a theatrical style that attracted public attention and clerical disapproval.[52] Ingersoll's first Canadian visit proved no exception. In Toronto, on the first evening of his two-night stand, he drew a good audience. But not everyone came to cheer. Along the streets leading to the Royal Opera House 'citizen evangelists passed out a pamphlet "A Warning Against the Fallacies of Ingersoll!"' That naturally provoked the American showman: 'Toronto allowed Ingersoll to speak,' he gloated. 'Scatter a little smallpox upon it.' Then he launched into his tirade on 'the gods,' pointing to the inconsistencies of the Bible, the horrors of religious history, and the wonders of rationalism: 'Free thought built the school house,' he summed up glibly, 'religion built the dungeon. Religion gave the thumbscrew, science gave the plough.'[53] So successful was his first oration that the following evening his audience was 'much more numerous than the previous evening and many more ladies were present.' His speech ranged over the myth of creation to the importance of the family, and included a few crude witticisms about Adam's rib. The meeting ended only after a motion was passed – with only one dissenter – condemning the *Globe* for failing to provide adequate coverage of the gatherings. The colonel then moved on to Ottawa, Montreal, Belleville, and Napanee, where he was no doubt warmly welcomed by Allen Pringle.[54]

Ingersoll's visit created a considerable stir. *Grip* dismissed Ingersoll as a man who 'came to Canada a few weeks ago on a purely business mission. He was engaged by responsible and respectable managers to do a certain amount of blaspheming for a certain amount of money.' *The Christian Guardian* was predictably outraged, and *The Bystander* defended Ingersoll's right to speak but deplored his vulgarity. Goldwin Smith then offered a defence of the clergy that may have made some of them wonder which side he was really supporting. 'In these times the position of the clergy is a most trying one,' *The Bystander* observed. 'Turned as their thoughts constantly are to these questions, and with the knowledge which they professionally possess, it is impossible that their minds should be free from general disquietude.' But if they disguised their doubts it was not, as Ingersoll had claimed, because they did not wish to relinquish their salaries. Rather, it was because they genuinely feared the 'general catastrophe' that would follow the triumph of unbelief, and because of their realization that 'scepticism is unable to devise any code of Ethics better than a rationalized Christianity.'[55]

The attacks on Ingersoll and even Goldwin Smith's attempt to defend rational religion offered Allen Pringle an opportunity to enter the debate once again. In a lengthy pamphlet entitled *Ingersoll in Canada* (the first edition of two thousand was rapidly exhausted) Pringle, 'amidst the pressure of farm work,' took on all comers: George R. Wendling, who had offered a 'secular reply' to Ingersoll; Archbishop Lynch; Goldwin Smith, 'Rationalist'; and the Reverend A.J. Bray, the liberal Protestant editor of the *Canadian Spectator*. Pringle attacked rational explanations for the existence of God, defended evolution by natural selection, ridiculed Christian intolerance, and set forth a position he called 'logical material-ism.' As for those who, like Goldwin Smith and the Reverend Bray, argued that much of traditional belief was no longer essential to Christianity, Pringle replied with scorn. 'Take away from it [Christianity] this obsolete theology (which "is opposed to all reason"),' he retorted, 'and there is nothing left of Christianity; for the morality Christianity contains does not rightly belong to it. It is Pagan ... There is not a single moral precept in the Bible but was taught before the book was written ... Therefore when you take away the dogmas of Christianity – "its obsolete theology" – you take away Christianity itself to all intents and purposes.'[56] The argument was a telling one, one that many orthodox Christians would have applauded, though nothing else in Pringle's armoury would have won their approval. But liberal Protestants would not have been impressed with Pringle's point, for they believed increasingly in Jesus the ethical teacher and social reformer, a Jesus liberated from the constraints of doctrine.[57]

Pringle's defence of Ingersoll against all comers earned him a new notoriety and a prominent place among the leaders of the Secular Union. When his pamphlet was denounced by *The Christian Guardian*, which resorted to a repetition of the design argument to refute him, Pringle penned a lengthy reply. When the Methodist paper declined to print his letter, Pringle published *'Design' in Nature. Replies to the Christian Guardian and the Christian Advocate*. Darwinian evolution had destroyed the design argument forever. 'From the lowest organism – the Monera, which are mere protoplasmic specks of mucous or slime – up to man, the ascent is so gradual as to be almost imperceptible, thus excluding for once and forever the idea of special creation or design.'[58]

The following year Pringle was asked to prepare a lecture for delivery before the Secular Union in Toronto. The then president, M.A. Pidding-ton, read it, and two thousand copies were printed for distribution. This

Archbishop Lynch, by J.W. Bengough. *Grip*, 22 May 1880

time Pringle took up the defence of Charles Bradlaugh against the unfair treatment he had been given in the *Toronto Mail*'s 'Saturday Sermons.' This piece of erudite ridicule included a certain amount of showing-off for the secularists in the Queen City: quotations from the latest English newspapers and the most obscure defences of materialism. Bradlaugh, he said, was a man of humble origins suffering persecution by the upper classes, who feared his appeal with the working classes. He then attacked the Toronto customs officer for confiscating a shipment of Paine's *The Age of Reason* and Voltaire's *Pocket Theology*, which the Yonge Street bookseller W.B. Cooke had ordered.

Now he was warmed up. His real object was to heap scorn on the Christian claim that without God there could be no effective sanction for the ethical system. What God did such people mean, asked Pringle. 'Besides Brahma and Vishnu, Siva and Chrishna, Osiris and Isis, Thor and Odin, Jupiter, Jove, Jehovah and Moloch and numerous other old Gods there are many comparatively young ones: which would you recommend? There is the Deist's God; the Theist's God; the Pantheist's God; the Materialist's God (Matter and Force); Spencer's God (the Unknown and Unknowable); the Positivist's God (a "nondescript con-glomerate called humanity"); Spinoza's God (an Absolute Substance); Fichte's God (the moral order of the world); Parker and Cope's God (the Soul of the Universe); the Spiritualist God (External Law); the God of the 39 Articles ("without body, or parts or passions"); Beecher's God (a "dim and shadowy influence"); Talmadge's God (who, according to his own account, is as nearly like a Mountebank as himself); the Calvinist's God (who has little infants not a span long roasting in hell); the Presbyterian God (who may not perhaps of late years have infants there but will ulti-mately have all there but the elect few); the Roman Catholic God (who generously divides power and honour with his Mother); the Methodist God (who is very emotional and slightly deaf); the Universalist's God, a benignant Father, who is, perhaps, the best of the whole lot, as he is, at least equal to his creatures in goodness.'

With so many Gods to choose from, Pringle prefered to choose none. Anyway, morality supported by religion was in fact immorality, an assertion demonstrated by the criminal history of Christianity. True morality could only be based on reason and science, never on faith and superstition. 'The dogmas, the creeds, may go and will go; but the Principles of Ethics, no less than the Principles of Mathematics, will remain ... The Rationalist may confidently look forward to the time when, in the higher and still higher development of man and the corresponding improvement of his environment, superstitious faith will have departed forever from the human mind, reason will sit supreme on its rightful throne, and a quietly superior practical morality will have attained the fruit of the awareness of Science and accumulated Experience.' Pringle closed his lecture with an almost Methodistical exhortation, calling on his fellow secularists to work for the coming day of emancipation and rationalism.[59]

The Toronto Secular Society used the publication of Pringle's lecture as another opportunity to disseminate both free-thought principles and its *Manual of Songs and Ceremonies.* Like any other religion, secularism had its hymns and rituals. Its creed read:

1 That the present life being the only one of which we have any certain knowledge, its concerns claim our primary attention.
2 That the promotion of the general good and of our individual well-being in this world is at once our highest Wisdom and Duty.
3 That the only means upon which we can rely for the accomplishment of this object is Human Effort based upon Knowledge and Experience.
4 We judge conduct by its issue in this world only; what conduces to the general well-being is right; what has the opposite tendency is wrong.[60]

From these principles followed the imperative need to defend civil and religious liberty and to maintain the absolute separation of church and state. 'A New Faith for Old' piously summed up the Society's hopes:

> Let superstition be destroyed,
>   And falsehood cast away,
> That liberty may be enjoyed
>   The truth hold sov'reign sway.
> ...
> Let love prevail o'er every breast,
>   And happiness abound;
> May all mankind be truely blest;
>   Humanity be crown'd.[61]

Throughout the 1880s and into the next decade the Toronto secularists continued to hold frequent meetings and publish *Secular Thought* and other occasional publications. In 1884 *The Week* reported that the annual convention was the occasion for a somewhat ideological ball: 'Secularists have now invaded the hall of terpsichore. The other evening a ball was given in Toronto to "Socialists [Secularists?] and their Friends" and the programme, which was in French, consisted of some two dozen dances named after the shining lights and dogmas of unbelief. The following are examples of the items on this extraordinary *carte du bal:* Voltaire's Waltz, Free Thought Polka, Ingersoll's March, Evolutionist's Waltz, Watts and

Putnam Lancers, Anti clerical Propaganda Circle, Secularist Women's Rockaway, the Atheist's Joy Schottische, Infernal Reel of Heretics, and the like.'[62]

Whether the French program was designed to frighten or to disguise was not explained. But the following day the assembled secularists turned to more serious matters, and English became the language of business. Charles Watts lectured on 'Freethought, Its Nature, Struggles and Achievements,' Phillips Thompson participated in a discussion of the 'Sabbath Question,' while Alf Jury, a prominent member of the Knights of Labor, made several interventions.[63] Goldwin Smith, ever watchful for new evidence of the dreaded spiritual unrest, reported that the conference concluded by approving a manifesto demanding the abolition of chaplains and prayers in Parliament, the removal of the Bible from public schools, the ending of public recognition of religious holidays, and the removal of religious oaths from the courts. The recognition of civil marriage and the repeal of Lord's Day legislation and all other laws that attempted to enforce morality were also demanded. The social order, the secularists insisted, should rest on secular and not religious sanctions, a claim *The Week* found quite unacceptable. 'Even Herbert Spencer,' that journal's editor remarked haughtily, 'has admitted the inexpediency of hastily pulling down religious systems.'[64]

In the 1880s Montreal − English-speaking Montreal − was the headquarters of an active secularist association, the Pioneer Freethought Club. Captain Robert Chambliss Adams, its founder, left the fullest testimony of the defeat of Christian faith by popular scientific claims of anyone in nineteenth-century Canada. Though he was an American by birth, his *Travels through Faith to Reason* and his twenty years of free-thought activity in Montreal make him an important figure in the history of religious and social thought in Canada. His ideas deserve examination not because of any particular originality, but because they reveal the relationship between the decline of religious orthodoxy and the development of social reform sentiment.

Robert Chambliss Adams was born in Boston in 1839, the son of the Reverend Nehemiah Adams, a prominent New England Presbyterian.[65] His understanding of the Bible, his knowledge of theology, and his awareness of the demands that Christianity made on the conscience of believers all resulted naturally from growing up in a home where Calvinist orthodoxy was part of the air he breathed. By the time he was eight, when his mother died, he had committed the *Westminster Shorter Catechism* to memory. Though he taught Sunday School, distributed tracts, and in every way fulfilled his family's expectations, he never experienced 'conversion.' Perhaps that explains his decision to go to sea at fifteen rather than to follow in his father's footsteps. For the next fifteen years he sailed the oceans of the world, eventually taking command of his own ship. But life before the mast rarely seemed to divert Adams's attention from religious questions. On shipboard he instructed his crew in the faith, and he read theology and biblical criticism in an effort to strengthen and clarify his own wavering belief. Ashore in foreign countries, he observed missionaries quarrelling and members of non-Christian religions living by what he had been taught were exclusively Christian ethical principles. 'A Calvinist who wishes to keep his faith,' he wrote years later, 'should never travel and never read secular books.' By the 1870s, when he gave up seafaring and went into business in Montreal, he was still searching for certainty, but his literalist interpretation of the Bible seemed increasingly untenable. Since his reading now included Thomas Paine, Herbert Spencer, Charles Darwin, and Ernst Haeckel, he was obviously on the slippery path to secularism. His interests were in 'especially what related to the genuineness and authenticity of the Bible, the laws of evolution and political economy and some social problems.' It was Darwin who finally supplied the new key to an understanding of the universe and allowed Adams to shake off 'the thralldom of tradition.' Not even the views of his fellow Montrealer, the anti-Darwinian Sir William Dawson, could save Adams for the faith: 'his religious objections did not satisfy me, and were overborne by the overwhelming list of the great scholars who have left him almost alone to support the theories of the past.'[66]

Having accepted evolution, Adams continued to study biblical history, theology, comparative religion, and social criticism. The conclusion that he reached by 1880 was that the Bible was a purely human document and religious belief the product of human imagination. Science, not religion, opened the secrets of the cosmos and pointed the way to human progress. As a one-time Calvinist now converted to scientific naturalism, Adams was unimpressed by the efforts of theological liberals to rescue Christianity by jettisoning as 'non-essential' those traditional forms of belief which modern, rational men found repugnant. 'The sermons which I read or hear from Orthodox pulpits show that most scholarly ministers are adopting the religion of evolution which scientists and liberal thinkers have propounded, and quietly ignoring miracles and dogmas; they add to this a sentimental and exaggerated estimate of the character of Jesus.' But attempting to put Christianity 'into a nineteenth century dress' was merely to admit that for eighteen centuries the church had taught lies. In reality it was an admission of defeat, an admission of Adams's contention that religion was a human formulation that could be adapted to the changing needs of different periods of history. 'The Bible statement, "God made man in his own image" is therefore rightly reversed, and we say, "Man makes God in his own image," and it is true that "an honest God is the noblest work of man"; for as man thinkest in his heart, so is he, and the conception each forms of the Deity shows the highest capacity and aspiration of his own nature.'[67]

Adams's emancipation was now complete. The pessimistic Calvinism of his youth gave way to a full-blown meliorism. 'The Bible says the world was made in six days by magic, man was perfect but sinned, Christ died to save a few, and soon God will destroy the world and punish the vast majority of men forever in hell. Evolution says the world is the product of a gradual development of matter, progressing through millions of years; man has risen from lower animals, and they form inferior orders of animal and vegetable life down to the single atom. Analogy teaches that man will continue to rise, and, through the operation of the same laws, attain to a far higher if not perfect development; for there must always be progress upward. So I have changed from a pessimist to an optimist and instead of ignoring this sin-cursed world doomed to destruction, I accept it as "the best world going," and one capable of improvement, it being my great aim to advance my nature and that of others that the world may be better for my life. Not the salvation of men's souls from hell, but the elevation of their hearts and minds, and the bettering of their social conditions, is now my desire.'[68]

Being something of a versifier, Adams summed up his new-found faith in these stanzas on 'The Pithy Creed of Rationalism':

> Jehovah ranks with Jupiter;
> The Bible's Hebrew literature;
> Confucius, Jesus, both were men;
> A future lies beyond our ken.
> A miracle do not expect;
> Seek nature's causes for each effect.
> From man have come all gods and creeds;
> Your only saviour is your deeds.[69]

The poetry was poor but the point important: the rejection of traditional religious teaching was the necessary step toward a secular religion of progress which substituted the hope of heavenly reward with a promise of worldly happiness.

Freeing man from the superstitions of the past, in Adams's view, ensured the flowering of a new moral man. No longer intimidated by the threat of eternal punishment, man would realize that morality must be the sum of man's experience of what is best for mankind. It would rapidly become clear that the problems of society do not result from human evil or imperfection, but are a consequence of inadequate material resources. 'Work and not prayer must be the instruments of reform.' The evidence seemed to multiply that a new and better society was evolving from the astounding technological advances of the nineteenth century. Time and space would soon be annihilated by telephone, telegraph, and airplane; machinery would abolish 'the curse of labor,' and science create an abundance of food; social science would point the way to a more equitable distribution of wealth and power. A new set of moral maxims would replace the old commandments of religions. Adams even ventured to suggest a few, offering a balanced mixture of rationalist and social reform ideals:

> Thou shalt give women equal rights with men.
> Thou shalt give a fair day's pay for a fair day's work and the laborers shall share with the capitalists the profit of their enterprises.
> Thou shalt not protect one industry at the expense of another, and thou shalt not refuse free trade with other nations.
> Thou shalt tax all property alike, religious or secular.
> Thou shalt not give religious instruction in public schools, nor force any to pay for the support of religious practices which they do not approve.
> Thou shalt not advance the price of merchandise by 'corners.'
> Thou shalt lay up treasure upon earth, but shall use it for the benefit of man.[70]

For free thinkers of Adams's temperament, rationalism was essentially an escape from the strict doctrines of orthodox Calvinism – 'the mind and the heart of the nineteenth-century revolt against those atrocious sentiments' of election and damnation. Yet he was determined that the moral values associated with Christianity should be preserved. He was even anxious to retain the church, in secularized form, as an educational institution. Adams believed that many Christian teachings, once drained of supernatural colouring, could continue to serve the new scientific humanism of rationalism. 'The arbitrary choice of men to be saved is irrational and immoral,' he maintained, 'and yet it is the perverted form of one of the most vital truths of nature – the survival of the fittest – the fact that fitness finds its sphere ... there is a natural selection, leading to the triumph of the best. The true "select" are the discoverers, the searchers, the earnest laborers who, in science, morals, education and benevolence are surely redeeming the world.'[71]

It is obvious that Adams, like other secularists, really could not escape the grip of a religious upbringing. Like the liberal Christians Adams so perceptively criticized, the secularists stripped Christianity of its more rigorous doctrines and put a simplified Darwinism in the place of traditional theology. Nor had they lost their expectations of the millennium; it would come as an inevitable result of evolutionary progress, as the triumph of a scientific social utopia. 'Modern progress is coincident with the advancement of science. It is knowledge of nature, not belief in God, that has elevated mankind.'[72] Virtually all Canadian free thinkers could have been included in the description of their more famous contemporary, Charles Bradlaugh, as 'a Puritan who has lost his way.'[73]

III

The Canadian secularist movement's chief significance was as an example of a radical aspect of a more general drift away from traditional Christian belief that was taking place under the impact of science, historical criticism, and the consequent growth of theological liberalism. Graeme Mercer Adam, the prominent literary journalist,[74] gave a somewhat complacent illustration of this point in his 1887 review of Francis Darwin's *Life and Letters of Charles Darwin*. Christianity, the editor of *The Week* contended, had suprisingly come safely through the years of controversy that followed the publication of *On the Origin of Species*. Heaven apparently had protected its own. 'But the controversy has taught us more than this,' he concluded; 'it has taught us more than ever to welcome Science as an ally, to distrust, if not discard, certain dogmas, and not to put too literal an interpretation on what most of us reverentially treat, in common with Nature, as a Divine, and in the main, to be spiritually apprehended revelation.'[75] To orthodox Christians a victory that conceded that much territory was hardly distinguishable from defeat.

In the melding of science and religion the line between rationalism and belief had nearly vanished. Or perhaps a common ground between the free thinkers and the liberal Protestants was gradually being uncovered. If, as Allen Pringle believed, 'polished and politic parsons' were no longer preaching 'old fashioned Biblical doctrines so odiferous of brimstone,' it was not merely because they had conceded the battle to rationalism, but also because they too had discovered the social question.

Perhaps the secularists were right in predicting that if the world was offered a stark choice between faith and works, the latter would be an easy victor.[76] The Reverend J.A. Macdonald appeared to agree. He urged his fellow Presbyterians to read Edward Bellamy's *Looking Backward* and other works of political economy; 'Christianity must vindicate her claim to Divine origin and her right to continued support, not by appeals to historic records or documents or creeds or confessions, but by showing her adaptability to present day human needs.'[77] By the end of the century, the Reverend Salem Bland, a young Methodist walking deftly through the intellectual minefields of the nineteenth century, pointed to a similar development with an almost audible sense of relief. 'In Canada, as in all English-speaking countries, social questions are enjoying increasing attention,' he told the Queen's University Theological Conference. 'Christianity is becoming primarily sociological which is a good deal better than if it should be regarded as primarily ecclesiastical or even theological.'[78] Secularists might have regarded that admission as at least a partial victory – by default.

Still, the free thinkers had by no means completely vanquished their religious foes. Whatever ground had been won, there were certainly still those – the majority – who rejected the sanguine ethical humanism of the secularists Allen Pringle and Robert Adams. Pringle, like Grant and his liberal Presbyterian associate, Agnes Maule Machar, attended the Parliament of Religions at the Chicago World's Fair in 1893. (Pringle had doubtless sat in on a competing event, the Congress of Evolution, presided over by his friend, B.F. Underwood.) All three had been greatly impressed by this ecumenical event; Machar noted approvingly that it called for a new emphasis on social problems.[79] Pringle concluded that it demonstrated how the religion of humanity, 'one of the highest products of the upward evolutionary process,' would be the religion of 'deeds instead of subscribing to creeds.' That was a view W.D. LeSueur had been advancing for nearly two decades.[80] But the Reverend Arthur Jarvis of St Margaret's Anglican Church, Napanee, demurred. He noted sharply that tolerance was dangerously close to indifference. As for the religion of humanity, it was simply one in which 'Christ may perhaps be allowed a seat beside Buddha, Confucius, Huxley and Joe Smith.'[81] That was hardly acceptable.

The universe unfolded, somewhat unkindly, and Jarvis was to have the final word. In July 1896, Allen Pringle, president of the Canadian Secular Union, died suddenly and prematurely of pneumonia. On the day of the funeral J.S. Ellis, the editor of *Secular Thought*, journeyed to Napanee from Toronto to deliver the eulogy. According to the *Napanee Beaver*, the Anglican church choir was also present, offering a rendition of 'Nearer My God to Thee' before the cortège moved off to the Napanee cemetery. The Reverend Jarvis, hastily and perhaps a little sheepishly, objected to that report. His choir had not sung for a 'professed agnostic.' And though it might seem 'invidious,' he felt 'compelled to make the correction not only to put myself right but also in observance to the request preferred by the authorities of the diocese.'[82]

As Msgr Bourget, twenty years earlier, had deconsecrated poor Joseph Guibord's Côte des Neiges resting place, so the Reverend Jarvis had denied Allen Pringle any final Christian consolation. Not that he would have wanted it.

5

Spiritualism, Science of the Earthly Paradise

'Is There Another Life?' was the title that Goldwin Smith, almost inevitably, gave to a lengthy chapter in his *Guesses at the Riddle of Existence.*[1] His answer recognized that he, like many Victorian intellectuals, was unable to respond with an easy, automatic affirmative. But even if he was unable to patch together from his substantial theological knowledge a convincing demonstration of immortality, Smith knew that the yearning for such reassurance remained strong. It was so strong, he had written twenty years earlier, that in 'twilight caused by the temporary eclipse of faith, physical or semi-physical superstitions are apt to abound.'[2]

Though spiritualism found no place in Goldwin Smith's quest for a rational religion, it is hardly surprising that Dr Maurice Bucke, who had little faith in arid rationalism, had a more sympathetic viewpoint. For Canada's leading psychiatrist, 'telepathy and clairvoyance' were signs of the gradual evolution of 'nascent faculties.' 'I place in the same class,' he told an audience at St Mary's Town Hall, where he opened an art exhibit in 1898, 'the phenomenon of what is often called spiritualism. The labours of the Society of Psychic Research have made it plain that these phenomena, as notably in the case of W. Stainton Moses, really exist.'[3]

Bucke and Smith were not isolated commentators on spiritualism in Canada in the late nineteenth century. There was a good deal of surprisingly open-minded discussion of the phenomenon in both religious and secular circles.[4] The Reverend Salem Bland, working his way gradually from Methodist orthodoxy to theological liberalism,[5] found the subject worthy of close investigation. Having read the work of the American spiritualist Jay Hudson entitled *The Laws of Psychic Phenomena,* Bland attended a seance in Quebec City in May 1894. His reaction was certainly not sceptical. Spiritualism, he recorded, was 'partly, perhaps mostly, humbug & imposture; partly spiritual agency, whether of good spirits or evil is a doubtful point.' But he did draw one firm conclusion: 'the appearance or manifestation of the departed dead is to me a proven fact. The only doubtful question, whether such manifestations could be, or should be sought at will.'[6]

The extent of spiritualist activities in Canada is difficult to measure. That those activities existed long before Mackenzie King discovered the consolations of the little tapping table or Stephen Leacock satirized psychic phenomena in his *Arcadian Adventures of the Idle Rich* is plain enough. The Fox sisters, with whom the spirit-rapping craze began in upstate New York in 1848, had come to Rochester from the Belleville area. It was there that Susanna Moodie at least temporarily fell under the influence of Kate Fox and other, local, spiritualists. By the 1850s in Canada, as in the United States and Great Britain, spiritualist activities had begun to arouse public interest.[7] Spiritualist lecturers, like itinerant preachers on virtually every other subject from secularism to temperance, crossed the intellectually undefended frontier with increasing regularity during the late nineteenth century. In July 1875, the same summer that B.F. Underwood brought his agnostic creed to the public in Toronto, local spiritualists joined hands with the Liberal Club (the secularists), to invite the Honourable Warren Chase and J.M. Peebles, both well-known American spiritualist writers and lecturers, to enlighten audiences in the Queen City. *The National*, always abreast of the unconventional, assured its readers that those speakers were thoroughly conversant with the philosophy, history and recent developments of the spiritualist movement.'[8] Peebles, author of *The Practise of Spiritualism: A Biographical Sketch of Abraham James and Historical Description of His Oil Well Discoveries in Pleasantville, Pa., Through Spirit Direction*,[9] had already visited Toronto two years earlier and had drawn the predictable condemnation from the Toronto *Globe*. Pure charlatanry accompanied by 'the usual and confidence inspiring adjuncts of ropes and bells, dark rooms and tables rickety with the divine afflatus' was the conclusion of George Brown's stern Presbyterian oracle.[10] A young independent journalist, whose name would be associated with virtually every radical cause in Canada over the next half-century, took serious offence at the *Globe*'s stand, as he did at so many of that paper's defences of the status quo. Phillips Thompson penned a sharp rejoinder, which the *Mail*, always glad to find fault with its competitor, willingly published. The letter was a typical Thompson mixture of knowledge, insight, vituperation, and calumny. He had been reading *The Debatable World between this World and the Next* (1871) by the utopian socialist and spiritualist writer Robert Dale Owen.[11] Thompson was completely convinced by the Englishman's arguments and urged others to take seriously the 'thousands of instances' of spirit return and, more particularly, the work of 'hundreds of private mediums who shun publicity and exercise their gifts without fee or reward.' But his most emphatic and revealing assertion – again following Owen – was that 'surely the affording of proof positive of existence after death, in this age of materialism, may be regarded as a benefit to mankind.'[12]

Thompson, who after a long and winding spiritual odyssey would himself embrace materialism, went to the heart of the matter when he spoke of 'proof positive' and 'materialism.' In the post-Darwinian age the only acceptable fashion of combating materialistic science was to provide scientific 'proof positive' of a credible alternative. That was what spiritualism and its close relative psychic research claimed to do. Many people – for the most part, those more orthodox than Dr Maurice Bucke and Phillips Thompson – were satisfied that such proof could be adduced. Noting the widespread interest in spiritualism, a writer in *The Week* asked, 'Can this movement be a mere reaction against the crude materialism which has swayed science so potently during late years, or is the theory of a future life about to receive scientific demonstration?'[13] Spiritualism can thus be understood in part as an effort, in a scientific and increasingly sceptical age, to demonstrate the validity of the traditional religious teachings about immortality.

For those who had moved some distance from orthodox Christian claims about the immortality of the soul, spiritualism offered an alternative to the threat of materialism. A. Russel Wallace was one distinguished scientist who followed that route.[14] Professor Daniel Wilson, after reading Darwin's *Life and Letters*, seemed tempted. 'The ultimate agnostic's creed,' he wrote to his friend, Principal William Dawson, 'and his passing into the great darkness, as though life were but a lamp, enkindled and going out, when its oil failed; with no replenishing, seemingly no hope of a hereafter; left in mind a shuddering sense of pain. The separation from our loved ones would be terrible indeed, if we could think that death meant such annihilation.'[15] Though Wilson did not follow the spiritualist path, it did not escape contemporary commentators – those who were not wholly hostile – that the growing interest in spiritualism arose out of exactly the feelings expressed by the University of Toronto professor.[16]

Ironic as it may seem, then, spiritualists, whose critics denounced them as gullible, naïve, irrational, and worse, often considered themselves to be part of a scientific enterprise. They were engaged in discovering scientific proofs for religious belief, having found traditional religious apologetics no longer convincing. That was certainly the burden of the testimony of a prosperous Collingwood, Ontario, Presbyterian named John Lawrence. Like most others who publicly proclaimed their conversion to spiritualism, Lawrence had experienced spirit return, telepathy, and other psychic phenomena. But he had also thought about his previous beliefs and had concluded that 'after seriously and conscientiously considering the doctrines and dogmas of the Old Theology, I find that they are founded largely on Paganistic legend, allegory, folklore and the most glaring irrationalisms of the childhood of the world, when reason, man's greatest endowment, which constitutes him a man was thrown to the wind. If a modern scientist with his keen rational intellect and analytical methods were to adopt such an erratic, haphazard system of science as men do in theology, his labours for the benefit of humanity would become useless.'[17] A similar testimony was offered by a Toronto man who, having tried Methodism, Presbyterianism, agnosticism, and materialism, was converted to the spiritualist persuasion on hearing a lecture by the leading British psychic researcher F.W. Myers on 'Heaven – What and Where Is It?' in Richmond Hall.[18]

To speak of 'conversion' is not inappropriate even while arguing that many spiritualists believed in the scientific character of their work. Reading the one hundred testimonies of 'conversion' gathered by the Reverend B.F. Austin for publication in 1901 – twenty-four were from Canadians, the remainder from Britons and Americans – there is an overwhelming sense that conversion often took place following the death of some close relative or friend. The experience of some psychic event evidently struck the observer with the same emotional impact as the outpourings of a revivalist preacher at a camp meeting might have affected a more orthodox convert. That parallel is a real one, for spiritualists gathered regularly for their own camp meetings, apparently most frequently crossing the border to western New York to participate in the Cassadaga Free Lake Association founded in 1879 (later rechristened Lily Dale).[19] In Canada, as in the United States and Great Britain, many spiritualists saw no contradiction between their 'new theology' of spiritualism and their 'old theology' of Christianity.[20] Descriptions of seances often included many of the rituals of Christianity, including the recitation of the Lord's Prayer and the singing of favourite hymns. It is therefore not entirely surprising to find *The National* – probably Phillips Thompson – urging Christians and spiritualists to co-operate in the fight against materialism. 'We have never been able to understand on what grounds professed believers in the Scripture can deny the possibility of spirit appearances and communications,' the editor remarked. 'The Bible in fact is full of spiritualism from Genesis to Revelations.'[21]

There were, of course, both spiritualists who rejected Christian doctrines outright and Christians – doubtless the majority – who condemned spiritualism as rank heresy. The careers of the Reverend Benjamin Fish Austin and Flora MacDonald Denison demonstrate the accuracy of that observation. They also provide some valuable insights into the varieties of religious experience in late nineteenth-century Canada.

I

In June 1899, after a highly publicized trial before the general conference of the Methodist church, the Reverend Benjamin Fish Austin, BA, BD, DD, was expelled from the ministry for heresy. For over twenty-five years Austin had served Methodism faithfully and energetically. He had occupied positions of substantial importance in the church's educational system and had in most respects been the very model of a modern Methodist divine. Only three years before his expulsion from his church Austin had been awarded a doctor of divinity degree by Victoria University in recognition of his exemplary services and, no doubt, as a sign of future expectations. Yet in 1899 the church's highest court judged Austin a heretic who subscribed to the beliefs and practices of spiritualism. Those beliefs were judged incompatible with Methodist doctrine.

Austin was born in Brighton, Ontario, in 1850. In 1877 he graduated from Albert College in Belleville, having earned a first-class honours degree in Oriental languages. Four years later he was awarded a bachelor of divinity degree. He served in the Methodist Episcopal congregation at Prescott before taking up a position as the first principal of Alma Ladies' College in St Thomas. His success as principal marked him as a rising man in the church who was building on a reputation already established by the publication of some early sermons, sermons which deviated in no detectable fashion from the standards of Methodism.[22] In 1884 he published a pamphlet entitled *The Gospel of the Poor vs Pew Rents*; in it he argued that pew rents created un-Christian distinctions among members of the church and were one cause of the growing estrangement of the working classes from Methodism. 'The Gospel of the Lord Jesus Christ,' he contended, 'with its doctrines of human brotherhood and human equality, has smoothed away those artificial distinctions of birth and fortune that have proved such terrible instruments of oppression to the poor in past ages.' That this hint of a social gospel was well within the four corners of Methodist teaching was made clear in a preface written by Bishop Albert Carman in which he warned against too close an association between the church and 'the men who have the money.'[23]

Six years later Austin joined many other Prostestant clergy in the equal rights crusade to keep Canada free from popery. His pamphlet, entitled *The Jesuits*, with an introduction by James L. Hughes (who in later years would share Austin's interest in spiritualism), advanced the well-honed argument that the presence of the Jesuits was a persistent threat to civil liberty. Austin viewed French in the schools as 'a barrier to the progress of Anglo-Saxon civilization.'[24] There was no hint of unorthodoxy or liberalism here.

In the same year, 1890, he edited and contributed several essays to a fat volume entitled *Woman: Her Character, Culture and Calling*, which revealed a more progressive cast of mind. As the principal of a ladies' college, Austin was naturally aware of the growing discussion of woman's place in higher education and more generally in society.[25] In his several contributions to this wide-ranging and generally liberal survey of woman's role, Austin emphasized two particular points. The first, indicating a somewhat advanced position, was that women had a right to education and training so that they could establish themselves as equal and independent individuals. 'No young woman should be placed in circumstances such as to make marriage an only refuge from poverty or dependence upon her friends or from a life of ennui,' Austin wrote. 'Having in her hands the power of self-support, she should be free to accept or reject the marriage lot, or, having accepted it, she would then hold in reserve a power that would, in times of worldly disaster, prove a life boat among the breakers.'[26]

Advanced as those sentiments were at the time – or even later – Austin was careful to hedge them in by a second, more traditional, attitude. Christian women, he held, had a special role that could best be played in 'the home, the school, the church – the three great pillars of modern civilization.' He concluded that 'if society is ever to become thoroughly permeated with the Christian doctrine and spirit, if the world is ever to become regenerated, it must be by the agency of Christian women.'[27] The 'regeneration' of society, that ultimate goal of nineteenth-century reformers, was in Austin's view closely connected with the full acceptance of the doctrine that 'Christ has recognized and declared woman's equality with man.'[28] Of the many roles and characteristics assigned to Jesus Christ by nineteenth-century liberals, that of feminist was by no means the most original.[29]

By the 1890s Austin, like many other Protestant clergymen, evidently was becoming increasingly preoccupied with social issues and their religious implications. His collection of speeches and articles, entitled *The Prohibition Leaders of America*, confirms this impression and also reveals one of the steps that Austin believed necessary along the path to regeneration.[30] But the development of Austin's social reform views was delayed in the mid-1890s by a personal and religious crisis that reached a climax in his heresy trial.

In 1897 Austin resigned the principalship of Alma Ladies' College and at his own request was left temporarily without a station. The exact reasons for his resignation are unclear; the newspaper reports stated that 'personal reasons are all that are given for his resignation.'[31] One personal reason might have been the death of his two-and-a-half-year-old daughter Kathleen in 1896. Another reason, offered later, was the development of 'liberal views' that raised questions about his orthodoxy. Austin's 1933 obituary noted that he had given up his post because 'he desired ... an unrestricted opportunity to investigate the subject of Spiritualism which had been thrust upon his attention by certain psychic developments among the college students who were eager to know the truth.'[32]

The nature of these 'psychic developments' remains obscure. Perhaps they referred to some earlier events of a mysterious nature which apparently had been witnessed by Austin. During his student days at Albert College in Belleville in the 1870s, Austin was doubtless aware of the astonishing career of a fellow student named Mary Merrill, whose academic brilliance and controversial death in 1880 were surrounded by hints of psychic powers. Her life was described in an unorthodox biography written twenty years later by her sister, Flora MacDonald. *Mary Melville: The Psychic*, published by the Austin Publishing Company in 1900, included a preface written by B.F. Austin which asserted that 'in all essential features, it is a genuine biography of a real and wonderful life.' By that date, of course, Austin had become a defrocked Methodist and a spiritualist evangelist. He had met Flora MacDonald at a Lily Dale spiritualist camp meeting, and they formed a lifelong friendship.[33]

Whatever the cause of his initial interest in spiritualism, Austin approached the subject in the manner of many other late nineteenth-century dabblers in psychic matters; his interest was both personal and 'scientific.' In his year free from clerical responsibilities he set out on an extensive investigation of psychic phenomena of all kinds. He became a

Rev. Benjamin Fish Austin and his family

psychic researcher. His findings were embodied in a five-hundred-page volume entitled *Glimpses of the Unseen*, a collection of accounts of psychic experiences gathered from published sources and from meetings with spiritualists mainly in the United States. The volume, prefaced and approved by the Reverend E.E. Badgley, professor of philosophy at Victoria University, was announced as a study of 'psychology' and especially of that 'mysterious region where mind and matter seem to meet, known in modern occult literature as "borderland."'[34] The work included chapters on dreams, telepathy, prayer, prophecy, Christian Science, apparitions, human prodigies, spiritualism, genius, and insanity. Of several prominent Canadians quoted as supporting these investigations, including James L. Hughes, a Toronto school inspector, none was more prominent than Austin's personal acquaintance, Dr Maurice Bucke.[35] Bucke's own version of evolution, which would soon blossom in his best-known book *Cosmic Consciousness* (1901),[36] offered the medical practitioner's imprimatur to spiritualism: 'The fact about these strange experiences is that the human mind is passing into a new phase ... The human mind has taken on one function after another and is going to keep on taking on new faculties. These sporadic instances of what is known as second sight are simply the signs of a new consciousness that is making its appearance.'[37]

Glimpses of the Unseen was a work of somewhat amateurish research and of popularization. It advocated no particular position other than appealing for open-mindedness on the topic of psychic phenomena. Given the confused state of psychological knowledge and thought and the continuing belief in mesmerism, phrenology, craniology, and mind-measurement in the late nineteenth century, Austin's book seems little more than the rather naïve but inoffensive explorations of a well-meaning but somewhat troubled liberal Protestant clergyman. Nevertheless, many of his Methodist contemporaries found his investigations threatening.

Austin himself had moved beyond the open-minded stage; he was satisfied that his glimpses of the unseen were glimpses of reality. But he was equally convinced that his new-found knowledge confirmed his Christian convictions. That was the theme of the sermon he preached at Parkdale Methodist Church on 8 January, 1899. No doubt this sermon, a commentary on the proverb 'Buy the truth and sell it not' was designed to meet criticisms of his spiritualist leanings. For the most part the message was a liberal defence of religious truth and man's need for it. It said little about sin, the crucifixion, or the atonement, but instead insisted upon what the preacher took to be the perfectibility of all men as the central promise of the Gospel and the progressive character of revelation in each age. These claims, while probably slightly objectionable to conservative Methodists, were only a lengthy prelude to a plea for the acceptance of new truth. Almost as though he anticipated trouble – even martyrdom – Austin reminded his listeners of the fate of Jesus, Luther, and Charles Darwin at the hands of the established religious authorities. Yet the truth of the messages brought by these men had ultimately been demonstrated. 'So it is with new truths in philosophy and psychic research,' he announced. 'The scientific truths of telepathy, clairvoyance, soul-flight, psychometry and prophecy are well established by incontrovertible evidence. But to mention them in certain church circles is to ostracize yourself.'[38]

Whatever immediate controversy the sermon stirred up, its subsequent publication (on the initiative of a friend to whom Austin sent a copy) in *Light and Truth*, a spiritualist publication in Columbus, Ohio, doubtless precipitated a powerful reaction. The Reverend A.H. Goring of Port Stanley, Ontario, preferred charges of heresy based on four claims:

Austin's sermon had denied the doctrine of eternal punishment, questioned Christ's divinity, denied the doctrine of Christ as God's final revelation, and finally upheld the fraudulent system of Spiritualism.' Claiming inability to attend his first trial, Austin submitted a written defence. He denied the first three charges outright and insisted that he upheld only true spiritualism, rejecting its fraudulent forms completely. The church court sustained all of the charges but the first – that Austin rejected the doctrine of eternal punishment.[39]

Austin then appealed his case to the annual conference, which met in Windsor at the beginning of June. There, before serried rows of Methodists, Austin spoke for three and a half hours – interspersed with interruptions and frequent heckling – in an effort to refute the charge of heresy and more particularly to establish the validity of spiritualist claims. He opened with a plea that the church should recognize the changes that were taking place around it. 'The period in which we live is evidently a period of transition,' he argued. 'This is seen in the fact that old interpretations of Scripture are giving place to new. Old conceptions of the method of creation are no longer popular.' Having thus paid homage to the higher critics and the theory of evolution, he moved on to assert that the church had failed to keep abreast of these changes. 'The creeds are not changing as rapidly as the beliefs of the people, nor as rapidly as most men of progressive mind desire.' Indeed, creeds had become an anachronism; as the popularity of Charles M. Sheldon's social gospel novel *In His Steps* demonstrated, the time had arrived to move 'from theological disputing to deeds of practical Christianity.'[40]

Nor should old dogma be allowed to stand in the way of acceptance of new scientific truths that could bolster Christian belief. Those scientific truths were the results of psychic research. Austin drew much of his evidence about these discoveries from the work of the British Society for Psychic Research, which had been at work since 1882. Sir William Crooks, the chemist, Alfred Russel Wallace, the biologist, and two leading British psychic researchers, F.W. Myers and Henry Sidgwick, were cited in support of his claims. On the Christian side he invoked as witnesses such American liberal divines as Dr Minot Savage, Dr Lyman Abbott, and the Reverend Joseph Cook. William James and even Sigmund Freud were also cited by the defence. All this testimony proved, Austin claimed, something John Wesley had always believed, namely, that spiritualism was genuine. Here was the nub of his defence: 'Now in the psychic phenomenon of our age we have a line of evidence that demonstrates the truth of those remarkable occurrences of the Old and New Testament

Scriptures, which occurrences, as we all know, form the great stumbling block to the acceptance of the Bible on the part of a large portion of the scientific world ... the Prophets of the olden time and the Psychics of today are one and the same.'[41]

With theological problems resolved scientifically, Austin believed, pastoral care would also benefit. 'I have found a truth that humanity needs,' he proclaimed, setting aside his role as a mere seeker after truth, 'that brings unspeakable joy to human hearts and homes, that brightens all the life, that assuages sorrow, that dispels care, that kills the materialistic spirit of our age and lifts manhood into noble thought and life.' And so on to the conclusion, which was a plea for liberty to interpret the Scriptures 'differently from what the Fathers did.' 'The night is far spent, the dawn of a new age is at hand.' On that thought he rested his case. Many of his peers doubtless agreed that the night was far enough spent, but they agreed with little else. All Austin's rhetoric, emotion, and erudition proved unavailing. Only one vote prevented the conference from unanimity in expelling Austin from the ministry.[42]

Austin's fate was hardly surprising. His liberalism doubtless offended many of the same Methodists who had applauded the removal of the higher critic Professor G.C. Workman from the Victoria theological faculty in 1891. And those who had demanded that 'holiness' leader Rev. Ralph Horner either conform to church discipline or depart – he departed in 1895 – were hardly likely to accept Austin's plea for liberty to teach what he pleased.[43]

Yet Austin's point of view was significant for what it revealed about the crisis in late nineteenth-century religious thought. His liberalism was the product of the new science, natural and historical. Like many others, Austin could no longer accept traditional religious dogmas that emphasized sin, divine retribution, and eternal punishment. Nor could he accept the materialistic conclusions of the Darwinians. Spiritualism seemed to provide the answer to both personal and intellectual problems. Communication with the spirit world and the evidence it provided of the afterlife allowed him to soften and even reject the harsher doctrines of orthodox Protestantism. In 1902 he wrote, 'by disclosing the true nature of death as a transition into a higher state, a change as natural and blessed as birth, by showing that it is not a penalty, a judgment, an arbitrary sentence but a resurrection and an ascension, in every sense a gain, Spiritualism has removed forever the gloom and sorrow and torment which humanity suffered through the false church teachings concerning death.'[44]

But the science of communication with the world of spirits was more than a personal consolation. As Austin had repeatedly insisted before the church conference, the evidence of contemporary psychic phenomena authenticated similar and otherwise inexplicable events in the Bible, thus 'making scriptural statements less difficult of acceptance by the sceptical and scientific mind.'[45] Science would confound science: psychic research, or rather its demonstrated results, answered the questions posed by scientific naturalism and the science of higher criticism. Christianity, having taken into account the progressive revelation of knowledge, remained intact. Materialism lay vanquished.

That Austin's spiritualism was an outgrowth of his theological liberalism is further confirmed by the fact that the social concerns he had earlier expressed on the matter of pew rents and women's rights continued to develop toward a more radical social gospel after his conversion to spiritualism. From a superficial viewpoint, the spiritualist's concern with the 'other world' might suggest indifference to the problems of the here and now. But in reality spiritualism emphasized this world's concerns to a greater extent than traditional Protestantism. The point of establishing contact with those who had departed was to provide consolation with those who remained in this world. Spiritualism, then, was a religion of instant gratification. But beyond that sentimental aspect of spiritualist claims there was the more fundamental insistence that spiritualism demonstrated that traditional Christian teaching about the separation of this world from the next was false. 'By showing us that the spiritual kingdom interpenetrates the physical and material, that heaven and earth are one locality, that our dead are not departed from us ... Spiritualism has become the world's consolation,' Austin maintained.[46] Or, as Phillipe Ariès has put it, spiritualism sought to create 'a new paradise ... an anthropomorphic paradise – which is not so much the heavenly home as the earthly home saved from the menace of time, a home in which the expectations of eschatology are mingled with the realities of memory.'[47]

By erasing the distinction between this world and the afterlife, Austin declared his acceptance of two essential concepts of modernist social gospel thought. First, he clearly believed in God's immanence in the world as opposed to the orthodox conception of divine transcendence. Second, and as a logical corollary, he erased the distinction between the sacred and the secular by insisting on the identity of heaven and earth, or, to use the phrase that became common coin among social gospellers, the kingdom of God was on earth.[48]

Austin's views of the state of the kingdom of God on earth reveal further and perhaps surprising affinities with social gospel thought. His modernism and liberalism made him reject exclusivist claims by any one denomination, or even religion, to a monopoly on religious truth. The 'new Science of Comparative Religion' and the higher criticism had, in his view, left all such claims open to doubt. 'We know as well as history and instruction can teach us,' he wrote, 'that *all religions are* one and the same – all the outgrowth of man's moral nature, differing only according to the intelligence and advancement of the people among whom they originated.' Those views echoed the conclusion of Austin's friend Dr Bucke. Since all religions were similar, then the emphasis of religious practice would be not on theological disputation but rather on ethical action – echoes of Edward Bellamy or Phillips Thompson. 'The first great work it [spiritualism] will do for society,' Austin claimed, 'will be a practical recognition of the claims of human brotherhood – resulting in equality of rights and privileges for all. Spiritualism will recognize the equal rights and claims of every man to nature's bounties. The earth, the air, the precious and useful metals, the treasures of wood and coal, of lake and ocean, belong of right to earth's inhabitants *in common*. They are not for the few but the *many* and society must be reconstituted, re-organized and regenerated.'

Austin felt constrained to deny that he advocated either anarchy or 'socialism as many understand it.' But he maintained that a 'new economic system' was an imperative spiritualist demand. He insisted even more vehemently that this preoccupation was a properly religious one: 'Such questions, you may say, are questions of sociology and not religion. We reply that true religion is the Kingdom of God here and now realized in happy hearts, pure homes and progressive and prosperous society. Spiritualism aims at heaven upon earth: justice, truth, equality, love peace, plenty, power and purity realized in human society here and now. Make heart and home and society right here: the future will look after itself. *Save thyself and thy brother man the Gods will save themselves.*'[49] To those sentiments Salem Bland, James Shaver Woodsworth, and Albert E. Smith – and perhaps the young Mackenzie King – could only have responded with a long amen.[50]

Austin's outline of what he called 'the mission of spiritualism' marked his evolution beyond his earlier Methodism. His liberalism had carried him toward an ecumenism in which the world's religions 'could lend and borrow the special good in each other's systems' in a fashion suggestive of the teachings of theosophy. His perfectionism led him to reject all thought of human 'depravity' and to attribute social problems to 'ignorance and wrong environments.' As for the church, it could only regain its lost leadership by turning itself into a school, especially of scientific thought, and its ministers and teachers into social reformers. In that new church – which seemed to anticipate the people's forums and labour churches of later years[51] – Tyndall, Darwin, Huxley, and Wallace would be recognized as 'prophets of a new age, priests of a newer and nobler religion, than the world has known before, divinely appointed interpreters of the Bible of our times, Nature.'[52]

It would be simple enough to underscore the contradictions, theological and scientific, in Austin's outlook. His resemblance to 'Mr Sludge, The Medium,' Robert Browning's satiric creation, is quite uncanny:

> As for religion – why, I served it, sir!
> I'll stick to that! *With my phenomena*
> I laid the atheist sprawling on his back,
> Propped St. Paul, or, at least Swedenborg!

Yet to dismiss Austin lightly would be to ignore the extent to which he exemplified the difficulties of people torn between the claims of science and religion. Men like Alfred Russel Wallace would have felt quite at home in Austin's pantheon of social reform prophets. So would the ornithologist Elliot Coues.[53] And that reveals a connection, logical enough, between the decay of traditional religious belief and the rise of social criticism. In Great Britain, spiritualism had its sympathizers among the prominent – Robert Blatchford and Keir Hardie, for example – and the less prominent members of the Independent Labour party, which was, naturally enough, among the heirs to Robert Owen. Similar alliances existed in the United States.[54] Karl Marx, despite an early interest in phrenology, found it difficult to accept the claim of an American feminist, free-love advocate, and spiritualist that the goals of spiritualism and the International Workingmen's Association were the same.[55] The Reverend B.F. Austin would certainly have understood what Victoria Woodhull meant, and so would his feminist friend, Flora MacDonald Denison.

II

On 7 April 1880, a twenty-two-year-old Belleville woman, Mary Edwards Merrill died of causes that produced, as the *Belleville Intelligencer* reported, 'a very wide divergence of opinion amongst the medical men.'[56]

Indeed, for two days there was serious disagreement about whether the young woman was dead or merely in some inexplicable state of suspended animation. Whatever the exact cause of death – and the doctors never did reach agreement – this mystery was apparently only the last of many. While she was a student at the Methodist Ladies' College (Alexandra College), Mary Merrill apparently had been a sickly prodigy of astonishing mathematical talents. Though the facts are difficult to establish with certainty – and Dr Cyril Greenland has made a substantial effort[57] – it is at least possible that at the age of eighteen she so impressed some leading mathematicians in the United States that they honoured her with the presidency of their society. Four years later she died.

At Mary Merrill's funeral, the Reverend Mr Turnbull, a Baptist, concluded his oration with this orthodox, if somewhat puzzling, admonition: 'The death of this young lady teaches us that there is no comfort but in the religion of Christ. Spiritualism and infidelity had not given her any comfort, but true religion would have achieved that end, for Christ is the friend of all. Ingersoll and his doctrines had added nothing to the happiness of Miss Merrill.'[58] *Mary Melville: The Psychic* might be read as an attempted refutation of the Baptist clergyman's claim. Released under the imprint of the Austin Publishing Company, this extraordinary book is a record of scientific and religious controversy in late nineteenth-century Canada. Among its cast of characters are the Evangelists Moody and Sankey and the equally well known free-thought lecturer Colonel Robert Ingersoll. Various theological doctrines are disputed, praises are sung to the achievements of modern science, and the entire work is founded upon a vulgarized version of Darwinism. The biography contains scraps of social and political criticism, but above all it presents a spiritualist message similar to the one advanced by Rev. Austin. As a story it is romantic and sentimental, but as a document in the religious and intellectual history of nineteenth-century Canada *Mary Melville: The Psychic* is filled, appropriately, with revelations.

Flora MacDonald Merrill was born in 1867 into a highly unorthodox family. Her mother was the daughter of a convert to Roman Catholicism. Her father was a brilliant schoolteacher turned failed prospector. Controversy over religious topics apparently was a staple of the family's intellectual diet. 'Bibles modern and Bibles ancient, church creeds and free thought for many months,' was the way that Flora MacDonald remembered her childhood.[59] At an early age she heard Colonel Ingersoll lecture, probably during his 1880 Canadian tour which included an engagement at Belleville.[60] At fifteen, two years after the death of her sister, Flora graduated from Picton High School and accepted a teaching post. But teaching, she recalled, 'was little more enticing to me than solitary confinement.' She moved to Toronto and became a seamstress, a business which did not flourish instantly. In a state of depression about her future, and suffering some temporary ailment, Flora had a psychic experience sometime in the mid-1880s. It took the form of a materialization of her deceased sister Mary, who, as frequently was the case in reports of such incidents, appeared first as a very bright light. As part of this experience came scenes of the past and the future which relieved Flora's depression and gave her confidence that the future was filled with promise for her. The meaning of the experience was clear: 'It convinced me that Mary was still living, and, under certain conditions, was able to make herself visible. It also proved to me that happiness can be prophesied years before. It also banished fear as to what might happen to me during this life or the life Mary was now living. It gave me confidence that all was well and that the apparent evils were only burnishings to bring out the good.'[61]

These recollections, set down nearly a decade after the events they purport to describe, are fuzzy and impossible to substantiate. But two observations are obvious enough. The first is that Flora MacDonald was to remain convinced of the reality of psychic experience throughout her eventful life. She participated actively in the Canadian Association for Psychic Research. In her later years her chief psychic interest appears to have been in making contact with Dr Maurice Bucke's friend Walt Whitman, whose 'democratic' philosophy she professed to follow.[62] The other, more significant, point is that the death of Mary Merrill at a very early age was a central experience in the life of Flora MacDonald. What needs to be emphasized about this otherwise obvious observation is that psychic experience, in Flora's case as in others, effectively erased the fear that something terrible was in store for humans after death. The experience of what was called spirit return destroyed the traditional Christian claim that hell-fire and damnation awaited many in the after life. Spiritualism was part of the sentimentalization of religion that is so evidently a feature of belief, especially liberal belief, in what has been called 'the Age of Beautiful Death.'[63]

While the claims of Darwinian science and the higher criticism raised doubts about traditional Christian teachings in the minds of educated and intellectual Christians, more immediate concerns shook the faith of everyday believers. Ethical rather than intellectual problems evidently were the cause of much doubt and uncertainty. In the increasingly liberal

Flora MacDonald Denison

and optimistic intellectual atmosphere of the late nineteenth century the Christian doctrines of eternal punishment and the substitutionary atonement themselves appeared immoral.[64] In no case did the immorality of Christian teaching seem more repugnant than when applied to children. By the late nineteenth century Canadian theologians, like their fellows elsewhere, were engaged in an effort to soften the application of the doctrines of human depravity and eternal torment of children.[65] It is precisely this issue which marks the starting-point for the discussion of the religious ideas contained in Flora MacDonald's *Mary Melville*.

The death of a very young child provoked a lengthy religious discussion at the beginning of the biography. It is not theology but rather a question of ethics that makes the most basic impact. 'It was not a case of dogma or of creed, but simply proved a grand truth, that above and beyond all superstition of the past, above and beyond all tradition and all religion, is the innate love for justice in the human heart; and the pleading blue eyes of an innocent infant were a stronger influence in favour of mercy and justice than all the arguments of bibles, preachers or priests.'[66]

If liberal ethics made traditional Christian teachings repulsive, the gap between Christian teaching and Christian practice offered another target for criticism. In Flora MacDonald's book a familiar series of charges against the church were presented in a dream sequence where, in idyllic surroundings, 'a tribe of strange, dark-skinned people' listened to a lecture on 'Christians in Christendom.' The lecturer, after outlining the ethical teachings of Christ, then turned to a description of inter-denominational feuding, hypocrisy, and worldly wealth. The speaker concluded: 'If half the energy spent on imposing ceremonies in palatial cathedrals were spent bettering the conditions of the people, there would be no starvation. If half the time spent in praying over and over the same prayers to Almighty God, who does not need them, were spent in education there would be no ignorance. If half the unused wealth were scattered with generous hands, Christendom might be a very heaven on earth. But such is not the case, a premium is put on wealth, power and influence, and so a rush and scramble, and fighting and wars, all to gain that end. Now these people call us heathens, because we do not know their Christ, who, they claim, has done so much for them. We work away, and all goes into the general coffers. We draw on that wealth as required for our support and comfort. One of our greatest crimes among us is to take more than we would give to our brother. The greatest virtue to Christians is to grab all within reach, and the more you are able to control, the greater will be the homage paid to you.'[67]

The moral indictment of Christian doctrine and practice advanced by secularists, spiritualists, and liberal Christians of various sorts was a powerful agent in the revision of Christian thought in the late nineteenth century. It contributed measurably to demands that the churches focus more of their energies on social questions and less on theological disputation. That was Flora MacDonald's outlook. It was part of what lay behind her conviction that in the progressive evolution of human spiritual consciousness the Christianity which taught that 'a poor little naked soul would burn in all eternity' was merely 'the missing link betwen superstition and reason.' That progressive evolution was the message of modern social and natural science. 'The plastic protoplasm, the feeling life, the man in the dug out, and then, up, up, up, brain cell after brain cell developing, the brow broadening, the face refining till reason, now our eternal birthright, dawned and Confucius, Buddha, Plato, Aristotle, Caesar, and on, and on, and on, Shakespeare, Newton, Burns, Huxley, Darwin – what a birthright.'[68]

But before the riches of this heritage could be fully claimed, old values, those represented by Moody and Sankey, had to be replaced by new ones. 'People must be educated up to moral standards of justice and learn through actual knowledge that to do wrong must hurt themselves.' In this the role of the free thinkers, such as Colonel Ingersoll, was critical. 'To my mind,' Mary Melville's father mused, 'he [Ingersoll] is not only a great man, but through him it will be possible for greater men to rise ... The old crazy superstition must be torn down. Dogmas and creeds must topple ... And this is what the Colonel is doing ... And when the errors of the past are levelled down, greater than Ingersoll will build on the ground he has left vacant.' Even liberal Christians, represented in *Mary Melville* by 'Dr World,' fail to 'comprehend' the demands of the new religion, condemning spiritualist manifestations as the 'work of the Devil,' as Salem Bland had done. And Ingersoll, for all of his virtues, was also found wanting, for his rationalism could no more explain Mary's psychic powers than the 'materialism' of orthodox medical practitioners could illuminate the curious events surrounding the young woman's death. It is an unorthodox doctor, a homeopath, who realizes that Mary Melville died so young because the world was not yet ready to accept what she represented as an example of the direction of human evolution or what she demanded as a social reformer. 'If we would benefit humanity,' the homeopath argues, 'if we would learn a lesson from this death, we should stand our shoulders to the wheel, and never cease turning it, till more men learn the lesson that humanity has evolved to a plane above the material body, and that if we would cure disease, we must be able to treat the mind.'[69]

The connection between religious heterodoxy and social reform is made quite explicit in the career of Mary Melville, even though the social reform element remains general and muted. There is throughout the book the repeated theme that orthodox Christianity with its emphasis on the afterlife and salvation removes man's responsibility for the secular world. 'I do not blame you,' Mary tells Rev. Moody; 'you are doing what you believe to be the uplifting of mankind, but you will never obtain that result until you teach men not to be dependent on anyone, be he Jesus Christ, Buddha, Confucius, Mohamet, but to develop their own powers, their own individuality, and know for themselves, that the power for good or ill lies within humanity, and not with an external God or an external personal Devil.' She believes a scientific, universal religion will emerge from the understanding that 'men are rising to a higher conception of human nature and the brotherhood of man.' More specifically, the social utopia that is outlined in *Mary Melville* includes a social order that would no longer allow the corrupt alliance of businessmen and politicians, where the right of women to equality would no longer be blocked by 'the Lords of Creation,' and where social injustice and inequality would be banished. 'The awful fact that while there was more wealth in the nation, still there were far more poverty-stricken ones,' Mary observes, 'shows the terrible lack in our civilization in allowing the wealth to accumulate in the hands of the few, and these an unproductive class.' In the future co-operative commonwealth of which Mary Melville dreamed, each would contribute according to ability and be sustained according to need.[70]

Throughout the remainder of her varied career, Flora MacDonald Denison – she contracted an unsatisfactory marriage in 1892 – combined feminist journalism, women's-rights agitation, and left-wing politics with spiritualism, theosophy, and the worship of Walt Whitman in about equal parts.[71] Her eclecticism was well illustrated by a summary she wrote of one year's activities in the Toronto Progressive Thought Club, one of the many organizations to which she devoted her energy after the turn of the century. 'The object of the club is to acquire knowledge and apply it wisely to life,' she reported. 'The books are along new thought, scientific and psychic lines ... All theories for social betterment were expounded and advocates of single tax, socialism, spiritualism, theosophy, Christianity could be heard any Saturday night at Forum Hall.'[72] Though this may seem a curious and even incompatible mélange of religious and socio-political nostrums, it really is not. What all these theories of 'social betterment' had in common was a rejection of the conventional beliefs of late Victorian Canadian society. The questioning of religious orthodoxy often, naturally enough, accompanied the questioning of social and political conventions. Spiritualism, then, was just one more manifestation of the decay of orthodox religious belief that accompanied attempts to integrate modern scientific, historical, and ethical demands into a new understanding of man's place in the post-Darwinian order.

III

The Reverend B.F. Austin, Flora MacDonald Denison, and their spiritualist brethren in Canada and elsewhere, having rejected traditional theology and dogma, were left with little more than 'a debased or sentimentalized supernaturalism, things that go bump in the night.'[73] Yet in responding to the impact of Darwinism and the higher criticism by attempting to formulate a science of earthly paradise they revealed a significant drift in religious and social thought in late Victorian English Canada. The direction of that drift was epitomized by Mary Melville's increasingly sceptical grandfather. Having tried St Paul, Luther, Calvin, Knox, and Roman Catholicism before his discovery of Darwin, he was led

to wonder: 'Was it not rather true that God was made in the image of man, than that man was made in the image of God?'[74]
    Or, as 'Mr Sludge' put it,

> Why, here's the Golden Age, old Paradise
> Or new Utopia! Here's true life indeed,
> And the world well won now, mine for the first time.[75]

6

Richard Maurice Bucke:
Religious Heresiarch and Utopian

Dr Richard Maurice Bucke, superintendent of the London Insane Asylum, was one of Colonel Robert Ingersoll's many acquaintances in Canada. In March 1892 the Canadian psychologist and the American free thinker both participated in a funeral service at Camden, New Jersey, for the controversial American poet Walt Whitman. Despite the colonel's celebrated atheism, he admitted that 'death is less terrible now than it was before, thousands and millions will walk into the dark valley of the shadow holding Walt by the hand.' There were other eulogies, including one by Bucke, interspersed with readings from Confucius, Buddha, Plato, the Koran, the Bible and naturally, *Leaves of Grass*.[1] The following year Ingersoll paid a visit to London, where he lectured on Shakespeare, a topic of growing interest to Bucke.[2] But for all that they had in common, Ingersoll the rationalist and Bucke the mystic were completely at odds on the most fundamental of questions. Bucke valued Ingersoll as a 'critic of life,' especially of 'the more or less worn out shell or bark of what we call Christianity.' But he recognized the American's limitations. 'He lived in the concrete,' Bucke wrote on Ingersoll's death, 'and had no sympathy with, perhaps no comprehension of, those who saw the objective world – as it appears to our senses – has no existence as a reality, but is a mere appearance – that the real world is other and elsewhere.'[3]

Bucke's entire astonishing intellectual life was an attempt to understand that reality, perhaps not so unusual a pursuit for a man devoted to the cure of the insane. His professional activities, his omnivorous reading, and his extraordinary personal experiences convinced him that there was a great deal more to reality than the narrow rationalism professed by free thinkers. Yet the conclusions which Bucke reached were if anything more unorthodox than those of the rationalists and secularists. For, like the

American psychologist and philosopher William James, with whom he shared many characteristics and interests, Bucke was deeply interested in the variety of religious experiences.[4] And his unconventional religious beliefs were complemented by a genuine, if vague, social utopianism.

I

In 1877, at the age of forty, Dr Bucke entered what was to remain his lifetime occupation: superintendent of the insane asylum of London, Ontario. In that position he earned for himself the reputation for innovative and humane treatment of the mentally ill. For these accomplishments and for his widely published writings Bucke won, within his profession and beyond, a reputation as a notable practitioner and investigator. Appointed professor of mental and nervous diseases at the University of Western Ontario in 1882, he was elected president of the psychological section of the British Medical Association in 1897, and the following year he became president of the American Medico-Psychological Association. His articles appeared in many of the leading professional journals in the English-speaking world, and he frequently lectured in Great Britain and the United States. In 1891 he was chosen to deliver a special lecture at the opening of the fifty-ninth session of the medical faculty at McGill, his alma mater.[5]

His major publications, the ones he valued most, reveal Bucke as something more than just an important alienist. *Man's Moral Nature*, published in 1879, was followed four years later by *Walt Whitman* and, in 1901, by his most famous work, *Cosmic Consciousness*. At the time of his accidental death in 1902 he had nearly completed a study which he was convinced would demonstrate that Francis Bacon was the true author of Shakespeare's plays. Given his growing reputation in a field still in its infancy, it is not surprising that when the Royal Society of Canada was organized by Lord Lorne in 1882 Bucke was among its original members – he was named a fellow in the English literature section. ('That is a great honour,' he told a literary friend in England, 'whatever else it may amount to.'[6]) These accomplishments and honours still lay ahead in 1877; what went before reads like an improbable combination of wild-west heroics and Victorian romance.

Bucke had been born in England in March 1837, the fifth son and seventh child of the Reverend Horatio Walpole Bucke and his wife Clarissa. Bucke's clerical father was the great-grandson of Sir Robert Walpole, the eighteenth-century prime minster, and the grand-nephew of Horace Walpole, the accomplished letter-writer. For obscure reasons Rev. Bucke uprooted his family in 1838, giving up his Church of England curacy near Cambridge in exchange for a pioneer farm a few miles west of London in Upper Canada. The senior Bucke had been educated at Trinity College, Cambridge, where together with theology he had studied three ancient and four modern languages. He concluded, quite sensibly, that his own library of several thousand books offered his children the chance of a better education than the rudimentary schools of rural Upper Canada.

His son Richard Maurice never attended regular school classes until, at twenty-one, he entered the McGill medical school. But his reading was both extensive and varied: natural history, poetry, religion, philosophy, and anything else that came to hand in any one of several languages. At fifteen or sixteen he read and was deeply influenced by Robert Chambers's *The Vestiges of the Natural History of Creation*, published anonymously in 1844. This work, which created a scandal among British theologians and scientists, was written by a Scottish journalist and bookseller, who had read widely in the scientific and philosophical literature of his time. In *Vestiges* Chambers advanced a theory of progressive evolution, moving from simple to complex phenomena. 'He actually put the pieces of the lost chart of Hutton, Cuvier and Smith together,' Loren Eiseley observed, 'and came up with the idea that organic as well as cosmic evolution was a reality.'[7] Chambers's ideas were closer to those of Lamarck than to those of Darwin, for his evolutionary scheme contained no hint of the natural-selection hypothesis.[8]

Toward the end of his life Bucke placed *Vestiges* first in a list of books that had influenced his thinking. 'It seemed to me to give meaning to the little I knew about the world, and my thoughts have ever since flowed in the channel then first traced. Later when I read the incomparably greater works of Darwin he only seemed to enlarge and deepen an impression already made rather than to teach me anything new or to sway me in a direction different from that already entered upon.'[9] Exactly which of Darwin's works Bucke later read is unclear, though *The Variation of Animals and Plants under Domestication* (1868) and *The Descent of Man* (1871) were certainly among them.[10] Whether he ever fully understood Darwin's most important volume, *On the Origin of Species*, is uncertain.[11] But what is certain is that Bucke adopted Chambers's progressive evolution rather than Darwin's evolution by natural selection. With his customary clarity Stephen Jay Gould emphasizes the distinction: 'Life is a ramifying bush with millions of branches, not a ladder. Darwinism is a theory of local adaptation to changing environments, not a tale of inevitable progress.'[12]

That Chambers so impressed the youthful Bucke is not surprising, for self-education had both opened Bucke's mind to wide-ranging speculation and left him deficient in the disciplined knowledge against which he could have measured the Scot's claims. Perhaps even at this early age those characteristics that were to exemplify Bucke's mature intellectual life, and which made him rather similar to Chambers, were already present: self-confidence in his own abilities, an insatiable desire for answers to fundamental questions, and a penchant for sweeping speculations and leaps of the imagination. These were his strengths, and his weaknesses.

Not long after absorbing Chambers's exciting explanation of life on earth, the first stage of Bucke's intellectual odyssey ended. But he had travelled a considerable distance. He had discovered and adopted progressive evolution. He had acquired a lasting taste for poetry, Shelley being among his earliest favourites. And, whatever his clergyman father turned farmer may have taught him, the son later recalled that 'he never, even as a child, accepted the doctrines of the Christian Church; but as soon as old enough to dwell on such themes, conceived that Jesus was a man – great and good, no doubt, but a man.' These youthful speculations about religion and life had an unusual intensity. 'He was subject at times to a sort of ecstacy of curiosity and hope. As on one special occasion when about ten years old he earnestly longed to die that the secrets of the beyond, if there was any beyond, might be revealed to him.'[13] If these recollections of later years did not modify the past too radically,[14] it is possible to see in this precocious teenager the seeds of the mature man. Science, poetry, and mystical religion would become his central preoccupations, though he rarely separated them.

The second phase of Bucke's education had little to do with books. In 1853, both of his parents having recently died, he left the farm and set out for the American west, working at whatever he could find. He was physically powerful and farm life had made him a jack of many unskilled trades – gardening, railway construction, farming, labouring as a deck-hand. In 1857 he left Fort Leavenworth as the manager of an ox-drawn wagon train destined for Salt Lake City. As he later recalled this five-month journey – the passage through Fort Carney to Fort Laramie, the buffalo, the Pawnee and the Sioux arrayed in a pitched battle with the Shosonee, the water shortage – his experiences seemed like an excerpt from a boy's western thriller. The final episode proved the most exciting and gruelling. Bucke decided to try his hand at prospecting in the Sierra Nevada. He joined two brothers, Allan and Hosea Grosh, who had already discovered what came to be known as the Comstock lode.

Returning to the site of their earlier strike with the intention of exploiting it, the party suffered a series of mishaps, including the death of Hosea, which left Bucke and Allan Grosh with no alternative but to set out on foot to cross the mountains into California during the storms of winter. After a month of slogging through deep snow and intense cold with almost no food, the two exhausted and frost-bitten wanderers finally stumbled on a miner's camp. Grosh died within two weeks. Bucke gradually recovered from his delirious state to discover that one foot had been so severely frozen that amputation was necessary. He also lost part of his other foot, and for the remainder of his life he endured severe pain from these injuries.[15]

The impact of these harrowing experiences on Bucke's development was enormous and enduring. He later told a friend that as he lay in pain in the miner's cabin in the late winter of 1857 'I was born again ... it cost me my feet, yet it was worth the price.'[16] Precisely what he meant is unclear, though the 'crisis' was evidently religious but not Christian. Certainly it turned his mind to his own future and perhaps resulted in the decision to follow two of his brothers into the medical profession.

Returning to Canada, he entered the McGill University medical school, where for four years he demonstrated that a lack of formal education was no obstacle to a brilliant and highly motivated student. In 1862 he graduated as a gold medalist. His prize-winning thesis, entitled 'The Correlation of the Vital and Physical Forces,' was published in the *British Medical Association Journal*.[17] What is perhaps most interesting about this essay is that it reveals that Bucke's medical interests were already focusing on psychological rather than physiological questions. His subject, he admitted, was 'not strictly medical,' but rather concerned the 'nature of life' which was at the root of all knowledge.[18]

As a medical student Bucke was already reaching beyond the conventional limits of medical knowledge in search of answers to larger problems. Medical science offered him a starting-point, but that was all. His extra-curricular reading during the McGill years led him far beyond his specialization. Darwin's *Origin* and Tyndall's *Heat* may have been part of the required readings (though at Dawson's McGill Darwin was hardly an officially approved writer). But Buckle's *History of Civilization*, whose emphasis on materialism and evolution left a permanent mark on Bucke, *Essays and Reviews*, dealing with Darwinism, higher criticism, and religious belief, and 'much poetry' were surely not part of the intellectual diet of most medical students.[19] Bucke's enthusiasm for these broader subjects continued and grew during a post-graduate year spent in Great Britain and France. The diary he kept and his lifelong correspondence with his friend H.B. Forman, the editor of Keats and Shelley, form the record of an omnivorous reader. He taught himself French in order to read Auguste Comte, Ernest Renan, and Victor Hugo, and German so that he could tackle Goethe's *Faust* in the original language.

Comte and Renan were especially important to his intellectual development. Comte's positivism appealed to his scientific bent and reinforced his belief that progressive evolution was the key to understanding human development. Though he never adopted positivism totally, Bucke remained convinced that Comte was one of the greatest philosophers. Renan's studies in religious history were of importance in confirming his belief that no single religion revealed absolute truth. (In Paris in July 1853 he recorded, 'Read in the course of the day 50 pages of V. de Jesus which gets better and better.'[20]) he especially liked to quote Renan's aphorism: 'la réligion étant un des produits vivants de l'humanité, doit vivre, c'est-à-dire, changer avec elle.'[21] It may even have been Renan's work that suggested, or at least confirmed, one of the central ideas of *Cosmic Consciousness*, namely, that history had witnessed many similar religious leaders; Bucke once asked his friend Forman if Renan had written anything about 'the rise of Christ's [sic] before Christ.'[22]

After his postgraduate year Bucke returned to Canada and established a private practice in Sarnia, having first returned to California as a witness in the Grosh brothers' claim to the Comstock silver lodes. In 1865 he married Jesse Gurd. But the small-town medical practice he built up over the next decade often seemed little more than a minor preoccupation. His letters to his English friends during these years were filled with requests for books medical, philosophical, religious, and poetic: Max Muller's translations of the *Sacred Books of the East*, Renan's latest works, volumes on Confucian and Taoist thought, contributions to the debate on the higher criticism, W.H. Mallock's *New Republic*, Matthew Arnold's books ('socially among the most advanced liberals'), and Herbert Spencer's *Psychology* ('damn poor stuff').[23] Mill's *Autobiography* evoked a revealing comment: 'I think he was the worst educated man I have read of and all the time he seems to think that his education was just the thing. The fact is his active and moral natures were not educated at all and only a small part of his intellectual faculty i.e. of abstract reasoning. I shall have his last work on nature and religion in a few days. It will be highly interesting to see what a man who has never had a religion has to say on the subject, but we had a very good example of that in Hume.'[24] That Mill's *Autobiography* was an admission of some of these criticisms apparently escaped Bucke, who found only the rationalist and knew what he disliked.

Indeed, since sometime in 1867 Bucke had known what he liked better than any other piece of writing. That year a medical friend drew his attention to the work of the American poet Walt Whitman. Almost immediate intoxication resulted, and it was to remain total and permanent. Bucke had discovered a new religion: Whitman was the prophet, *Leaves of Grass* the holy scriptures. Before long Bucke had assumed the role of the Apostle Paul to the new Christ; or, as others might prefer, he had become the leading Whitmaniac. The parallel with Paul and the burning bush on the road to Damascus is not exaggerated. During a visit in 1872, to Great Britain, where he had begun to promote Whitman's writing, he underwent what William James later described as 'a typical onset of cosmic consciousness.'[25] The experience was so central to Bucke's life that his own description alone can do it justice. He wrote: 'It was in the early spring, at the beginning of his thirty-sixth year. He and two friends had spent the evening reading Wordsworth, Shelley, Keats, Browning, and especially Whitman. They parted at midnight, and he had a long drive in a hansom (it was an English city). His mind, deeply under the influence of the ideas, images and emotions called up by the reading and talk of the evening, was calm and peaceful. He was in a state of quiet, almost passive enjoyment. All at once, without warning of any kind, he found himself wrapped around as it were by a flame-coloured cloud. For an instant he thought of fire, some sudden conflagration in the great city; the next, he knew that the light was within himself. Directly afterwards came upon him a sense of exultation, of immense joyousness accompanied or immediately followed by an intellectual illumination quite impossible to describe. Into his brain streamed one momentary lightning-flash of the Brahmic Splendor which has ever since lightened his life; upon his heart fell one drop of Brahmic Bliss, leaving thenceforth for always an aftertaste of heaven. Among other things he did not come to believe, he was and knew that the Cosmos is not dead matter but a living Presence, that the soul of man is immortal, that the universe is so built and ordered that without any peradventure all things work together for the good of each and all, that the foundation principle of the world is what we call love and that the happiness of everyone is in the long run absolutely certain.'[26]

Much of the next thirty years of Bucke's life was devoted to explaining and propagating his understanding of this 'illumination.' Though he never mentioned it later, it is likely that the experience was only a crystallization of thoughts and intuitions that he had been gathering for many years, perhaps since his youth: speculations about life and death and what existed after death. His wide reading had been directed toward answering those concerns and (not surprisingly, given Bucke's temperament), his purpose was at least as grand as that which had motivated Robert Chambers when he composed his *Vestiges*. Several months before his mystical experience in London, Bucke told a friend about a book he was trying to write and the difficulties he was having with it. 'It will be nothing less than a new theory of all art and religion and I am sure a *true* one. It will furnish a sound basis for poetical and other art criticism, not that but taste and ability will be needed to work on this basis. It will supply a new theory of the universe and of man's relation to the external universe and while being as a religion as positive as positivism and [sic] will supply more hope for mankind and will not shut up man's faculties in the known and present in the same way that positivism does.'[27]

That a young doctor in Sarnia, Ontario, should harbour such ambitions might at first blush seem truly astonishing. Yet such grandiose speculations were not that uncommon among Bucke's post-Darwinian contemporaries – Sir Charles Lyell, Benjamin Kidd, Edward Carpenter, William James, Ignatius Donnelly, John Fiske, Francis Galton, and Madame Blavatsky, to name only the best known. Perhaps the only astonishing fact about Bucke was his physical place of residence. Intellectually he lived in the wide world of Victorian speculators, seers, and religious heresiarchs.

Before Bucke published his first attempt to fulfil his mighty ambition, he moved from private medical practice to the public practice of what today would be called psychiatry. In his day that distinction would not have been made, since the specialized treatment of mental and emotional disorders was in its infancy. What prompted Bucke's move is unclear. For one thing, Sarnia's climate did not suit him. More important, his intellectual interests pointed in the direction of work with the mentally ill. His connections with the Ontario Liberals – and he was a partisan Liberal of the continentalist variety[28] – probably helped him to gain the superintendency of the newly opened Hamilton Asylum in 1876. A year later he transferred to the more familiar territory of London. In the evolution of his thought and practice as an asylum superintendent can be seen something of Bucke's more far-reaching cosmological speculations.

Probably because of his own peculiar psychological experiences, Bucke had a natural curiosity about and sympathy for his patients. In a paper published in 1880 he argued that there was no clear-cut distinction between sanity and insanity; sanity was merely a conception of reality that conformed to the definition of the majority. The insane were, in a sense, merely nonconformists. Perhaps he had his own case in mind when he concluded that 'doubtless there was more truth in the old idea of a special connection between mania and spiritual illumination than we prosaic moderns accept to think. And the reasoning of Plato in the Phaedrus – the contention for the innate superiority (from some points of view) of madness over sanity is not yet obsolete.' Bucke's interpretation of evolution also contributed to his explanation of insanity. Man's mind, he argued, evolved from the 'imperfect sensation of the worm' through 'thousands of generations of placental mammals' to human consciousness. Since mind was a recent acquisition it was more subject to instability and breakdown than were organs of more ancient origin. This conclusion he drew from Darwin's *Animals and Plants under Domestication*. With his characteristic penchant for sweeping applications, he included man's mental faculties. 'The large number of mental breakdowns,' he wrote, 'commonly called insanity, are due to the recent and rapid evolution of those faculties' which 'the more progressive families of the Aryan race' had acquired.[29] Insanity, therefore, rather than being an unnatural condition was closely linked to sanity through the evolutionary process.

These views determined Bucke's attitude toward asylum administration. His guiding principle was that patients should be placed in as normal an environment as possible. Though he began as a convinced believer in restraint and seclusion, he quickly admitted that he was wrong. Restraint was discontinued. By 1882 he had abolished the use of alcohol, which only stupefied and contributed nothing to cure. 'I am even satisfied,' he wrote in his 1883 report, 'that the use of alcohol either in sickness or in health is always a mistake and often a fatal one.'[30] Instead of confining the inmates, he opened the doors of the asylum to allow freedom of movement. He put his patients to work in the fields and harvested an excellent vegetable crop. For relaxation the asylum provided a band, a cricket club, drama, minstrel groups, and regular sports days. Non-denominational church services were held regularly, and Bucke, whatever his unorthodoxy, often preached, once using a story by Charles Kingsley in his sermon.[31] Like Philippe Pinel in France and William Tuke in England nearly a century earlier, Bucke was a 'moral manager' concerned to redress the emotional imbalance of his patients.[32] Whitman visited the London Asylum in 1880 and, though not a completely detached witness, left a reliable enough account. 'His method is peaceful, uncoercive, quiet, though always firm – rather persuasive than anything else. Bucke is without brag or bluster. It is beautiful to watch him at his work – to see how he can handle difficult people with such an easy manner. Bucke is a man who enjoys being busy – likes to do things – is swift of execution – lucid, sure, decisive. Doctors are not in the main comfortable creatures to have around, but Bucke is helpful, confident, optimistic – has a way of buoying you up.'[33]

One aspect of Bucke's attitude to 'curing' the insane revealed that like many other alienists who practised moral therapy he also accepted much of the medical orthodoxy that attributed mental disorders to somatic causes. Gynecological operations on women and attempts to prevent masturbation by male patients, using a primitive wiring technique, resulted from that belief. Though the experiments on men were terminated once their ineffectiveness became evident, in the case of women Bucke refused to accept the negative evidence. The operations may have given the women some physical relief, but even within the context of the limited medical and psychiatric knowledge of the time these experiments were crude and inhumane, especially in the light of Bucke's generally compassionate attitude to his patients.[34]

By the mid-1880s Bucke's philosophy of treatment had matured, though the dubious operations still lay in the future. He set out his views in his 1884 report. 'The object of treatment in the case of insanity is (to my mind) not so much the cure of disease as the rehumanization of the patient,' he wrote. This would be achieved by 'kindness, management, hygenic measures ... regular work, amusements, properly ordered mental exercise ... I am certain the greatest achievements so far in the direction of liberty and employment are only short steps in comparison with the great strides that are yet to be made; in a word I believe in the possibility of rehumanizing – of recivilizing – the lunatic *as a lunatic*, where recovery is out-of-the-question, and so rendering his life on the whole comfortable, if not happy, and financially nearly or quite self-supporting.'[35] Those were modest goals, but they reflected his broad view of the role of a medical man and his concern that doctors take account of more than the immediate physical causes of disease. Medical education, he argued at the opening of the McGill medical faculty in 1891, meant 'the study of *man*. But in order to study man we must study his surroundings, that is, the world in which he lives.' There was also a larger environment that had to be comprehended. 'The great value of the study of medicine,' he told the students, 'is not the cure or even prevention of disease, but the liberation of the human mind.' For Bucke that meant the study of psychology, 'the science of the evolution of the human mind.'[36]

II

The study of the evolution of the human mind was both Bucke's day-to-day preoccupation at the asylum and the subject of three books and a flood of shorter publications that he began to produce in the 1880s. Each of his main works was an attempt to utilize scientific knowledge and

Dr Richard Maurice Bucke

evolutionary theory to explain his own 'illumination' and to justify his conviction that Walt Whitman represented a new level of human consciousness. Whitman's place in Bucke's life and thought was, then, both central and complex.

Bucke's first meeting with the American poet took place at Whitman's home in Camden, New Jersey, in 1877. The impact of that meeting on the Ontario doctor was almost as great as the 'illumination' five years earlier. 'I hardly know what to tell you about W.W.,' he wrote to Forman afterwards. 'If I tried to say how he impressed me you would probably put it down to exaggeration ... He seems more than a man and yet in all his looks and ways entirely commonplace (Do I contradict myself?). He is an average man magnified to the dimensions of a god ... I not only felt deeply in an indescribable way towards him – but I think that that short interview has altered the attitude of my moral nature to everything.' Though Bucke remained somewhat ambiguous about Whitman's 'human or divine' status[37] he had undoubtedly discovered in the poet and his writing a living exemplification of his own mystical philosophy. Sometime in 1879 he told the London (Ontario) Literary and Scientific Society that 'Whitman promises moral elevation to all who will put their minds in relation to his, and this moral elevation means a greater amount of faith, a greater power of loving and a consequent reduction of the liability and capacity to hate ... Walt Whitman does not teach or found a religion but gives moral elevation, which is religion itself.'[38]

What Bucke meant by 'moral nature' and what that revealed about his own 'illumination' was the subject of *Man's Moral Nature*, which he dedicated to Whitman, 'who of all men past and present that I have known has the most exalted moral nature.' Bucke attempted to explain man's conscious states – his intellect and his emotions – by relating them to his physiological condition, an approach which might suggest that Bucke was a materialist. He argued that man's intellectual nature was rooted in the cerebral-spinal nervous system, while his moral nature was located in the sympathetic nervous system. What Bucke meant by 'moral nature' was the emotional make-up of man. Moral states were 'faith,' 'love,' 'fear,' and 'hate.' Both of man's natures were subject to the laws of evolution: physical adaptation increased man's ability to cope with the material world, intellectual evolution provided man with a growing understanding of his immediate world, and the evolution of his moral nature led toward the triumph of faith and love over fear and hate. To support this contention he appealed to the history of religion as a demonstration of progressive evolution. 'I need not insist upon the fact that, speaking generally, all the religions which have originated subsequently to Buddhism, and which have been held by the foremost races of men, such as the various forms of Christianity and Mahometanism, all differ from Buddhism and Zoroastrianism in these two essential particulars – first they declare the good power or principle in the government of the universe stronger than the evil power; and, secondly, that they represent the state beyond the grave to be, for the good of man, more to be desired than feared. The meaning of this, of course, is that with the advanced nations in modern times, that is, speaking generally, the last two thousand years, the scale has turned and faith is now in the human mind in excess of fear, and, consequently the ideas projected in the unknown world by man's moral nature are, on the whole, a plus quantity, instead of being, as in the lower races, a minus quantity, or simply equal to zero.'[39]

Bucke's progressive evolutionism, his conviction that evolution produced both more complex organisms and a morally improved mankind, had much in common with the theological liberalism that was radically altering Protestant thought. But Bucke went well beyond modernist Protestantism which, at least in its more widely accepted formulation, continued to insist upon the centrality of Jesus Christ. For Bucke, Christ was merely one among a number of religious figures who had shown the world the way to an expanded moral consciousness. In an unpublished essay in 1882 Bucke argued in favour of life after death and contended that 'all the greatest teachers of the race, the men who in all ages have gained more credence from their fellows, the men of supreme genius, the loftiest poets, the religious founders, have never rested their convictions upon the intellect, but always upon the dictates of the moral nature.'[40]

Man's Moral Nature was typical of Bucke's writings. It demonstrated extensive reading, it asserted its scientific character, but in reality it was a highly personal, even mystical, statement. Romantic that he was, he repeatedly insisted on the superiority of the 'moral' over the 'rational' understanding. Progressive evolutionist that he was, he insisted that just as man's active and intellectual natures had evolved toward perfection, so too his moral nature would continue this ascent toward the highest plane where love and faith would completely conquer hatred and fear. In the final analysis 'religion, morality and happiness are three names for the same thing – moral elevation.' As man's active nature developed, so did his control over the material environment. Intellectual development brought greater understanding of the universe. The expanding moral nature resulted in fuller communion with the meaning of existence, in which 'everything is really good and beautiful,' in which 'infinite faith and love are justified.' Though he was not yet prepared to apply the term, he was clearly describing the state he would finally call 'cosmic consciousness.'[41]

Increasingly, Bucke came to believe that Walt Whitman represented the contemporary 'Christ figure,' the man whose moral nature pointed to the future. This was the essential point of Bucke's biography – hagiography – of Whitman, published in 1883. By that time Bucke had come to worship Whitman not just as a poet or as an unusual man, but as a godlike figure. He read, reread, and memorized *Leaves of Grass*; he defended Whitman against every real and imagined criticism; he corresponded with the poet regularly and provided Walt with medical and financial assistance in his last years. He even affected a Whitmanesque style: baggy suit, floppy hat, and bushy beard. That there was something curious and unexplained in this sycophantic relationship is evident both in the correspondence and in Bucke's writings about the poet. Certainly Mrs Bucke did not share her husband's enthusiasm for Whitman or his erotic poetry. She firmly and successfully forbade a second visit to her London home after the long four-month sojourn of 1880. Perhaps she suspected, as Edmund Carpenter and other friends of both Bucke and Whitman did, that the poet was a homosexual.[42] Whitman himself, though obviously pleased with the London doctor's adulation and assistance, sometimes found it suffocating. At any rate, while actually writing part of Bucke's *Whitman*, Walt convinced his London disciple to leave out some sections in which Bucke used his subject to exemplify a godlike moral nature. Indeed, to the end of his life Whitman remained very cagey whenever Bucke attempted to obtain explicit accounts of his religious views.[43]

Bucke simply could not be restrained. The Whitman biography was a thoroughly uncritical celebration of the 'great grey Poet,' whom Bucke presented in the manner of a Holman Hunt portrait of Christ. *Leaves of Grass*, he wrote adoringly – and Whitman let it stand – 'belongs to a religious era not yet reached, of which it is the revealer and herald. Towards that higher social and moral level the race was inevitably tending – and thither even without such an avant-courier, it would still eventually have reached. This book, however, will be of incalculable assistance in the ascent.'[44] Later, as Whitman's collected works began to appear, Bucke told his friend that 'it is the bible of the future for the next thousand years, and after that (superseded by even greater poems) to live as a classic forever.' Whether old Walt thought a mere millennium was enough is unknown. Bucke, at least, was more than content; he was 'dazed' to find himself at the centre of 'the largest thing of these late centuries ... of spiritual upheaval.' When the old poet finally expired in 1892, Bucke was both desolate and uplifted, for he knew that his redeemer still lived. 'Over and over again I kept saying to myself: the Christ is dead! Again we have buried the Christ!' He told two of the poet's English disciples. 'And for the time there seems to be an end to everything. But I know that he is not dead and I *know* that this pain will pass.'[45]

Whitman's death in 1892 may have precipitated the final formulation of the scientific and religious ideas which Bucke had been developing for a quarter of a century.[46] *Cosmic Consciousness* might best be read as the final apotheosis of Walt Whitman, who, together with Gautama the Buddha, Jesus Christ, Mohammed, Francis Bacon, William Blake, and Edmund Carpenter, was pronounced an unmistakable example of the phenomena under study, though Walt had never admitted categorically to any 'illumination.' Nevertheless, Bucke now asserted that 'Walt Whitman is the best, most perfect example the world has so far had of the Cosmic Sense.'[47] But the book was more than just another example of Bucke's uncontrollable urge to beatify the author of *Leaves of Grass*. It was also, and more significantly, an example of many late nineteenth-century attempts, by William James and others, to use scientific methods to demonstrate the validity of religious experiences.[48]

Bucke subtitled his book *A Study in the Evolution of the Human Mind*, suggesting a work of science or at least of psychology. He set up an evolutionary scheme designating four distinct stages: the perceptual mind, which received sense impressions; the receptual mind, the first stage of consciousness responding to sense impressions; the self-conscious mind, capable of formulating concepts from received sensations; and finally the intuitional mind capable of 'cosmic consciousness.'[49] The intuitional mind was obviously connected with what Bucke had earlier designated man's moral nature. Yet the achievement of cosmic consciousness was equally obviously a religious experience beyond the reach of most men's moral natures, at least at the existing stage of evolutionary progress.

Cosmic consciousness, in so far as Bucke could either define or describe it, was consciousness of 'the life and order of the universe.'[50] It was, in short, really nothing more – or less – than an experience of an illumination of the sort that Bucke had undergone in 1872. And it was that experience which he now used as the standard in his search for other examples throughout history. Given the nebulous character of the concept, the use of such a personal measurement was doubtless inevitable. But it was also the major reason that the concept failed to be convincing either scientifically or even in comparison with other mystical experiences.[51] It is, however, evidence of Bucke's independence, not to say eccentricity, that at a time when liberal Protestants were turning away from 'conversion experiences' and seeking rational historical and sociological defences of religious belief, Dr Bucke, the scientist, insisted that the mystical and emotional were the essence of religion. Bucke's gnosticism, like that of Madame Blavatsky and the theosophists, is best understood as the product of an age convinced that science and religious belief could be reconciled.[52] In Bucke's view, science could explain religion but it could not explain it away.

Bucke's science of religion was essentially the application of his version of evolutionary theory to the history of religion. And here, as in earlier writing, the concept of progressive evolution was the key: not only was a contemporary, Walt Whitman, the most advanced example of cosmic consciousness, but the large number of other examples drawn from modern times indicated that one day all men would achieve nirvana.[53] Bucke was convinced that this spiritual evolution, evidenced by the emergence of new religious leaders, was not surprising and did not require supernatural explanation. It was simply another example of the working-out of evolution as he had learned it from Chambers's *Vestiges* long ago. 'So came, doubtless yet will come, among plants and animals, new varieties and species; and in the world of men, new religions, philosophies, politics, social arrangements.'[54] Every day, in every way, evolution brought improvement.

By the 1890s Bucke's progressive evolutionism and his religious mysticism gave birth to a new, though not wholly unexpected, feature of his thought: social utopianism. In so far as Bucke had any orthodox political sympathies, they were on the Liberal side. He was a continentalist for whom a reading of Goldwin Smith's tract *Canada and the Canadian Question* (1891) confirmed his conviction that 'union with the States is the only solution of the very ugly knot existing now.' Indeed, like Smith, he looked forward to the reunification of Anglo-Saxondom, with Walt Whitman as 'the prophet of world empire and imperialism.'[55] But in addition to these somewhat eccentric ideas, Bucke had also given some thought to broader social issues. In 1895 he attended a lecture by Henry George, and later had supper with the American social critic and a number of members of the London Labour Council. Moreover, he was a reader of the Christian socialist Charles Kingsley and of Edward Bellamy.[56] It also seems likely that his association with Edward Carpenter, a militant if idiosyncratic socialist, and some other British acquaintances may have led him toward social radicalism.[57] In 1894 he predicted a coming revolution in Great Britain whereby 'the present useless and worse than useless drones who have too long lived on the labour of others ... must work or die.' In one of his characteristic oversimplifications he divided all history into a 'parallelogram of two forces: liberalism and socialism,' and identified progress with the socialist cause.[58]

It was, apparently, only in *Cosmic Consciousness* that Bucke allowed his utopian imaginings to run free. 'The future,' he predicted confidently, 'is indescribably hopeful,' chiefly because of the progressive spread of cosmic consciousness. But the coming technological revolution that would accompany the invention of aerial navigation was another reason for optimism. That, he believed, would destroy national boundaries and make huge, crowded cities unnecessary, returning men and women to the pleasures of decentralized, but not isolated, country living. 'Space will be practically annihilated, there will be no crowding together, and no enforced solitude.' And the technological revolution would be accompanied by social transformation. 'Before socialism,' he wrote with Bellamyite assurance, 'crushing toil, cruelty, anxiety, insulting and demoralizing riches, poverty and its ills will become subjects for historical novels.'[59] Bucke later sketched in one final detail of his anticipated utopia, one which again suggests the influence of Edward Carpenter: the institution of marriage would disappear. In the meantime, the development of cosmic consciousness in women would 'merely deepen their spiritual life and make them better wives, mothers, friends.'[60]

These far-reaching prophecies Bucke left without much elaboration. But then he had long believed that 'knowledge of the mind' must precede any understanding of social evolution.[61] He also insisted, with the fervour of an old-fashioned Methodist 'convert,' that what he called 'cosmic consciousness' had to be widespread before a new social order could come into being. Indeed, there was more than a little of the old-fashioned Methodist, as well as a telling portion of new-fashioned religious modernism, in the London mystic's vision of the world to come. 'In contact with the flux of cosmic consciousness all religions known and named today will be melted down. The human soul will be revolutionized. Religion will absolutely dominate the race ... Religion will govern every minute of every day of all life. Churches, priests, forms, creeds, prayers, all agents, all intermediaries between the individual man and God will be permanently replaced by direct unmistakable intercourse. Sin will no longer exist nor will salvation be desired. Men will not worry about death or the future, about the kingdom of heaven, about what may come with and after the cessation of the life of the present body. Every soul will feel and know itself to be immortal, will feel and know that the entire universe with all its good and with all its beauty is for it and belongs to it forever. The world peopled by men possessing cosmic consciousness will be as far removed from the world of today as this is from the world as it was before the advent of self consciousness.'[62]

III

Despite Bucke's unorthodoxy and the extravagance of his ideas, visions, and prophecies, his outlook was not entirely foreign to the spirit of his times. Nor were his similarities only with spiritualists, theosophists,[63] and the other seekers after new religions whom Goldwin Smith identified as harbingers of religious decay. Bucke, like the liberal Christians who were increasingly influential in Canadian Protestantism, wanted to simplify religion, to bring God, man, and society closer together, to humanize religious belief. Bucke rejected the idea of divine transcendence, and insisted on God's immanence – that is what Walt Whitman taught him.[64] Struggling to clarify the meaning of cosmic consiousness, he wrote shortly before his death that 'the emotional state of man after illumination is not easy to describe, but it may be said positively that what may be called love of God becomes so overwhelming that it absolutely drowns out most ordinary emotions. It does not drown, but intensifies, sexual love, though it certainly lifts it to a higher plane or largely or entirely frees it from physical relations.'[65]

Here was the mystic state of nirvana – or salvation. Bucke adapted the Christian account of man's fall from innocence, having sinned and been made to labour, to fit his own progressive evolutionary scheme. Man's predecessor experienced only simple consciousness and therefore, in Bucke's view, could not conceive of sin. With the appearance of self-consciousness man acquired a sense of his nakedness and his sinfulness. Only then did he realize that he had to work to survive. But salvation and the kingdom lay at the end of the long process of evolution. 'For weary eons this condition has lasted – the sense of sin still haunts his pathway – by the sweat of his brow he still eats bread – he is still ashamed. Where is the deliverer, the Saviour? Who or what?' Here is the rhetoric of the revivalist preacher, the millenarian prophet. And the promise of future or immediate salvation is as powerful as it is inevitable: 'The Saviour of man is Cosmic Consciousness – in Paul's language, the Christ. The cosmic sense (in whatever mind it appears) crushes the serpent's head – destroys sin, shame, the sense of good and evil as contrasted one with the other, and will annihilate labour, though not human activity.'[66] Scientific investigation is here swallowed up in religious enthusiasm; the medium becomes the message.

The whole of Bucke's effort to join the scientific knowledge of the nineteenth century with man's religious experience was directed not toward denying religion but rather toward reinforcing it. But to reinforce religion Bucke, like so many liberal Protestants preoccupied with the place of religion in modern society, was determined to shatter the traditional distinction between the sacred and the secular. Bucke's conclusion was that the progress of evolution led inevitably toward a society where all life was religious. A world of cosmically conscious men and women, living in a socialist utopia, thriving on the benefits of advanced technology: that was Bucke's kingdom of God. It was emphatically on earth.

Bucke, then, exemplifies, in an exaggerated fashion, the connection between religious unorthodoxy and social criticism. He resembled a growing number of English Canadian intellectuals in the late nineteenth century in his belief that religion, in order to be meaningful, had to express itself as a social philosophy applicable to the here and now. Individual salvation and social regeneration had become largely indistinguishable. A new view of God as immanent in this world led to the conviction that this world would be the place of God's kingdom. That a 'social gospel' was a concomitant of a theology of immanentism was well understood by Richard Maurice Bucke. As a disciple of Renan, he believed that man's religious practices followed from his conception of God. An ancient sun-worshipper rose at sunrise and retreated at sunset. 'Her idea of religion,' Bucke wrote, 'was to imitate as well as she could the actions of God; and after all that is about all the religion any one has.'[67]

7

Toward a Christian Political Economy

That Dr Maurice Bucke should have been invited to meet Henry George when the famous American social critic visited London, Ontario, in 1895 was entirely appropriate. It was not just that Bucke was the city's most illustrious intellectual and reformer, though that counted for something. More important was the two men's shared conviction that Christianity had to adapt and evolve to meet the scientific and social challenges of a rapidly changing world. George would almost certainly have agreed with Bucke's belief that God should be made in the image of man, for that was merely a rather blunt way of expressing the modernist view that the sacred and the profane were one. That same idea was frequently expressed as the urgent need to reinterpret Christian teachings to bring them into closer touch with the requirements of modern man. Those needs were almost automatically assumed to be the consequences of the social dislocation of modern industrial and urban society. A Christian God would surely have devised a Christian political economy. Bringing God into the economic system was, of course, nothing new. In Goldwin Smith's cosmos God was the prime mover in the political economy of Manchester liberalism.[1] As doubts grew about the justice and equity of laissez-faire capitalism, so too did doubts about God, or at least about the way he was utilized by liberal political economists.

The extent to which orthodox political economy and orthodox Christianity were identified with each other naturally encouraged the growth of both religious and social dissent. The reinterpretation of Christian teachings was part of an effort to discover a social ethic and a political economy that would challenge the injustices of the emerging capitalist industrial order. But the reform of society meant more than just a satisfying and comfortable material existence. It also meant, for many, building a society wherein Christianity could truly be lived. That was what the Reverend Hugh Pedley – whose earlier worries about the church's ability to meet the challenge of secularism had by the 1890s been replaced by fears concerning the church's ability to meet the social crisis – meant when he said that the growth of socialism 'will drive us back to Christ.'[2] If for conservatives God could assume the appearance of Adam Smith or Richard Cobden, then by the end of the nineteenth century radicals began insisting that he bore a striking resemblance to Henry George.

God's place in the political economy of social reform was fully revealed in the session of 'Our Social Club,' the regular discussion group that met in the columns of *The Palladium of Labor*, the Hamilton Knights of Labor weekly, during the autumn of 1883. That discussion group also made plain the important role played by Henry George's *Progress and Poverty*, published in 1879, in the evolution of the new Christian political economy. From first to last, explicitly or implicitly, *Progress and Poverty* was the focus of the group's attention. At the club's first meeting Frank Harcourt, an Oxford graduate, bookseller, and social reformer, summarized George's view and, while objecting to land nationalization, accepted the contention that in the existing economic order progress brought both enormous wealth and grinding poverty. If progress, the growth of industrial society, caused such misery, one member asked, would not a return to the pre-industrial order be best? Not at all, retorted Alfred Freeman, the young Canadian carpenter; 'it is not machinery which is the cause of the trouble – it is the wrong system of distribution – it is monopoly of opportunities.'[3]

As the discussion continued during subsequent weeks it moved through the whole range of economic and social problems. Various proposals for reform were considered. Freeman insisted that government support for business established a precedent from which labour would benefit, since more, not less, government intervention would become a necessary feature of modern society. A more equitable social order would only arrive after labour recognized its international solidarity and exposed 'patriotism' as a disguise for monopolistic exploitation. Currency reform, votes for women, a curb on land speculation, and other issues occupied the club's attention. And in the midst of these disputes the question of the role of the church in industrial society was taken up.[4]

Clergymen, Freeman contended, too often had closed minds; their training turned them into little more than apologists for dogmas that had been handed down from on high. That 'habit of mental dependence,' once formed, led clerics almost automatically to become defenders of all forms of established authority. 'They are apt to accept the current views of political economy, and the opinion of the class with which they associate, on questions of work and wages just as unquestioningly and implicitly as they do their religious dogmas.' In adopting this position the clergy were conveniently forgetting that 'Churchism is not Christianity,' for the latter was simple, forthright, and radical. 'Christ was the greatest social reformer who ever lived.' Were he to appear on earth again he would find new scribes and pharisees to denounce: 'usurers, land grabbers, monopolists and tyrannical employers.' Freeman concluded his interpretation of Christian teachings as a program for social reform with the observation that 'there is a growing class who are neither Christians of the fashionable modern type – nor yet Infidels. They believe in God and the future life and accept Christ as a type of high moral excellence. Further than this they do not dogmatize – and are repelled by the hypocrisy and sham of Churchism. Why should not a religious society recognizing the Fatherhood of God and the Brotherhood of Man, and insisting on justice to the toiler, be the outcome?'[5] If a place and date for the birth of the social gospel in Canada was required, *The Palladium of Labor* for 27 October 1883 could make a serious claim to that distinction. A central part of the new doctrine was drawn from the writings of the American political economist Henry George. By the 1880s George's ideas and panaceas were being propounded from pulpits and platforms by clergymen, social critics, and labour reformers in Canada.

I

On 4 August 1884, the Hamilton Knights of Labor held their annual demonstration. It was a gala affair beginning with a colourful and noisy parade of trade unions, bands, athletic teams, and even a group of Tuscarora Indians, all led by a grand marshal on horseback. Sandwiched between a delegation of unorganized workers and the True Blues Fife and Drum Band rode a hack bearing the day's leading attraction, the celebrated American social critic, Henry George. It was an occasion that, according to one report, attracted an estimated 10,000 people, and that evening the Crystal Palace bulged with the throngs eager to hear the great man's words.[6]

George's message, warmly received by his Canadian audience, was the same one that he had been preaching on two continents, and with increasing impact, ever since the publication of *Progress and Poverty* in 1879. That message, delivered with typical evangelical fervour, was that despite enormous material progress the modern world suffered an increasing burden of poverty and distress. The cause and the cure were George's discovery. 'All over the world,' he declared, 'the private ownership of land has been the great cause of serfdom ... I hold that an equal right to land is an inalienable right that attaches to every human being that comes into the world.' How could man's God-given right to the land be restored? By a taxation policy that would give society that unearned increment now pocketed by the landlords. Land values increased as a result of social causes, particularly population pressure, and not from anything a land-owner did to the land. Therefore society, not the landlord, should be the beneficiary of increased land values. True value, George told his readily convinced audience of working people, came from labour, which deserved a full return, and not from land ownership, which, through high rents, caused the oppression of the working classes.[7]

In his Hamilton speech, as in all of his writings, George spoke at great length about the inequities and miseries of urban industrial life. His emphasis and the tone of his interpretation is best summed up in a well-known passage from his famous book: 'unpleasant as it may be to admit it, it is at last becoming evident that the enormous increase in productive power which has marked the present century and is still going on with accelerating ratio, has no tendency to extirpate poverty or to lighten the burdens of those compelled to toil. It simply widens the gulf between Dives and Lazarus, and makes the struggle for existence more intense. The march of invention has clothed mankind with powers of which a century ago the boldest imagination could not have dreamed. But in factories where labour-saving machinery has reached its most wonderful development, little children are hard at work; wherever the new forces are anything like fully utilized, large classes are maintained by charity or live on the verge of recourse to it; amid the greatest accumulations of wealth, men die of starvation, and puny infants suckle dry breasts; while everywhere the greed of gain, the worship of wealth, shows the force of the fear of want. The promised land flies before us like the mirage. The fruits of the tree of knowledge turn as we grasp them to apples of Sodom that crumble to the touch.'[8]

These sentiments touched the hearts of a considerable segment of Canada's working-class population because they described the realities of their often miserable lives.[9] But to explain the conditions he described so graphically, George turned from the city to the country, attacking land monopoly and urging the simple cure-all of taxation of unearned increment. With land costs lowered by the removal of the speculative element, he believed that more of the people huddled around the dark satanic mills could take up rural occupations. That in turn would reduce the labour pool and force capitalists to pay higher wages. To the Malthusian dilemma he proposed a frontier solution, and in a period of transition from pre-industrial to industrial society he was not alone in believing in the need for balance between country and city.[10] As one of George's Toronto friends wrote in 1892, 'The only people who have any interest in seeing Toronto doubled or quadrupled in size are the handful of monopolists who would profit directly from the special privileges conferred upon them, or those who have land to sell or rent. To the labouring masses and those engaged in trade the increased concentration of population at any point brings no improvement in their condition ... If Toronto were the size of New York or Chicago we should have more millionaires but we should also have a larger proportion of men and women in abject poverty than we have now.'[11]

George's message was ambiguous, and that at least partly explains its popularity. In fact, his ringing denunciations of the emerging industrial order apparently influenced the thinking of many who paid little attention to what later became known as the 'single tax' panacea. But even the single tax, a term which George did not coin and which only came into use in 1887,[12] was far from clear in its meaning. Was it merely a taxation policy, or did it mean land nationalization? As late as 1891 Principal G.M. Grant distinguished between George and one of his disciples: 'Mr. George's remedy is land nationalization, and Father Huntington's, the single tax.'[13] And George, at least in the early years of his campaign, was apparently willing to take supporters where he found them – single-taxers, land nationalizers, labour reformers, Christian socialists, Fabians, and others. Consequently, the Georgeite movement was composed of a motley crew, attracting both support and criticism from many quarters in Canada and elsewhere.[14]

George himself was an attractive, if fanatically single-minded, reformer. He spoke with fervour, wrote powerful prose, and was the master of the arresting example. Certainly he seems to have succeeded in impressing his Hamilton audience in August 1884 and infecting at least some of them with the zeal he felt for his cause. The editor of *The Palladium of Labor*, a Georgeite and a Knight of Labor who may have played a part in getting George to visit Canada in 1884,[15] was carried away on the wings of the American reformer's oratory. 'Henceforth and forever more,' he wrote, 'the ideas of Land and Labor Reform are one and inseparable. The days of aimless agitation are over. The days of partial and temporary remedies, political quackeries, industrial war, blind and despairing struggles against conditions which must ever co-exist with monopoly are drawing to a close. The watchword from this time out is 'Land for the People.' In that sign we shall conquer. Free land means free men. Land monopoly means industrial slavery.'[16]

For a decade and perhaps longer, Georgeism was as central to the discussion of social questions in Canada as it was in the United States and Great Britain. George's influence on late-Victorian radicalism deserves greater emphasis than it has so far received, partly because Georgeism has too often been made synonymous with the single tax.[17] Yet it was his analysis rather than his cure that appears to have impressed many of his readers. 'George had aroused the British social and political conscience during the 1880's as no one else had done,' one historian has written, and that is certainly attested to by no less a figure than George Bernard Shaw.[18] A similar assertion about George's importance in Canada is suggested by the extent to which his views were discussed in the 1880s and 1890s.[19]

Many Canadians were acquainted with George's ideas and his campaigns well before he visited Hamilton in the late summer of 1884. He had held moderately successful meetings in 1881 in Toronto and Montreal, where he concentrated on the Irish land question,[20] and his British campaign had been fairly fully chronicled in the Canadian press. But the Hamilton visit, which followed on the heels of another well-publicized British tour, made him the centre of a good deal of Canadian attention. In the next decade he was the subject of newspaper editorials, speeches, and articles in secular and religious periodicals. In 1885, when the Toronto *Globe* serialized George's *Protection or Free Trade*, the editor claimed that 'Henry George is, without exception, the most widely read of modern writers ... He is the man to whom the workingmen of the Anglo-Saxon races are looking for comfort and inspiration.'[21]

George's ideas played a major role in at least two Canadian novels, and it was his philosophy that informed the drawing, writing, and speaking of J.W. Bengough, one of the country's most brilliant caricaturists. At least one candidate ran for Parliament on a Georgeite platform – though Major Edward Eustace, who described himself as a Georgeite and a socialist, managed to garner only twenty-seven votes against his rather more notorious opponent, Sir John A. Macdonald, in the 1891 election.[22] Almost every respectable intellectual felt called upon to state his position on *Progress and Poverty*, and even young Mackenzie King was tempted by the Georgeite heresy, though his caution, as usual, overcame his enthusiasm. Having heard David Mills lecture on George in 1895, King wrote: 'Though I would not like to declare myself in favour of single tax I would like to see more clearly how it would benefit the classes it is intended to, viz. the poor and labouring classes.'[23] George was certainly widely discussed, and one prominent writer on social and political questions, Morley Wickett, believed that the growing interest among Canadians in political economy could be attributed both to the condition of the Canadian economy and 'in certain quarters to the writings of Marx, Henry George and also Edward Bellamy.'[24]

Not surprisingly, Goldwin Smith and W.D. LeSueur, who always kept a close eye on international controversies, were among the earliest to respond to George's ideas. Smith's reaction, which came in a July 1880 review of *Progress and Poverty*, was predictably negative. In Smith's judgment, George was inaccurate about the increase in poverty, wrong about the causes of the limited economic distress that did exist, and positively immoral in urging what amounted to the confiscation of private property without compensation. In a widely circulated polemic entitled *False Hopes*, Smith lumped George in with socialists, Greenbackers, labour unionists, and other troublemakers, and grumbled angrily 'that such views can be propounded anywhere but in a robber's den or a lunatic asylum, still more, that they can find respectful hearers, is proof that the economical world is in a state of curious perturbation.' Smith retained those views about George and other 'prophets of unrest' until the day he died, for he never gave up his firm conviction that the laws of economics, sanctioned by divine imprimatur, should not be criticized or tampered with by agitators and cranks. Man's lot was hard but it was improving slowly, though perfection was hardly to be anticipated. 'Injustice is human, and where inequality is the fiat not of man, but of a power above man, it is idle, for any practical purpose, to assail it as an injustice.'[25]

Smith's view of man and his world contrasted sharply with that of Henry George. *Progress and Poverty* exuded optimism about man, locating problems in the social order rather than in human nature. George believed in a moral progress that would ultimately result in equality and justice. In his Hamilton speech he struck out at the gloomy 'Bystander,' and the crowd cheered. 'Men of a certain type seem to think as if slavery were the natural lot of man – they wish to console us with the idea that, though things are not today what they should be, yet the masses should be contented when they look at their forefathers. This is all humbug. The natural state of man is that of freedom.' There was no real meeting-

Very Much Alike. HENRY GEORGE: I don't see any difference between slavery and – slavery. *Grip,* 23 July 1887

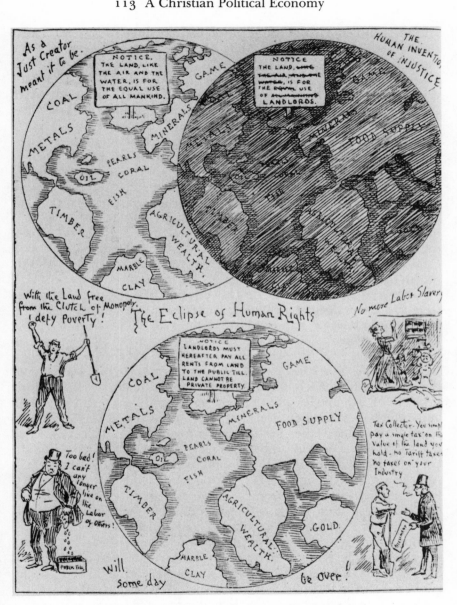

The Eclipse of Human Rights. *Grip*, 19 May 1888

ground between George and Smith, though their differences were fundamental to an understanding of late nineteenth-century social thought.[26]

Less predictable than Goldwin Smith's views was W.D. LeSueur's response to *Progress and Poverty*, a copy of which George had presented to the Canadian positivist. LeSueur was a follower of Comte, and his writings on literature, science, religion, philosophy, and history expressed a theoretical radicalism that was rarely applied to social questions.[27] His defence of *Progress and Poverty* in 1881 was designed not so much to uphold George's reformist ideas as it was to assert that the American's thinking fitted into evolutionist conceptions. It was George's general philosophy and method rather than his specific proposals that LeSueur approved, and that because he perceived correctly that George questioned dogmatic religious and ethical teachings as much as he himself did.[28] For this reason LeSueur was much closer to Henry George than Goldwin Smith; the American was quick to proclaim his Canadian disciple 'worth half the college professors in the United States.'[29]

Numbered among George's most enthusiastic supporters in Canada were the leaders of the struggling trade union movement, which was beginning to develop national links in the 1880s. There was a natural affinity between the Knights of Labor, which made such a powerful impact on central Canadian workers in the 1880s, and George's teachings. Indeed, George was a member of the Knights.[30] At the initial meeting of the short-lived Canadian Labor Congress in 1883 delegates debated the problem of monopolies and the land question. In moving a successful anti-monopoly resolution, Delegate J.R. Brown urged all members to study *Progress and Poverty* for 'the land question was at the bottom of all labor troubles.' He held, 'with Henry George, that land should be the property of the community.'[31] The presence of such labour leaders as Alf Jury, A.W. Wright, and D.J. O'Donoghue from Toronto and P.J. Ryan and Redemond Keys from Montreal, as well as Jennie Hepburn and Marie Joussaye of the Working Women's Protective Association, ensured that Georgeite sentiments were aired and single-tax resolutions frequently passed at local and national labour meetings in the late 1880s and early 1890s. 'The earth, with its lands, forests, mines and other natural opportunities,' the Trades and Labor Congress resolved in 1893, 'is the gift of nature not to a part, but to the whole of humanity.'[32]

Many of these same labour intellectuals promoted Georgeite doctrines through the columns of the radical weeklies that sprang up in the last decades of the century. These papers – *The Labor Union*, *The Palladium of*

Labor, The Labor Advocate, The Canada Farmers' Sun, The Social Reformer, Grip, and *Citizen and Country* – were all in some measure associated with the Knights of Labor, the Patrons of Industry, the Anti-Poverty Society, the Toronto Conference on Social Problems, the Toronto Trades and Labour Council, nationalist and single-tax clubs, and suffragist groups that harboured whatever radical and quasi-radical ideas existed in late nineteenth-century English Canada. Only *The Palladium of Labor,* which claimed the title of George's first Canadian exponent, *Grip, The Social Reformer,* the Anti-Poverty Society, and the single-tax clubs fully espoused Georgeite doctrine. The others provided only partial support or at least platforms for single-tax advocates. J.W. Bengough, William Douglas, J.W. Dawkins, and Samuel T. Wood (known to his friends as 'Single Tax' Wood) were thoroughgoing Georgeites. But they could almost always count on support from a broader group of social reformers and religious dissenters, people like W.H. Rose, A.W. Wright, Phillips Thompson, and George Wrigley, and even suffragists like Dr Emily Stowe, Dr Margaret Gordon, and others.

The members of this group and their followers were united by at least two convictions which provided a link with Henry George. All of them believed that the emerging industrial order in which they lived contained growing injustices that were unacceptable: monopoly and tramps, poverty in the midst of plenty, child labour, slum housing, low farm produce prices, discrimination against women. They were equally convinced that the economic laws proclaimed in orthodox circles were not laws at all, but rationalizations. Finally, all were somewhat unorthodox in religious belief – either critics within Protestantism like Bengough and Wrigley, or seekers who had moved out of the orthodox churches to theosophy or Unitarianism, like Thompson and Stowe. They would probably all have agreed that 'the son of the Carpenter was the greatest social reformer that ever lived' and that 'if Christ were to come to earth today and speak against usurers, land grabbers, monopolists and tyrannical employers, as he did against the Scribes and Pharisees, they would lock him up as a criminal or a lunatic.' In that, at least, they agreed with Goldwin Smith. Their creed was well summed up in W.H. Rowe's *Labor Union,* a Knights of Labor paper, which criticized defenders of the status quo, saying: 'They quote scripture to prove that Almighty Wisdom intended from the outset that man should prey upon his fellows; or, if they belong to the modern materialistic school, they quote science to show that it is in accordance with natural law that the stronger should prey upon the weak. It may be that an effectual scheme for the mitigation of poverty and the prevention of that flagrant injustice by which one soulless avaricious man can possess himself of a superfluity through the labor of others, has not yet been devised. It is difficult to tell until the attempt has been made but there is every reason to believe that a good deal at any rate could be accomplished by the nationalization of land according to the scheme of Henry George. Be that as it may what we wish to point out is that the obstructives who do nothing but pooh-pooh any proposition for ameliorating social conditions virtually endorse the libel on Divine wisdom that these evils are either natural or necessary.' Their goal, almost always expressed in religious metaphors, was to build a society where the ethics of the Sermon on the Mount could be practised.[33]

What is important to emphasize is that among Canadians influenced by the writings of Henry George only a few accepted what J.W. Bengough labelled 'the whole hog' solution of single tax and free trade.[34] But many others accepted all or part of his analysis, and particularly his insistence that while the rich grew richer in industrial society, poverty was also on the increase. As *The Labor Advocate*, whose editor, Phillips Thompson, had moved on from the Georgeite analysis to a Bellamyite socialist solution, put it in 1891: 'We have made great progress of late years – great strides in the direction of material development and national prosperity. And as a natural, inevitable consequence under the system of monopoly of land and capital and competition among workers, we have chronic pauperism, soup kitchens and the bitter cry of the unemployed and disinherited who, though they may not know it, are poor because they have been robbed.'[35]

It was exactly those sentiments that were expressed in a memorial presented by a joint committee of the Knights of Labor, the Single Tax Association, the Trades and Labour Council, the Women's Enfranchisement Association, the Eight Hours League, and the Nationalist Association to the annual meetings of the Anglican, Methodist, Presbyterian, and Congregational churches in 1891. The memorial called upon the leaders of these churches to raise their voices against the oppression of the poor by the rich. The Anglicans and Methodists rejected the petition, while the Congregationalists and especially the Presbyterians expressed a willingness to take the matter under study. This response was not entirely surprising, given the known attitudes of leading churchmen to the doctrines of Henry George.

The Christian Guardian, edited by the Reverend Dr E.H. Dewart, had proclaimed George's doctrines misleading and dangerous. Repeatedly these 'communistic theories'[36] were condemned, for the *Guardian*'s editor viewed society in a manner much closer to Goldwin Smith than to Henry

George. Commenting on the Toronto Anti-poverty Society, which sponsored a visit by George to Toronto in 1889,[37] the *Guardian* remarked sourly that 'the best anti-poverty society is an association of men who would adopt as their governing principles in life, industry, sobriety, economy and intelligence. Any theory that promises wealth without regard to character is a snare and a delusion. The lazy and shiftless cannot become wealthy in an honest way.'[38]

The main Presbyterian response was a few degrees more positive and a good deal more thoughtful. That church's most eminent spokesman on social and political questions was Principal G.M. Grant. Like many other Canadians in the 1880s, he had some thoughts on *Progress and Poverty*. Perhaps more perceptively than any other observer he detected the religious character of George's writings and the attitude of his followers. 'Nothing short of remarkable qualities in a book could give rise to such bibliolatry,' he wrote. Yet most of the qualities were remarkable only for their falseness, Grant believed. He disagreed with George's contention that most men's living standard was worsening, rejected the labour theory of value, and denied that land monopoly was the central evil. Yet he was satisfied that George had identified a real problem, one that orthodox political economists like Goldwin Smith had failed to answer. 'For convince the masses that the doctrines of the orthodox political economist are the whole truth, and Karl Marx's conclusions will be accepted by them,' Grant observed shrewdly. The old political economy of individualism was outdated, and Henry George, for all his failings and oversimplifications, at least realized that.[39]

Grant returned to the fray on other occasions, admitting that a tax on land speculation would be a good measure, but growing increasingly emphatic in his rejection of George and his Canadian disciples. A speech given by the Presbyterian divine at Trinity College early in 1891 brought an immediate counterattack from Reformers, who usually viewed Grant as something of a friend. J.W. Bengough, who was certainly an admirer of Grant, believed that the Queen's principal had so distorted George's position that only a sarcastic parody could serve as an adequate response. 'We understand that Mr. Henry George intends delivering a lecture at Queen's College, Kingston, in which he will completely refute and demolish Newton's theory of gravitation. He has given long and earnest study to the subject and feels confident that he will be able to prove the fallacy of Newton's idea that the earth is kept in orbit by the periodical falling of green apples. Principal Grant has secured a reserved seat for the occasion.' S.T. Wood and the Single Tax Association took a more serious line, one that they thought should be especially telling. 'Has your address added to the respect for Christianity,' they asked, 'or has it aided to intensify the feeling of hostility and contempt with which, unfortunately, so many of the toiling masses regard the Christian ministry?' Grant delivered his reply in a lecture at the Kingston city hall, once again rejecting George's theories and dismissing his critics as men with 'a comical conception of Christianity.'[40]

Yet George's influence on Canadian Protestantism appeared to be growing by the 1890s. One piece of evidence was the warm reception accorded to the Reverend J.O.S. Huntington, a radical New York Episcopalian, Knight of Labor, and Georgeite,[41] who visited several Canadian cities, including Toronto and Kingston, in January 1891. (His visit may in fact have been the cause of Grant's renewed denunciations of George.) He delivered several speeches and sermons in Toronto, including one entitled 'Religion and the Single Tax,' in which he had a few uncharitable words for the principal of Queen's University. But just as interesting as his speech was the composition of the platform party. The usual single-taxers and representatives of the Trades and Labour Council were there, but they were far outnumbered by a large group of reverends, rural deans, and doctors of divinity. Perhaps not all of these men of the cloth found themselves in full agreement with their ecclesiastical Georgeite visitor, but their very prominent presence gave his ideas a new respectability.[42]

Clerical approval of Father Huntington's Georgeite message was not unanimous by any means. One clergyman, writing anonymously in *The Week*, reacted in tones at once of astonishment, disgust, and even fear. Why were clergymen who knew nothing of the real conditions of working people now being heard clamouring to have the American priest in their pulpits? Had they failed to comprehend the revolutionary implications of Father Huntington's message, which was 'setting class against class ... stirring up discontent among the poor?' And what would the single tax achieve? 'It means the speedy destruction of all estate in real property. It means the nationalization of the land. It means that those who have put their earnings into real estate, under the laws of the land, are to be robbed of those proceeds of their earnings. We confess that these are strong measures to be advocated by the clergy.'[43] The spectre of Henry George obviously haunted some property owners' imaginations.

An important sign of the compatibility of Georgeism and Protestantism soon appeared in *The Canadian Methodist Quarterly*. The July 1891 issue of that periodical, more liberal but much less widely circulated than *The*

Christian Guardian, carried a long article by one of Methodism's most powerful leaders. The Reverend Albert Carman entitled his piece, which had probably begun life as a sermon, 'The Gospel of Justice.' In it he made no bones about his belief that the church too often allied itself to the rich and attempted to anaesthetize the poor. 'Should the suddenly rich, the monopolists, those who have filched the savings of the people, all who live by the labour of others, meet in secret council to frame a religion under which they would like the world to live, what better could they enact than that the oppressed would bear with Christian humility their oppression, and the wronged would live on with silent lips, looking for right only beyond the grave? And yet that is in practical effect the Gospel heard today in many an upholstered pew.' As Carman rolled on in the sepulchral tones of an Old Testament prophet, he paid his respects to Henry George for his 'tremendous persistence in drawing to the world's attention the evils of land monopoly.' Like many a single-taxer before him, Carman reminded his readers of the twenty-fifth chapter of Leviticus: 'The land shall not be sold forever, for the land is mine; for ye are strangers and sojourners with me.' 'If that chapter is not inspired,' declared this traditionalist in biblical interpretation, 'the Old Testament must be thrown away.'[44] George could not have received a more forceful endorsement.

Carman's contention that Henry George's teachings were nothing more than an updating of biblical ethical imperatives was a point that single-taxers themselves repeatedly made. One advocate of the 'New Crusade' argued that the single tax was simply an application of the Golden Rule, and, since 'Christ was no mere idle dreamer,' it was a practical measure. A young Presbyterian minister, who described George as 'the greatest political economist the world has ever seen,' claimed that the American offered a Christian alternative to the political economy of the agnostic John Stuart Mill. 'I can understand how an atheist might write a treatise on botany, chemistry or geology,' he wrote, unconsciously siding with Darwin over Principal Dawson, 'but not on political economy.' And 'Single Tax' Wood sought to confound his clerical opponents by declaring that 'our aim is to emphasize the doctrine of the Fatherhood of God, the Brotherhood of Man, the equal right of every one of God's children to the common bounties of a common father.' That same message was the theme of two social gospel novels published in the 1890s: *Roland Graeme: Knight,* written by the Presbyterian feminist Agnes Maule Machar, and *The Preparation of Ryerson Embury,* whose author, Albert R. Carman Jr, was the son of the general superintendent of the Methodist church. In these novels Christian ethics and Georgeite economics became indistinguishable.[45]

That George should play the role of a regenerator in communities where Protestant Christian values were embedded in the culture is not surprising. The explanation is found in the final chapter of *Progress and Poverty*. Odd as it might seem in a book on political economy, the concluding section, entitled 'The Problem of Individual Life,' was devoted to a discussion of man's immortality. It was a chapter about religious belief. George observed that though the yearning for a future life remained powerful, religious faith 'among men on whom mere creeds have lost their hold' had grown feeble. The explanation, he argued, was not so much 'the revelations of physical science' as it was the harsh teachings of orthodox political economy. 'It is difficult to reconcile the idea of human immortality with the idea that nature wastes men by constantly bringing them into being where there is no room for them. It is impossible to reconcile the idea of an intelligent and beneficent Creator with the belief that the wretchedness and degradation which are the lot of such a large proportion of human kind results from his enactments.'[46]

Since George's book claimed to demolish Malthusian population theory and laissez-faire orthodoxy, it also restored hope in the future. *Progress and Poverty* was a work of theology as well as of political economy – though George would not have made such a distinction. And that explains its wide appeal. In arguing that the source of religious doubt and the decline of faith lay in social circumstances and false economic arrangements rather than in the intellectual climate, George pointed Christians away from theological concerns and toward social criticism. For him the resolution of both sacred and secular problems required the same prescription. Once the new theology, or political economy, was adopted and applied, social and individual salvation would be assured. The essence of George's message was to transform the traditional idea of Christian salvation and immortality into the rhetoric of social regeneration. 'With want destroyed,' he proclaimed, 'with greed changed to noble passions; with the fraternity that is born of equality taking the place of the jealousy and fear that now array men against each other. With mental power loosed by conditions that give the humblest comfort and pleasure; and who shall measure the heights to which our civilization shall soar? Words fail the thought. It is the Golden Age of which poets have sung and high raised seers have told in metaphor! It is the glorious vision that has always haunted men with gleams of fitful splendour. It is what he saw whose eyes at Patmos were closed in trance. It is the culmination of

Christianity – the City of God on Earth, with its walls of Jasper and its gates of pearl. It is the reign of the Prince of Peace!'[47] That, quite simply, was the apocalyptic vision of the social gospel. For Henry George, as for many spiritualists, the Christian promise of perfection in immortality was made mundane.

II

In Canada as in the United States, Henry George was a seminal figure in the development of the social gospel. Where Goldwin Smith, *The Christian Guardian*, and conservative Protestants rejected George as a threat to both society and religion, liberal Protestants perceived that his views were entirely compatible with their desire for modest reforms. To Protestants whose theology was under attack from historical criticism and science on the one hand, and who were frequently criticized for failing to be relevant to the social needs of the times on the other, George provided an answer. That answer was a moralistic rhetoric combined with a reform proposal that promised a maximum of utopia with a minimum of change. Social salvation through works seemed easier than individual salvation by faith to a growing number of Protestants.

But Henry George performed another task. As Ryerson Embury put it, '*Progress and Poverty* – lays out the orthodox ideas on political economy with a flail.'[48] Just as George challenged traditional Protestants to face up to the demands of social suffering, so he forced others to question the dogmas of orthodox political economy. 'Political Economy has been called the dismal science,' he wrote, 'and as currently taught, *is* hopeless and despairing. But this, as we have seen, is solely because she has been degraded and shackled; her truths dislocated; her harmonies ignored; the word she would utter gagged in her mouth and her protest against wrong turned into an endorsement of injustice. Freed – as I have tried to free her in her proper symmetry, Political Economy is radiant with hope.

'For, properly understood, the laws which govern the production and distribution of wealth show that the want and injustice of the present social state are not necessary; but that, on the contrary, a social state is possible in which poverty would be unknown, and all the better qualities and higher powers of human nature would have opportunity for full development.'[49]

As Goldwin Smith and others recognized, once the accepted ideas about the economic order were questioned, especially those concerning property, a large hole was opened in the established order. There was no reason to believe that the single tax would be the stopping place. Phillips Thompson, who had thought his way out of Christianity, realized that he could go beyond George, too. 'The Single Tax movement is doing excellent work in breaking ground for Socialism by causing people to think of the evils begotten by land monopoly and the way to remedy them,' he wrote. 'There is no tariff on ideas, nor any conceivable method by which those who have cut loose from conventional opinions so far as to realize that the landlord instead of being a social benefactor is a spoliator and a parasite, can be prevented from carrying the principle to its logical conclusion and condemning all forms of unearned increment.'[50]

A Phillips Thompson in Toronto, a Henry Harvey Stuart in Fredericton, a Salem Bland in Winnipeg began with Henry George and then moved on to a more thoroughgoing radicalism. There were others who did not – J.W. Bengough, F.J. Dixon, Nellie McClung, and T.A. Crerar. But George's writing opened the eyes of many Canadians to the idea that social and economic arrangements were not forever sanctioned by divine or scientific laws beyond the powers of man to change. 'The old days of slavish acquiescence to whatever is uttered with an air of authority and fortified with a scripture text or a passage from Adam Smith have gone by forever,' one Canadian social critic wrote. 'The monopolists and their advocates have been compelled to make the attempt to meet the arguments of George and the other noble minded Labor Reformers.'[51]

In a nutshell, Henry George's contributions to the discussion of the progress of poverty in late-Victorian Canada was to arm social critics with a doctrine that fitted snugly into the emerging modernist Protestantism. 'Henry George set out to find the cause of poverty in the midst of plenty,' W.A. Douglas, a leading Toronto Georgeite, explained, 'and he accomplished something manifold better, he gave humanity a Christian science of political economy.'[52]

8

'A Republic of God, a Christian Republic'

John Wilson Bengough, editor of *Grip*, the superb weekly magazine of caricature, light verse, puns, and satirical paragraphs, subscribed fully to Henry George's 1897 creed: 'My republic is the republic that is coming; not a republic of tramps and millionaires; not a republic in which one man has the power of a czar; not a republic where women faint and go hungry; but a republic of God, a Christian republic.'[1] That republic would be reached through the application of Christian ethical teachings, and in Bengough's view Henry George had showed the way to do that, too: the single tax. Henry George probably had no more faithful follower anywhere than the Toronto journalist and entertainer.

I

Bengough was a self-taught journalist and caricaturist. Lacking the financial resources that might have sent him to university, he had turned to a trade that required his intellectual and artistic talents – printing. 'His best education was received in that modern university, the printing office,' an admirer later wrote.[2] First at the Whitby *Gazette* and then at the Toronto *Globe* he worked as both a printer and a reporter, experiencing a growing frustration at not being able to practise his drawing skills. Then, in May 1873, still only twenty-two years old, he founded *Grip*, where for the next two decades he almost single-handedly edited, drew, versified, and punned outrageously for a growing audience of admirers. Though sales probably never exceeded 7,000 copies at the peak of *Grip*'s popularity in the mid-1880s, its readership was doubtless larger.[3] Bengough's influence went beyond his subscription list, for he attracted large audiences to his public lectures. His 'chalk talks,' combining witty discussions of public issues and public men with instant cartoons, were popular entertainment in Canada and abroad in the years before the radio and the movies. (In the 1920s, just before his death, Bengough turned to movie-making as part of an anti-smoking campaign.) By the turn of the century his drawings appeared in newspapers in Canada, the United States, and Great Britain, in both single tax publications and the more orthodox mass circulation press – the Toronto *Globe*, the *Montreal Star*, the *Single Taxer*, the *Weekly Templar*, the *Square Deal*, the *Daily Express*, the *Morning Chronicle*. W.T. Stead, who shared many of Bengough's reform goals, described the Torontonian as 'one of the ablest cartoonists in the world.'[4]

Though caricature was Bengough's finest talent – and even that was somewhat weakened by his urge to fill his frames too full – he also wrote serious and comic poetry[5] and devised puns and dry satire. Goldwin Smith, he once wrote, had made a New Year's resolution 'to start a new Bystander one of these days, as soon as his indignation against women suffragists, Home Rulers, labor men, prohibitionists, etc., had accumulated near the bursting point.' His puns were sometimes sophomoric, as when he defined the Fenian scare as 'a threatened lack of whiskey,' or as in his suggestion that the national spirit could best be cultivated by growing barley. He could even be a little risqué: 'Absinthe,' he maintained, 'makes the heart grow fonder.' Typical of his style and outlook was 'Fresh from College.'

ETHEL: I think that Henry George is just a dear, good man.
MAUD: Why, Ethel, for shame! He's a horrid nihilist, isn't he?
ETHEL: I don't care what he is. He is in favor of the 'Single Tax,' and I believe that is the only thing that will bring bachelors to their senses.[6]

But for all of his determination to make people laugh, Bengough was not satisfied just to puncture the pompous and ridicule the powerful. He was a Victorian and a Protestant for whom even a pun had a serious purpose. *Grip*'s view, he explained in 1888, 'is that the legitimate forces of humor and caricature can and ought to serve the state in its highest interests, and that the comic journal that has no other aim than to amuse its readers for the moment falls short of its highest mission. *Grip* has sought to play the part of educator, though dressed in the motley, and upon questions with a distinct moral bearing he has always striven to be on the right side.' While he defined his politics as 'strict, unswerving independence,' that meant 'upholding the party which is right.' Morality,

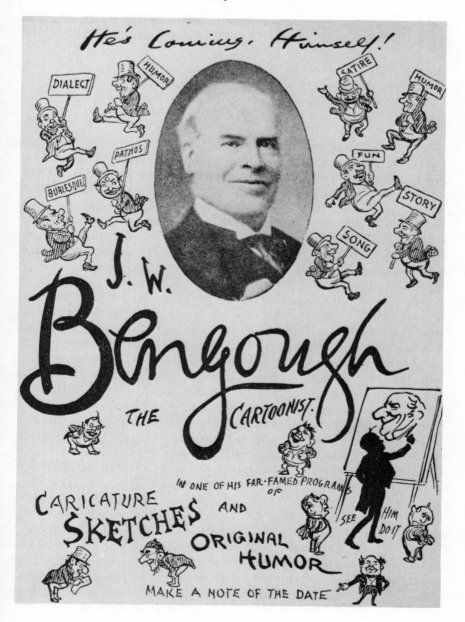

public and private, was his chief concern, as was clear in a 'New Nursery Rhyme' written on the occasion of the Pacific scandal investigation:

> Sing a song of scandal, the Premier full of rye
> With half a hundred Tories knotted in a pie;
> When the House was opened, quite small they had to sing,
> And went back to Hugh Allan, the Great Pacific King.[7]

Grip's first success was a by-product of the Pacific scandal. 'The whole country was at once aflame with interest and excitement,' he later recalled, 'and an absorbing theme adopted to keep *Grip* going for many issues had been supplied at the right moment.'[8] Since Bengough had first become interested in political cartooning as a result of his early admiration for the work of Thomas Nast in *Harper's Weekly*, the Pacific scandal was obviously tailor-made. As Nast had excoriated Boss Tweed and the Tammany Tiger, Bengough could now go after Sir John A. Macdonald, whose face was a caricaturist's dream, with enthusiasm. Nast's influence on Bengough was enduring, and some of the Canadian's drawings were inspired directly by his American counterpart. For example, Nast's Republican elephant, which first appeared in 1874, surely provided the model for *Grip*'s National Policy elephant, which appeared often in the following year. More striking, perhaps, is the similarity between one of Bengough's most famous cartoons, entitled 'Ancient Tory Tactics,' which depicts the Conservatives entering the National Policy Trojan horse just outside the walls of office, and Nast's 1872 drawing of Horace Greeley and the Liberal Republicans boarding a similar apparatus.[9]

Those similarities are striking, but the differences between the two cartoonists were no less important. While Bengough drew workingmen who resembled Nast's and adopted the 'Ragbaby' that symbolized the Greenback movement for Nast and applied it to Canadian soft-currency advocates (inevitably known as 'beaver-backers'), the intention was different. The Toronto cartoonist sympathized with labour and monetary reformers; the American ridiculed them. Though each man established his reputation fighting for political purity and against corruption, they were temperamentally quite unalike. Nast's caricatures reveal an almost humourless Germanic outlook that imagined gloomy, fierce, and frightening images. Bengough preferred humour, exaggeration, and ridicule. 'The pun,' he characteristically contended, 'is mightier than the sword.' Both men were patriots, and there is some similarity between Nast's bloody Unionist cartoons during the American Civil War and

Bengough's celebration of the Canadian cause during the Northwest Rebellion in 1885.[10] Yet Bengough was only occasionally a flag-waver; he preferred to lampoon rather than praise the patriotic pretensions of politicians and businessmen. Perhaps that explains why Nast received a minor consular post from Theodore Roosevelt, while Bengough's appeal to Laurier for a Senate appointment resulted only in 'sympathetic consideration.'[11]

If some of the forms of Bengough's cartoons were drawn from Nast's example, the spirit and mood had other sources. The title *Grip* was taken from the raven who constantly accompanied the feeble-minded Rudge in Charles Dickens's 1841 novel *Barnaby Rudge*. 'Strange companions, Sir,' Dickens has Varden, the locksmith, remark. 'The bird has all the wit.' *Grip*, with its 'croaks and pecks,' puns, sallies, verses, and cartoons played that role, and, for a brief period at the beginning, Bengough even listed 'Barnaby Rudge' as editor. Dickens appealed to Bengough, as he did to many other Victorian reformers, because without being radical he expressed a powerful Christian sympathy for the lower orders and society's outcasts.[12] Bengough's own origins were modest and his upbringing evangelical Presbyterian, a product of the revivalist atmosphere of mid-century Canada. It is impossible to understand his social views without emphasizing his religious sentiments.

Introducing Bengough's *Caricature History of Canadian Politics* in 1886, Principal Grant, whose own religious views were only slightly more sophisticated than those of the cartoonist, described the artist as 'at times utopian ... In the best sense of the word, he is religious.'[13] It was an accurate assessment, given Grant's view that religion was a practical ethical matter. Bengough was inspired by a vision of dissenting Protestantism which looked forward to the future fulfilment of God's kingdom on earth through the implementation of a few simple reforms. In religious matters he was somewhat conservative or, perhaps more accurately, evangelical; emotional rather than intellectual. His reading was sufficiently extensive to inform him in some considerable detail of the claims that the higher criticism and Darwinian science were making against Christian orthodoxy. His poem, entitled 'The Higher Criticism,' demonstrated both his understanding of contemporary biblical scholarship and his rejection of it. It began:

> I saw a Higher critic, looking scholarly and cool,
> As he stood beside the portals of the new Negation
>   School.

Any Thing to Get In. You can't play the old Trojan horse game on Uncle Sam.
By Thomas Nast

Grip, 6 July 1878

The poem described the higher critic's list of biblical weaknesses and inconsistencies and his attempt to replace 'comfortable faith in Christianity' with 'modern doubts and theories.' Bengough responded by reaffirming the beliefs he had learned at his mother's knee: 'She told me 'twas from God direct.' He concluded uncompromisingly:

> I have no quarrel with learning – wise doctors have
>   their place –
> But the scalpel of the scholar cannot dissect God's grace.[14]

Naturally, the proponents of free thought and agnosticism had even less success with Bengough than the higher critics. One of his finest clerical creations – and there were many – was a Professor E. Volushin, who preached a gospel remarkably similar to that of W.D. LeSueur's defence of modern thought. The satire was broad but effective. One of the professor's 'Saturday Sermons' took up the question 'What Is Life?' The message was plain: 'We must try to solve the problem of life aside from Christianity, because our theory demands that we exclude the idea of God from the Universe. Happily we *can* solve the problem. Modern thought *has* solved it. These are the glad tidings I am commissioned to preach, beloved friends! I have to tell you today that the vilest malefactor may be regenerated by gazing upon the masterpieces of classic art; that the impure mind may be cleansed by the contemplation of the lily; that domestic infelicity may be purged away by the gracious offices of bric-a-brac, and that, in short, the sin and misery of life may be cured by Culture. Next week I shall give you a discourse on Hope. A special collection will now be taken up to supply a bereaved family with a volume of Homeric poems, of which they are very much in need.'[15]

Other sermons dealt with such topics as 'Human Nature Is All Right' and 'Natural Morality Is the Thing.' The message might well have been directed at Colonel Ingersoll or his Napanee disciple, Allen Pringle: 'It is my business to be in collision with the Church. The Church is wrong. It is unscientific and shockingly credulous ... [It claims] that human nature is created by an Intelligent Being and *did not evolve itself* ... where is the necessity – the scientific necessity – of a Creator, when one is able to evolve oneself ...? Human nature today is what it has become through its own efforts, and therefore it is right.'[16]

Such spirited satirical defences of orthodoxy against the onslaught of secularism did not arise out of any complacency about the church's monopoly on truth and virtue. Indeed, Bengough saved some of his sharpest barbs for what he identified as the self-satisfaction of the major Protestant denominations. Another of his creations was the Reverend Diaphanous Dixie, D.D., who regularly preached self-serving sermons for the satisfied and admonished his parishioners on the need to fill the collection plate to overflowing. In Bengough's eyes the association of the church with the wealthy was a particular evil. That association could compromise the church's moral authority by making it the handmaiden of the powerful. *Grip*, like Dr Albert Carman, heaped scorn on the idea of the 'gospel of wealth' and took particular pleasure in attacking the Massey family's ostentatious acts of public charity. 'There is joy in the ranks of Methodism,' Bengough wrote in 1892, 'over the donation of $40,000 by Mr. H.A. Massey to endow a theological chair in Victoria College ... The hard working people of this country have voluntarily by legislation made Mr. Massey a wealthy man by taxing themselves on the machinery they use to put money into his pocket. A world minded or careless man might have dissipated his accumulations or lost the opportunity of making any by paying his employees something more than subsistence wages, which they would no doubt have squandered in beer and riotous living. It is

A Hundred Years Later. SHADE OF WESLEY: 'And this is Methodism! I should hardly have known it!' *Grip*, 21 March 1891

obviously better for the world that capitalists should brave the censure of the unthinking, and, while exacting by means of combines the highest price from the public with one hand and manfully cutting down wages with the other, acquire the means of being charitable and munificent on a grand scale.' Methodists like the Masseys, Eatons, Coxes, and Flavelles would eventually destroy the original spirit of the church. In a burlesque on 'Suksessful Preechers, or, How to Get the Best Kalls,' Bengough made his point in slapstick fashion. The 'preecher' told his flock: 'Let the Methodist people adopt pew rents everywhere, and we shall soon be as respectable as the other churches, and the poor trash will have to go to the *Salvation Army.*'[17]

Bengough's admiration for the Salvation Army revealed his belief that Christianity should stress social action and practical charity. In sentimental poems like 'The War Cry,' which contrasted a Salvation Army woman's self-sacrifice with the cynicism of a group of businessmen, and 'Made Whole,' in which a clergyman welcomes an ex-convict into his home, he displayed his admiration for 'practical Christianity.' In 'Modern Religion' he contrasted the new, up-to-date, 'higher critic' preacher

> Then up rises the preacher, the preacher of today,
> Expounding points of scripture in a very clever way,
> And gives so many meanings to words both great and small,
> That he makes you quite decided that the text has none at all

with what he believed was the essential Christian message:

> When shall we find the churches teach what their founder taught –
> To deal with each man justly, and pay each other what he ought?
> To scorn hypocrisy, although its wealth be what it may?
> When shall faith as given at first be taught in modern day?

For Bengough, then, right conduct, not doctrinal scrupulosity, was the correct test of religious faith, a contention that he shared with more liberal, social gospel Christians. Bengough's formulation of that position was unusual, simple, and direct. He criticized churches 'Whose preachers preach theology a deal more than they should, / And try to make men wise, when they should try to make them good.'[18]

Once again anticipating the strategy of the social gospel, the Toronto satirist insisted that only by focusing on moral and social issues could the church again make itself relevant. That the church was in trouble

Miss Canada, Barmaid. When will the country be 'ripe' to get out of this partnership? *Grip*, 9 July 1887

The Workingman's Position (On the Sunday Street Car Question). 'Here I stand and here I rest!' *Grip*, 10 August 1889

Bengough had no doubt. He summed up that conviction in a judgment made all the more acute by its sarcasm. In a paragraph captioned 'Clerical Retreats,' he wrote, 'Pressed as the clerical element is in modern time, by assaults of infidelity, the attacks of non-conformists, the faiths, the desperate in their dying agonies, the trouble of their flocks, the troubles of getting flocks, the difficulty of watching and especially of shearing flocks when got – the health, spirits and strength of the worthy clerics decay to an alarming extent.'[19] By taking up social questions the church, so obviously in retreat, could once again march forward.

It was perhaps inevitable that Bengough, as a Protestant moralist, should become the exponent of two typical causes: prohibition and sabbatarianism. But what is notable about *Grip*'s advocacy of these causes is that it was couched in terms of the needs of the working classes. The moral evil of drink, in Bengough's view, though an affliction felt by all classes, wrought the heaviest toll on working people and their families. That is the message of 'Miss Canada: Barmaid.' So too he opposed liberalizing the Sunday laws; he believed that an open Sunday would lead to open factories and longer working weeks. To those who claimed that Sunday streetcars would carry people to church, he retorted that even more would find their way to the park or the workplace. When the Toronto *World* maintained that Sunday cars would improve church attendance, *Grip* replied with a mixture of sabbatarianism, moralism, and concern for working people. It was not getting to church that concerned the workingman, he began, but preserving a day of rest. 'Human nature in Toronto is the same as human nature in Chicago and, under similar conditions, will work out similar results. In the latter city, by gradual stages, Sunday has been abolished as a day of rest, and now thousands of men are glad to work seven days in the week for wages they would otherwise get for six. Whatever guarantee is there that, once the start is made by even so trivial a thing as Sunday streetcars Toronto will not ultimately end with Sunday papers, Sunday saloons, Sunday business of all kinds...? Better go without church services than to go to them in streetcars which open the way to the destruction of the day itself. 'The Sabbath was made for Man' – and the workingmen of Toronto are determined to keep it sacred for labor as one of the few things that grasping monopolists have left them.'[20]

Though the rhetoric of prohibition and sabbatarianism was negative, it contained much that was to become part of the standard vocabulary of Canadian reformers: suspicion of big business – 'monopolists' – the

Woman's Sphere. THE ATTORNEY-GENERAL, ONTARIO: 'Er – personally, I may say, I regret it, and you see the Legislature is still of opinion that woman's proper sphere is to look after the babies, and not to vote.' SUFFRAGIST: 'So it is, and yonder are a couple of political babies that require looking after in the worst way, but we must be enfranchised before we can take charge of them!' *Grip*, 16 March 1889 virtue of working people, and the corruption of the 'old' political parties. Moreover, the reforms advocated necessitated the use of the state to achieve moral and social improvements. This was the plain implication of a statement in one of Bengough's prohibition tracts. 'It is oft said by the Gin Mill crew that you cannot make men good or pure by law, and no one said you could. To make a man pure you must get at his Heart. But though you cannot make Folks pure, you can make them drunk by Law, and that is what is now done, and it is the thing we wish to stop. It is the true sphere of the law to keep the Path of Life clear, and to make it hard for men to go wrong.'[21]

The desire to banish King Barleycorn led Bengough and many other prohibitionists into the camp of the women's suffrage movement. His conversion to this cause was part of a more general change that overcame *Grip* in the early 1880s. In the previous decade he had expressed scepticism about the 'Female Righter,' but, as the caricature 'Woman's Sphere' reveals, he became convinced that women voters would hasten the arrival of a dry Canada. 'The domestic realm is, of course, woman's special charge,' he explained, 'but there are babies in the political world too, that require looking after in a motherly fashion.' He also supported coeducation and the right of women to enter the learned professions. A decision by the Ontario benchers ('the Lawyer's Trade Unions') to refuse a woman admission to the bar in 1892 provoked one of Bengough's best satirical poems. 'The Lady and the Law,' by Ananias Limberjaw, Q.C., concluded:

> Praise to the benchers who have stood
> Against the innovating flood,
> To save us and our ample fees,
> From tribulations such as these.[22]

The established political parties, especially the Conservatives, were viewed by Bengough as vehicles of hypocrisy and corruption interested only in winning and holding power. In *Flapdoodle: A Political Encyclopedia and Manual for Public Men*, he defined party as 'a word of such significance that in the minds of some politicians it stands for country, friends, family and sometimes even self-itself.' And when Young Canada asked its guardian about the benefits which his National Policy had promised to farmers and workers, Sir John A., Bengough's archtypical politician, replied:

Some Exhibits That Ought to Find a Place in an 'Industrial Show.' *Grip*, 21 September 1889

> My child, I will now explain to thee,
> The motive of our Policy.
> The N.P. cry was just the thing
> Our party back in power to bring;
> This Policy, my verdant elf
> Was to turn out the Grits and get in myself;
> That's all, that's all, my child.[23]

Though Bengough had obvious sympathies for the Liberals – especially when they were out of power – he was, as a moralist, a natural oppositionist, a third-party man. By the mid-1880s he was urging the formation of a new party especially to fight the prohibitionist cause. 'The Tory oligarchy is now, and always will be, solid for whiskey, for the pure love of evil,' *Grip* complained: 'the Grits and their Hamlet-like leader, have as usual hesitated and halted until their chance is gone, and richly deserve the demoralization that is in store for them.' In 1888, when the Third Party was established and led by the Methodist Dr Alexander Sutherland, *Grip* gave it full support. But this ephemeral movement, which brought together those who hated alcohol and those who hated Honoré Mercier's Jesuit Estates Act, splintered into bits, and died almost as quickly as it was born.[24]

Had Bengough gone no further than to support such moralistic measures as prohibition and Sunday observance, his reform credentials would be slight. He would not have found it possible to work with such radicals as Phillips Thompson, who by the 1880s had become a leading proponent of the Knights of Labor and Bellamyite socialism, and who certainly did not share Bengough's opinion of drink or Sundays. What brought radicals like Thompson and Bengough together was the common conviction that the economic system developing under the umbrella of the National Policy produced wealth for a handful of monopolists and misery for the multitude. *Grip* summed up the problem in an 1889 cartoon entitled 'Some Exhibits That Ought to Find a Place in an Industrial Show.' In the 1870s Bengough had joined in the general nationalist demand for a protective tariff, but by the early 1880s he had become a crusading free trader. While wealthy businessmen waxed, poverty and unemployment increased, and all John A. did was to go into 'hiding from the Great Unemployed,' who cried:

> Fee-fo, fi fum
> I fail to hear the N.P. hum
> Where's John A., the man who said
> We'll all have plenty of work and bread?[25]

'The Workingman's Delicate Position' made the point in another way: the N.P. elephant supported the monopolist against foreign competition, while leaving the Canadian worker to compete for low wages against cheap imported labour. In short, the protective tariff was blatant class legislation, a 'system of sneaking robbery of the masses for the benefit of the classes' under which farmers and labourers were 'plundered.' When the 1891 census revealed a stagnating economy and a declining population, Bengough summoned all of his considerable talent for simplification to describe 'Cause and Effect': 'It is said that the use of intoxicants will stunt the growth of a child, and it is beyond all question that the stimulant put into the hands of Miss Canada in '78 has had this effect. Protection has been a good thing – and will continue to be a good thing – for a certain number of gentlemen engaged in certain industries, but it makes the country a cheap one for the rich to live in and a dear one to live in for artisans, while it imposes the heaviest burden on the farmer, lumberman

The Workingman's Delicate Position. *Grip*, 19 July 1884

The Consumer Consumed. In the eyes of protectionist statesmanship, the chief function of the consumer is to feed swine. *Grip*, 21 January 1888

and fisherman who, if common sense ruled our councils, ought in Canada to be the most lightly taxed of our citizens. The fact is this stimulant is a rank poison and if we don't give it up right away, and take steps to get the baleful effects of it out of our system, we are doomed. Fools and boodlers may continue to shout for the great N.P., but natural law will vindicate itself against the puny forces that seek to set it at naught.'[26]

Repeatedly *Grip* pilloried the monopolies which Bengough believed flourished under the National Policy. 'A Giant for Jack to Kill' appeared on 25 February 1888, and it hardly needed an explanation. 'Sugar Combine' was lettered on the side of a barrel; 'robbing the Canadian consumer of 1¼ cts. per lb. or $200,000.00 annually, for the benefit of a few refiners who pay less wages than any other industry in Canada, in proportion to capital and profits.' 'The Consumer Consumed' was nearly as graphic, but Bengough nevertheless took the occasion to explain to anyone who might have missed the point that 'even the body of consumers represented on the payroll of Protected Manufactories, profit nothing by an increased tariff.' Nor did *Grip* leave its audience in the slightest doubt about the method by which the political system ensured that protection of monopolists could wield more power than the oppressed public at large. In one of his many shots at the profiteers of patriotism, Bengough drew on his limited classical knowledge in 'The Protected Manufacturer Bleeding for His Country': 'Dulce et Decorum est pro Patria bleedi – as the poet hath it – So Shell Out!'[27]

For *Grip*, then, free trade was part of the solution to what Victorians called 'the Labour Question.' Though thoroughly hostile to annexation and completely unsympathetic to Goldwin Smith's well-known answer to the Canadian Question, he supported the Liberals' unrestricted reciprocity proposal and later ridiculed Laurier's attempt to straddle the tariff fence. But more was needed than tariff reform if the condition of the working classes was to be improved. Bengough knew that under the existing system working people were nearly powerless to protect themselves against employers. 'It is simply a disgrace to civilization,' *Grip* announced, 'that manufacturers can be found who are capable of this cruelty of reducing the wages of their employees below the living rate that their profits may be swelled. The explicit curse of Heaven has been against those who grind the faces of the poor, and no invective of ours can add to the weight of that denunciation.' But what was the solution?[28]

By the 1880s Bengough had become a missionary for what he called the 'whole hog' remedy. That remedy was free trade plus the single tax, Henry George's well-known elixir. As late as 1882 Bengough was still

Grip, 12 February 1887

spoofing George's book, but shortly thereafter he fully absorbed its message, and stuck to it until the end of his life. The appeal of the single-tax philosophy to Bengough, as to many others of his generation, was religious. Society, he maintained, was deeply divided between rich and poor, the millionaire and the pauper. 'Is there a city on this continent,' Bengough asked a group of Protestant ministers in 1892, 'in which we do not witness extraordinary disparities in society, poverty appalling in the midst of aggregations of avarice – hovels of wretchedness within a stone's throw of palaces gorgeous in their luxuriousness?' Here was a social sore which, if left to fester, would lead eventually to 'a cataclysm of ruin.' In his 'chalk talk' on 'The Social Question,' which Bengough delivered to hundreds of audiences, he could think of no harsher way to describe modern industrial society than 'this travesty on Christianity; this satire on the doctrine of the Fatherhood of God and the Brotherhood of Man.'[29]

This was essentially the same simple message contained in *Progress and Poverty*. It fitted exactly into Bengough's evangelical Protestant view of the world, for Georgeite doctrine 'contained nothing antagonistic to the spirit of the Christian religion.' Henry George thus became the infallible prophet of social and moral regeneration and the single tax the theme of an endless stream of cartoons. Landlordism came to represent 'The Eclipse of Human Rights,' and Bengough repeatedly denounced 'in the name of God and Humanity this legalized system of heathen robbery.' Wage slavery and legal slavery, as he captioned a cartoon showing Henry George flanked by a worker and a black slave, were 'Very Much Alike.' His commentary read: 'Mr. George's elaborate and able work "Progress and Poverty" was an attempt on his part to answer the elaborate question: *why in spite of the increase in productive power do wages tend to a minimum which will give but a bare living?* That such is the tendency of wages at the present time, when the productive power of labor is greater than it ever was before, is unquestionable. Mr. George's reply is, in brief, that the laborer comes out short because the landlord gets more than his share, as a result of laws now in operation, which are radically wrong and unjust ... it will hardly be denied that nowadays, in many classes of society labor cannot hope to do more than secure the absolute necessities of life – food, clothing and shelter – and this takes no account at all of the unemployed. Now these things are what slavery guaranteed to the slave in exchange for his toil, and it follows therefore that, so far as the comforts and pleasures of this life are concerned, the laborer is literally in a state of bondage.' Bengough believed that George's ideas would eradicate these injustices: a tax on unimproved land values would destroy land monopolists as free trade would destroy business monopolies.[30]

What Bengough and other late nineteenth-century Protestant moral reformers were aiming at in the advocacy of the single tax was the recognition of the community's responsibility and right to ensure social justice. The lack of social justice in modern society resulted from the community's failure to protect its common rights against individual greed. The community had the right to all value created by nature or God – land values, natural resources, and franchises related to the development of those values. What was created for all should be taxed for the benefit of all, the community. Distinct from 'land values' were 'labor values,' the things which men by their effort created: houses, furniture, clothing, and machinery. These should be tax-free. 'Now it seems obvious to me,' Bengough argued, 'that the free gifts of nature to the community ought to belong to the community, and the fruits of labor to those who do the work or give a full equivalent for it.' The failure to recognize this principle explained the ills of society. The tax system invaded both public and private property, literally breaking the commandment not to steal – or at least legalizing theft by allowing 'monopolists' control of what properly belonged to the community. The religious foundation of Bengough's panacea was most directly expressed in a poem entitled 'Restitution,' which restated the biblical account of the expulsion of the money-changers from the temple in Georgeite terms:

> But Christ has not forgotten, and wolfish human greed
> Shall be driven from our heritage, God's bounties shall be freed;
> And from out our hoary statutes shall be torn the crime-stained leaves
> Which have turned the world, God's temple, into a den of thieves.[31]

The key to social peace, even social utopia, was a simple combination of free trade and the single tax. At the time of the violent Homestead strike in the United States *Grip* asserted that 'the land question is at the bottom of the trouble. Why do workingmen struggle with one another to get a job ... at almost any wages ...? Because they are not free to employ themselves. Why? Because they can't get access to land by which they might live. Why? Because the land is now owned by monopolists who hold it at a premium beyond the reach of poor men. The single tax would destroy this monopoly and by doing so would render such scenes as those lately enacted at Homestead impossible.' Those who rejected the single-tax prescription were regularly lampooned in *Grip*. Goldwin Smith,

The Very Obtuse Professor; (Or, in other words, the professor who professes to be very obtuse). *Grip*, 21 December 1889

who saw Henry George as a proponent of confiscatory laws, became a 'Very Obtuse Professor.' Bengough's friend Principal Grant also found himself out of the raven's favour. In fact, since George's single-tax idea found little support from academic social critics and political economists, Bengough had many opportunities to excoriate the 'Scholastic Muck-rakers.' It was only when Mackenzie King published his *Industry and Humanity* in 1919, by which time Bengough had become a regular supporter of the Liberal party, that Bengough could hope that he had

The Schoolmaster Schoolmastered. HENRY GEORGE (to Principal Grant): 'I'll teach you to criticize "Progress and Poverty" before you know the first thing about it.' *Grip*, 31 January 1891

found an influential fellow believer. He drew King an original caricature which he believed illustrated the similarity between their views. Mr King, who knew a good cartoonist, to say nothing of a supporter, when he saw one, agreed that the sketch revealed a common concern with 'this most important of all problems: namely, the right distribution of all the fruits

The Scholastic Muckraker. The Political Economist who devotes himself to a microscopic search for the cause of social unrest and the cure of poverty amongst the sticks and straws, while the palpable explanation is to be seen if he would but look up!

of industry, and the best methods of ensuring this end.' He said nothing about solutions.[32]

II

There were other planks in *Grip*'s 'Solid Platform': independence under a republican government; alliance of all Anglo-Saxon nations; public control of monopolies 'to be worked by the government in the interests of the whole people'; separation of church and state; and one official language. The latter point revealed that Bengough, like many other nineteenth-century reformers, had little use for either the Frenchness or the Catholicism of Quebecers. A good inoculation of British ideas and the English language were what they needed. But the centre-piece of the platform was the free-trade single-tax panacea. As G.M. Grant had observed, Bengough was utopian in his belief that these measures would resolve the critical social problems of a developing industrial capitalist society. In the final analysis he was a Protestant moralist, like many contemporary reformers, rather than a systematic radical theorist. For such critics social and economic problems were moral questions for which the Christian ethical code offered sufficient answers.[33]

For Bengough, then, Henry George provided the essential prescription for social criticism and social reform. It was a religious prescription, for, as Bengough maintained, Georgeite economics was simply 'the earthly side of the Gospel.' When George died in 1897 Bengough composed a poem hailing the American reformer as 'the Seer of our age,' comparing him to Moses. George's crusade would come to be seen as equal in importance to the role played by John Brown in the abolitionist movement. As blacks revered Brown, 'so Labor kisses Henry George, who 'gainst a blacker slavery stood.' So, too, George's crusade would go marching on:

> His cause undone? nay, sprung anew!
> His cause was God's – his prophet call,
> 'God made this fruitful earth for all,
>   Not for the few!'
> The sun is up and lights the world, and men have seen,
>   and truth is true![34]

The moral urgency and religious certainty of Bengough's position were more impressive than its intellectual depth. Nevertheless, there was considerable justice in the observation *Grip* made at the beginning of

1891: 'I think I can claim to have done this much – I have made it clearer to a greater number than ever saw it before, that the existing system *won't do*.' Bengough's friend Phillips Thompson was correct in arguing that for many reformers the single tax was merely a transitional point. Once the community's right to tax the unearned increment on land was admitted, its right to a much wider degree of control over economic and social development was a logical implication.[35]

Bengough did not take the road that eventually led Thompson and others to socialism. But his active Christian conscience, his fruitful imagination, and his skilful pen nurtured the growth of social criticism in late Victorian Canada without much of that humourless self-righteousness that so often characterizes reformers. Instead, he took it as his personal mission to proclaim that self-congratulation was the opiate of the society in which he lived. In doing so he deftly punctured the pomposities of politicians, poets, prelates, and professors – and even of single-taxers. In a gentle satire entitled 'The Ragged Reformer' he perhaps had the last word on his own career:

> He's kind and philanthropic,
>   Full of plans both wise and great,
> To raise the sunken level
>   Of humanity's estate;
> With wisdom overflowing,
>   With kindness as a stream –
> But how to pay his butcher's bill
>   He doesn't dare to dream.

> You hear him on a Sunday,
>   A-spouting in the Park;
> And spell-bound hundreds list to hear
>   His simplest least remark;
> He preaches Anti-poverty
>   From morn till even's close;
> But he hides his feet behind a seat –
>   His boots are out of toes!

> While National Economy
>   Employs his mighty mind,

Economy his wife must use
  Of the domestic kind.
The law of wealth he knows full well,
  And learnedly displays it;
But he must pawn the coat he's on
  Each once in a while, to raise it!

Democracy he preaches, too,
  All thrones would trample down;
And you'll observe, consistently,
  His hat has lost its crown.
Consistent? No, well hardly so,
  For, while 'No Rents' he teaches,
I must alas! confess he has
  A dozen in his breeches!

So treads he on through shade and sun,
  The world's cold winds defying,
Though through each hole, from head to sole
  Its arrows keen on prying.
A crank? Yet let no harsh word hurled
  His expectations dim;
Though he may not remould the world,
  This hope is joy to him![36]

9

'The New City of Friends':
Evolution, Theosophy, and Socialism

'The Single Tax movement,' Phillips Thompson wrote in *The Labor Advocate* in 1891, 'is the Unitarianism of political economy – a half-way house where the investigator may find rest for a breathing spell, but not a permanent abode.' A few months later he asserted that Canadian reformers were divided into two distinct camps: single-taxers and socialists. He challenged his readers to a public discussion of the two options. He must surely have known that one of the first to enter the lists would be *Grip*'s editor, J.W. Bengough, who naturally championed the single-tax cause. But that defence, predictable as it was in its insistence that the single-tax–free-trade panacea remain at the top of the reform agenda, actually admitted that this was only the beginning – Thompson's point. Once the single tax was implemented, 'all the rest,' presumably meaning socialism would follow 'in due course.' Bengough certainly knew that while he could count on Thompson's support in the campaign for Georgeite justice, his friend and frequent collaborator in reform causes had long since left 'unitarianism' far behind.[1]

If Bengough had a rival as a satirical journalist and hot gospel social reformer in late nineteenth-century Toronto, it was without question T. Phillips Thompson. In the cartooning event Thompson did not compete. But he was a better versifier than *Grip*'s editor and at least a match as a humourist, and he took second place to no Canadian as a mimic and satirist. Thompson was better informed than Bengough, more intelligent, and angrier about the injustices he saw around him. In politics, social thought, and religion Thompson was a radical, Bengough a reformer. In the small intellectual community of late nineteenth-century English Canada there were few radicals, but Thompson was always delighted to defend his unpopular causes against the intellectual establishment of professors, clergymen, and assorted literary figures. 'The able editors and cultured professors against Labor Reform!' he once sniped. 'Of course,if they were not they could not be editors or professors for long.' Thompson could write with the clarity and bite of Goldwin Smith, the passion of Principal Grant, the humanity of Agnes Machar, and the erudition of W.D. LeSueur. He shared Dr Bucke's admiration for Walt Whitman and Whitman's religious heterodoxy. 'The pen of a revolutionist,' E.E. Sheppard wrote of Thompson in *Saturday Night*, 'and the heart of a gentle, loving woman.'[2]

Phillips Thompson's career was a kaleidoscope of late Victorian intellectual nonconformity. In 1880 *Grip* described 'An Evening with the Toronto Literati': 'At the head of the table sits a man with a high forehead, Roman nose, and straight sandy whiskers, a tall, thin, ungainly figure. It is Phillips Thompson of the *Mail*, at one time on the *Telegraph*, afterwards of Boston; now pres. of the Free Thought Association; the "Jimuel Briggs of Coboconck University," the writer of satirical poems, the composer of National Currency, Rag Baby songs. A stalwart Beaver-backer, an uncompromising atheist, a profound thinker, and a genial, jovial gentleman.'[3] Even in 1880 that description hardly did justice to Thompson's already varied activities, though it accurately suggested that much still lay ahead. Thompson's active career stretched from Confederation to the Great Depression, though the most creative years were lived before the Great War. During that time he engaged in virtually every debate – religious, political, and social – that took place in the English-speaking world. So, too, he backed a multiplicity of radical causes, occasionally running for public office himself – without success. At the heart of all of his controversies and causes was a concern, typical of social critics of his time, with ethical questions and the relationship between religion and social values.

Born of Quaker parents in Newcastle-on-Tyne in 1843, Thompson arrived in Canada at the age of fourteen. After studying law (he was never called to the bar) he discovered his true calling: journalism, especially dissenting journalism. In 1864, having just reached his majority, he entered the debate over the proposed federation of the British North American colonies with a forceful attack on the idea that the new nation should be a monarchy. Far better to start with a clean slate by establishing an independent republic, which would be in keeping with Canada's North American character, 'the progressive spirit of our people, and the age in which we live. This is the nineteenth century – the age of progress.' He advocated legislative union based on representation by population rather than a federal system. That, he agreed, meant the assimilation of French-speaking Canadians. But progress and Canada's 'glorious destiny' demanded the sacrifice, Thompson believed. 'The question is this: shall one fourth of the people of British North America, of *foreign* descent, speaking a foreign language, having laws and institutions of the sixteenth rather than the nineteenth century, be suffered to bar progress and prevent the advancement to national greatness of the British portion of the community – or, in case they see fit to separate from them, to block the pathway to the ocean, and interpose a barricade to their free communication, in a *British* colony, won by *Britons* at the mouth of the canon and the point of a bayonet?'[4] That militantly patriotic question was obviously rhetorical.

Thompson, like Bengough, remained a lifelong republican, a fairly characteristic stance for a nineteenth-century radical. But unlike most radicals and reformers in English Canada Thompson gradually developed a strong sympathy for French Canada. In 1885 he publicly defended Riel's rebellion as a people's attempt to defend itself against 'spoliation at the hands of land grabbers and rascally government agents.' Having no representation in Parliament, they had no alternative but to resort to force. He recognized and admired the anti-imperialism of French Canadians at the time of the Boer War and, though a secularist, defended separate schools on the ground that they, unlike the public schools, were not teaching imperialism. 'If children must be taught to worship anything,' he wrote during the 1905 controversy over separate schools in the new prairie provinces, 'it is better that they should adore the Virgin Mary of Mr. Sarto of Rome than prostrate themselves before the great god Jingo or the flag that is the emblem of class and caste rule at home and pillage and spoliation abroad.' Indeed, by the 1880s he had concluded that it was not the French Canadians but rather the Orange Lodge that posed the most serious threat to Canadian well-being. When his friends Bengough and Sheppard joined in the general hue and cry against Premier Mercier's settlement of the Jesuit estates question in 1889, Thompson eloquently attacked the Orange Lodge and the equal rights movement. 'Corruption in politics is bad, but race and creed war is infinitely worse ... Class supremacy in any form is a hateful thing, but if it must be – if the feeling between Catholic and Orangemen is so intense and deep-seated that no *modus vivendi* can be arrived at other than the ascendancy of one or the other – the Catholic, the "Jesuit" if you will, is on the whole preferable to the Orangeman. The Jesuit is at least a gentleman and a man of the world. The Orangeman is too often either a fanatic or a self-seeker affecting fanaticism to serve his personal ends. Either party, of course, having power may be expected to abuse it. But it is less disagreeable to be met by the "stand and deliver" of a gentlemanly and courteous highwayman of the Claude Duval type, than to be garroted by Bill Sykes.'[5] It was probably his familiarity with Ireland as much as his natural sympathy with minorities that explains the change in Thompson's attitude to French Canada.

During the early 1870s Thompson worked as a reporter for the *Telegraph* and the *Mail*, where he developed his reputation as a witty political critic. His sharp satire, frequently directed at George Brown, the Grits, and the *Globe*, was carried under the pseudonym Jimuel Briggs. As correspondent for the Coboconk *Irradiator*, Jimuel described the *Globe* as 'a joint stock company which is Brown, but he would scorn the idea of limited *lie-ability*. His ability in that direction is unlimited.' In 1873 he collected some of his satirical columns and published them as *The Political Experiences of Jimuel Briggs, D.B., Graduate of Coboconk University*. It sold for the modest sum of five drinks. His degree was as bogus as his alma mater, standing for 'Dead Beat.' The humour was broad, but the points it made were often telling. A good example is the account of Thomas Moss's campaign in 1873 for election on the 'Canada First' platform. Jimuel set out with Moss and the young men of 'Canada First':

We assembled in the Masonic buildings that evening. There were fully twenty of us involved with the idea of Canadian nationality. Previous to our proceeding to business, one of those moved that we should wet the New Party, a proposition that was wildly encored. 'I move,' continued he, 'that we order a dozen bottles of Bass, or perhaps the party would prefer some hot Irish whiskey?'

I rose with concentrated indignation in my glance, and proceeded to excoriate the cuss. 'Do I hear aright? Have we then already a traitor to the cause in our midst? Is it possible that any one of those here assembled to vindicate the glorious cause of Canadian nationality is so lost to manhood, so degraded and servile a being as to advocate the use of such derogatory foreign beverages as Bass and Irish whiskey?'

'Never! Never! shall I be so false to our glorious motto "Canada First" so as to endorse such a proposition. Let us have *Canadian* old rye, hot and sweetened with the extract of the maple – the noblest tree of the forest to whose trunk the emblematic *Moss* clings as tightly as our candidate does to the principles of Canadian nationality – and some lemon in it – beg pardon, gentlemen, I retract the lemon, I forgot that was a foreign ingredient.'

My motion carried *nem con* and the being who proposed the un-Canadian beverages wilted into a corner.

That night, under such auspicious circumstances, the Canadian Party was

'Jimuel Briggs,' by J.W. Bengough. *Grip*, 30 December 1882

formed, the germ of its existence being stimulated into growth by Canada's national beverage.

We passed resolutions declaring that we were actuated by truly Canadian sentiments, that we deplored the virulence of party warfare, that anyone who deprecated the formation of such a party was a scoundrel, a thief and a traitor to the best interests of the community, and finally that Thomas Moss, Q.C., having never had any experience in political life, had, on that account, a first class claim to the suffrage of the electors.

We again moistened the roots of the Maple and adjourned.[6]

Thompson had been involved in 'Canada First' though, predictably, somewhat outside the mainstream. In 1874, with H.R. Smallpiece, he embarked on his first venture in independent journalism. *The National*, a weekly, was 'Canada First' and anti-George Brown in sentiment: it carried general news of political, social, and religious discussion and activity. Much of the news it found fit to print was either ignored or buried in the back pages of the daily press. At least at the beginning the editor's intention appears to have been to support William Foster, Goldwin Smith, William Howland, and the other Canada-Firsters who had established the sedate, respectable journal, *The Nation*. Thompson's sheet had no ambition to be sedate or respectable. 'The utterances of *The National* will be characterized by snap and spice – vim and vigor,' the editor announced. 'Untramelled by journalistic conventionalities and bound by no slavish deference to English or American models it seeks to promote the growth of a healthy, indigenous Canadian literature, racy of the soil, and reflecting Canadian sentiment.'[7]

The alliance between the bohemian 'dead beats' who ran *The National* and the clubby élite that formed 'Canada First' was an unstable one. 'Canada First,' in Thompson's view, had to be transformed from an intellectual coterie into a popular movement – a new, principled, perhaps even radical, political party. *The National*, for example, found the outlook of organized farmers – the Grange – attractive: 'they have our strong sympathy on social and political grounds – despite the slurs of political economists, literary dilettanti, and the organs of the non-producing class.' The paper also expressed support for the developing working class, even though it did not yet fully recognize the need for collective organization. Nevertheless, *The National*'s political economy remained fairly orthodox: like a growing number of Canadians in the depressed 1870s, the paper argued that tariff protection would solve the country's economic ills. But to that Thompson added support for currency reforms similar to those advanced by the Hamilton merchant, Isaac Buchanan, and to those of the 'Greenback' monetary reformers in the United States.[8]

Even when he dropped his 'Jimuel Briggs' disguise (he continued to use it for occasional contributions to *Grip* where, writing about a temperance convention, he described himself as a 'moderate drinker ... for it ain't very often we exceed our ten or a dozen nips every day'), Thompson's writing was often strident and sensational. He had little respect for conventional standards, and allowed his dislikes to serve foolish as well as defensible causes. His contention that George Brown had fathered an illegitimate child proved silly and groundless, but his defence of the proponents of free thought was courageous. He was himself an active member of the free-thought movement, and he recognized the social and political significance of the religious and scientific debates of the 1870s. He was only sorry that so many Canadians appeared oblivious to these controversies. 'The great intellectual conflict,' he remarked, 'now in progress in other countries between the old theology and the new ideas has made scarcely a ripple upon the smoothly flowing current of our plodding unintellectual existence. Our people have generally but the crudest ideas of the important changes in the views and modes of thought that are taking place in other places – of the vast upheaval which is shaking the moss-covered structures of antiquity to the foundations, and causing the solid earth to tremble beneath men's feet.' He did what he could to stir up interest by participating in the Toronto Secular Society and by ensuring that free-thought events like Allen Pringle's Napanee debates were fully reported in *The National*.[9]

Attitudes like these ensured that a break with 'Canada First' would almost inevitably take place. Goldwin Smith and his friends seemed happy to settle complacently into the newly established, very English, National Club. The boisterous group at *The National* wanted to launch a popular movement. Goldwin Smith's hostility to women's suffrage was symptomatic. 'Instead of projecting bold, radical measures,' Thompson complained, 'they are content to give utterance to reiterated platitudes.' By 1875 he pronounced the 'Canada First' leaders a 'fraud': their entire course had been 'a succession of stupid blunders and disgraceful deceptions.'[10]

By 1875 Thompson was restless; the parochial, conservative, conformist Toronto milieu frustrated him. 'Moral cowardice,' he wrote in an essay on the unprogressiveness of Canadian literature, 'is the leading vice which permeates alike our society and our politics, our religion and our literature ... In no English-speaking community ... is there more blind and bigoted intolerance of all that conflicts with conventional opinion and sham respectabilities of the age than in Canada.' Thompson was never a man of qualified judgments.[11]

Sometime in the next year or so, with *The National* on the edge of financial collapse, Thompson decided to test his fortunes in the United States. There the social ferment of the 'gilded age' doubtless appealed to his critical temperament. Settling in Boston, he found work with several newspapers, sent dispatches home, and contributed to such humorous publications as *The American Punch*. Boston, according to Henry James, had more than its share of 'witches and wizards, mediums, and spirit-rappers and roaring radicals,' and Thompson no doubt went the rounds of unconventional gatherings as he had done in Toronto. It was probably during these years that his naturally critical turn of mind absorbed some of the ideas that were to mark his writing over the next few decades.[12]

The most striking evidence of the direction in which his thoughts were moving was revealed in the publication of perhaps his finest poetic satire. It was directed at the American adaptation of the ideas of the English philosopher Herbert Spencer. Promoted by such publications as E.L. Youman's *Popular Science Monthly* (where W.D. LeSueur's defence of Spencer against Goldwin Smith had been carried on Spencer's recommendation), social Darwinism had won considerable approval among successful businessmen and leading academic social philosophers. Thompson, who had never been attracted to laissez-faire economics or to the view that the survival of the fittest was a valid principle of social organization, published his judgment on Spencer in *The National* in 1878. Entitled 'The Political Economist and the Tramp,' the poem made its point so effectively that Thompson used it on several later occasions and included it in his book *The Politics of Labor*.[13]

> Walking along a country road,
>   While yet the morning air was damp,
> As unreflecting on I strode,
>   I marked approach the frequent tramp.
>
> The haggard, ragged, careworn man,
>   Accosted me in plaintive tone:
> 'I must have food —' he straight began;
>   'Vile miscreant,' I cried, 'begone!
>
> "'Tis contrary to every rule
>   That I my fellows should assist;
> I'm of the scientific school,
>   Political economist.
>
> 'Do'st thou not know, deluded one,
>   That Adam Smith has clearly proved,
> That 'tis self-interest alone
>   By which the wheels of life are moved?
>
> 'That competition is the law
>   By which we either live or die?
> I've no demand thy labor for,
>   Why, then, should I thy wants supply?
>
> 'And Herbert Spencer's active brain,
>   Shows how the social struggle ends;
> The weak die out — the strong remain;
>   'Tis this that Nature's plan intends.

'Now, really, 'tis absurd of you
　To think I'd interfere at all;
Just grasp the scientific view –
　The weakest must go to the wall.'

My words impressed his dormant thought.
　'How wise,' he said, 'is nature's plan!
Henceforth I'll practice what you've taught,
　And be a scientific man.

'We are alone – no others near,
　Or even within hailing distance;
I've a good club, and now right here
　We'll have a "struggle for existence."

'The weak must die, the strong survive –
　Let's see who'll prove the harder hittist;
So, if you wish to keep alive,
　Prepare to prove yourself the fittest.

'If you decline the test to make,
　Doubting your chances of survival,
Your watch and pocketbook I'll take,
　As competition strips a rival.'

What could I do but yield the point,
　Though conscious of no logic blunder?
And as I quaked in every joint,
　The tramp departed with his plunder.

Thompson would attack Spencer many times in later years, but never
again with such deftness.

By 1880 Thompson's Boston sojourn was over and he was back in
Toronto. After a short stint with the *Mail*, he moved over to the *Globe*,
George Brown's death apparently having erased past enmities. He was
called a 'descriptive writer,' and one of his first assignments was to cover
the Irish Land League agitation. In a series that ran regularly between 16
November 1881 and 10 January 1882, he demonstrated a superb talent
for careful, detailed, objective reporting. Nevertheless, the plight of the
Irish peasants aroused his sympathy and convinced him that Ireland was

ripe for violence. 'Everything,' he concluded, 'points to a prolonged and bitter conflict during the winter, to continued evictions and renewed outrages, to a continuance of the Land League in one shape or another with the aid of the funds which have come so freely from America. With American money comes American ideas ... Revolutions never move backwards. The longer it continues the more radical will be the ground taken by the popular party. And so, in spite of blunders, and crimes and defeats – in spite of the greed of the self-seeking and the ambitions of the demagogue – through bloodshed and tears, and suffering, the cause of the people will prevail by slow degrees; and the accumulated and buttressed wrongs of centuries will be overthrown.' In typical Thompson fashion, he finished off with a doctored version of a gospel hymn:

> And the night so dreary and dark and long
> At length will the morning bring:
> And over the hills the ransomed song
> Of the ninety and nine shall ring.
> And echo afar from zone to zone
> Rejoice for labour has gained its own.[14]

Thompson's readers would have realized that his reference to 'American ideas,' in part at least, meant the ideas of Henry George. His visit to Ireland had coincided with George's campaign on behalf of the Irish Land League. Thompson, who was apparently already familiar with *Progress and Poverty*, interviewed the American reformer over 'punch and cigars' in Dublin. George described his horror at the conditions he found in Ireland and explained his solution – land nationalization. That solution, George maintained, would spread to the rest of the civilized world once it was fully understood that land monopoly was the source of social injustice and inequality everywhere. George was unprepossessing at first, Thompson told his readers, but 'the longer the interview the more the visitor will be impressed with his extraordinary intellectual grasp, his large comprehensive views and his forcible, incisive way of putting things.'[15]

Thompson's meeting with Henry George added a new element to his growing and highly eclectic reform portfolio. He was already an active participant in the 'Land, Labour, and Currency League' which was led by William Wallace, a Tory MP for Norfolk, and supported by A.W. Wright and Louis Kribbs, two of Thompson's fellow journalists of radical persuasion. To currency inflation he added the Georgeite panacea of the single tax on unearned increment. Georgeism was one of many causes supported by a new labour reform newspaper established in Hamilton, *The Palladium of Labor*, to which Thompson became a regular contributor in 1883, at about the same time as he went to work for E.E. Sheppard at the *Toronto News*. Thompson had become a member of the Knights of Labor whose cause the *Palladium* served.[16]

When the Knights brought Henry George to Hamilton in 1884 Thompson was on hand to address the crowd (one report said 10,000 people attended) between the sporting events and the great man's appearance. Thompson probably expounded on the need for 'a new political economy' as he had done a few weeks earlier at a meeting of the Toronto Secular Society. 'We must place Man before Mammon,' he had told an appreciative audience on that occasion, uttering a sentence that summarized the message he would repeat in various forms for the rest of his life. Thompson was doubtless the author of the *Palladium*'s feature called 'Our Social Club,' wherein the Georgeite perspective was brought to bear on a variety of social problems. So, too, he wrote as 'Enjolras,' setting out a social philosophy that took George as the starting-point but moved quickly to somewhat more radical ground. In one column he expressed his conviction that land monopoly was only part of a much bigger problem. 'What law, pray, that can be passed in Ottawa or Toronto has such vital, all-absorbing interest for Labor as the unwritten, arbitrary law which says, you, wage slave, have produced us, your master, so much wealth that we are in fact suffering from over production. Therefore it is decreed that the factory is closed until further notice. What law duly assented to by the governor-general in fully panoply of cocked hat, laced coat, knee breeches and sword is one tenth part the importance to the toiler as the silent, informal decrees of landlordism "whereas the necessities of the public for accommodation have increased, therefore rents are increased henceforth twenty percent." Where is the law duly incorporated on the statute book in good set terms and legal phraseology that affects the toiling masses like the machinations of speculators who put up the prices of coal and wheat and pork? What are the government taxes to the exactions continually levied on industry by the usurer and the landlord and the profit monger and the capitalist?' Freeing the people from the oppression of the omnipotent 'money power' would require more radical remedies than Henry George's simple proposal. In fact, Thompson feared that George's doctrine was becoming so watered down as to suit the interests of middle-class reformers.[17]

Though Thompson was only beginning to develop an all-embracing prescription for reform by the mid-1880s, he thought that he saw in the Knights of Labor the makings of a mass movement of social protest that would succeed in ridding society of the beneficiaries of unearned increment and capitalist profits. The Knights, whose spectacular rise in the United States in the 1880s spilled over into Canada, called for the organization of all 'workers of hand and brain' with the ultimate goal of reorganizing society along co-operative lines. Only lawyers, gamblers, bankers, and bartenders were judged 'non-producers' and excluded from membership in the Knights, whose philosophy was a heady mixture of trade unionism and the Christian social gospel. Thompson, a 'brain-worker,' belonged to the appropriately named Victor Hugo Assembly in Toronto. The assembly included many of Thompson's journalistic colleagues. It was from that base that Thompson worked in the late 1880s and early 1890s to establish a Canadian 'Populist' party of workers and farmers, which would crusade for the regeneration of Canadian society. Among his contributions to that crusade, as befitted an 'intellectual worker,' were his social analyses and political commentary in the Knight's press, speeches to meetings organized by the Patrons of Industry, his book, *The Politics of Labor*, and, by no means least, twenty-six sets of lyrics for the movement's hymnal, *The Labor Reform Songster*.[18]

By the 1880s, then, Thompson had become a prominent spokesman for a little band of Toronto radical regenerators who, through such organizations as the Single Tax Association, the Nationalist Clubs (Thompson was an executive member of both of these organizations), the Anti-poverty Society, the Trades and Labour Congress, the Knights of Labor, the Patrons of Industry, the Toronto Suffrage Association, and the Toronto Conference on Social Problems, agitated for social reform. It was a disparate group which differed over means but agreed that society was out of joint and had to be set right by the adoption of policies based on humanitarian principles. For many of these reformers – J.W. Bengough and George Wrigley, for example – that humanitarian system was founded firmly on Protestant ethical teachings. But for others, Christianity was part of the established order and needed reform as badly as society itself. Phillips Thompson had long been a critic of established religion – indeed, having been born a Quaker, he had never been an orthodox Christian. But he had a persistent interest in religious questions, writing sympathetically about spiritualism and participating actively in the free-thought or secular movement. Yet even in the latter activity

Thompson seemed less concerned with attacking the churches' doctrines from a militantly rationalist point of view than with emphasizing the failure of Christians to live up to their own teachings. He contended that the church was a social institution to which people belonged for reasons of social respectability. Therefore, the way to get rid of the church was not to argue about doctrine, but rather to change the social order that made religious organizations socially acceptable.[19] His criticism of the church and its ministers was put most effectively, as was often the case, in poetry. He composed a pointed satire entitled 'Always with You':

> 'The poor ye have always with you.'
>   What a true and consoling verse!
> It is so ordained from the outset
>   It is part of the primal curse.
> God wills that some should be wealthy,
>   And others their lot endure,
> And learn to suffer in patience,
>   For they were meant to be poor!
>
> The preacher put it so plainly
>   In his sermon last Sunday night,
> His talent for exegesis
>   Never showed him in a better light.
> These Socialist agitators
>   Who are kicking against the rod,
> Are trying to war with Nature
>   And combat the will of God.
>
> 'The poor ye have always with you.'
>   It is part of God's gracious plan
> To show forth his wisdom and justice,
>   And humble the pride of man.
> We must banish all vain delusions,
>   And meekly accept what's given.
> What's earthly dross? If we bear the cross
>   We shall get our reward in Heaven.
>
> Now that's what I call sound preaching,
>   Such talk goes right to the point.

When infidel Socialist doctrines
　　Are putting things out of joint.
But I fear that Dr. Sleeker
　　Has another church in view:
'A wider sphere of influence,'
　　And a larger salary, too.

I reckon we'll have to see him,
　　And go one better to keep
This faithful shepherd from leaving
　　To the wolves his straying sheep.
He'll stay if we put up a grand new church
　　And give him more 'earthly dross.'
Well, the hands at the mill shall foot the bill,
　　I cannot afford the loss.

They can stand a cut in wages,
　　Say another ten percent.
And those tenants of mine in the corn block
　　Must pay me an increased rent.
'The poor ye have always with you.'
　　Makes my duty as plain as day,
What God ordains is not for us
　　Rebelliously to gainsay.

I should be an unfaithful steward
　　Of riches which God has given,
Did I fail to garner the golden store
　　And hold it in trust for Heaven,
I give to the Church and mission schemes
　　Fully ten percent or more,
And by charity organization strive
　　To succor the starving poor.

The girls in the mill they tell me
　　Will frequently go astray.
I can only afford to pay them
　　About forty cents a day.
There are plenty to work for that figure.

And were I to give them more,
We never could pay the dividend
We always paid before.

But a Magdalen Asylum
Has been founded by my aid
And soon to the topmost storey
'Twill be crowded I'm afraid,
For the poor we have always with us
Ah! sad that such things must be,
But I'm no infidel scoffer to scout
The justice of God's decree.

In Thompson's view, the organized churches had corrupted or twisted the teachings of Christ 'who was himself a working man and a socialist,' and had naturally lost contact with the working class. Worse, some workers remained under the influence of 'a perverted Christianity which disparages sublunary matters as of little moment, and blasphemously regards the consequences of human greed and oppression as Heaven-sent afflictions which must be borne in patience, holding out a prospect of a "home beyond the skies" as an incentive to contentment under unjust conditions here.' There were some exceptional ministers. Thompson praised Dr Albert Carman for his espousal of Georgeite views, but he noted that other Methodists attacked 'Christian Socialism.' He expected little practical response from the established Christian denominations.

Yet for all of his scepticism about Christianity and his active role in the free-thought movement, Thompson was not ready to abandon religion completely. Indeed, he appears to have discovered that some free thinkers were as reactionary as Christians. When Colonel Ingersoll declared his support for Carnegie during the Homestead strike in Chicago, Thompson wrote bitterly:

At your unfaith let others rail,
I have no care for forms or creeds;
The point at which you always fail
Is when you pass from words to deeds.
I mete you by no Christian test,
But by the standard of your choice,
Your sympathy for the oppressed
Extends no farther than your voice.

By the early 1890s Thompson had joined a religious movement that had a certain popularity among radicals, namely, theosophy. He may have discovered this syncretic religion, which strongly emphasized ethical action, during an unsuccessful attempt to establish himself in England in 1888–9. There he doubtless observed and came to admire Annie Besant, who turned to theosophy after a lengthy and spectacular flirtation with the free-thought movement of Charles Bradlaugh. Like Besant, Thompson's adoption of the new religion coincided with a growing social radicalism. But it is also important to underline the association between theosophy and Bellamyite nationalism or socialism, which influenced a number of Toronto radicals in the 1890s. Edward Bellamy's *Looking Backward*, published in 1887, made a substantial impact on Canadian reformers, both Christians and those whose views were more unorthodox, apparently moving some single-taxers along the road to socialism.[20]

In Canada, as in the United States, theosophists and Bellamyites were, at least for a time, almost indistinguishable.[21] At the meetings of the Toronto Nationalist Association, Thompson and other prominent reformers discussed the teachings of Edward Bellamy and Madame Blavatsky. Like spiritualism, theosophy at first seems a strange religion for reformers to adopt. Its connection with Eastern mysticism and the superficial appearance of extreme other-worldliness make it appear an even stronger 'opiate' than Christianity. But on closer examination theosophy bears many similarities to that liberal Protestantism that eventually led to the social gospel. Theosophy, while rejecting Christian theology, claimed to combine the best elements of all of the world's main religions and to reconcile or transcend the gulf between science and religion by adapting evolutionary thought to religious faith. As a writer in the *Week* accurately remarked, theosophists 'argue that the tendency of science is towards a blind and helpless materialism, and that their mission is to preach and to prove the existence of a spiritual world surrounding, pervading, and guiding man until he shall attain the highest conceivable destiny.'[22]

Theosophy also denied the traditional Christian distinction between the sacred and the secular, insisting on the immanence of God in the world. Mrs E. Day Macpherson, the women's editor of Phillips Thompson's *Labor Advocate*, emphasized this point in a speech entitled 'Theosophy Considered in Relation to the Great Social Problem' at a meeting of the Nationalist Association in Toronto early in 1891. Man's history, she maintained, was one of spiritual evolution characterized by repeated reincarnations guided by the law of karma. Karma, she continued, was the law of cause and effect, which meant that man's actions and thoughts in this incarnation determined the nature of his next life. Good works and thoughts would lead to a higher spirituality. Here then was a statement of the doctrine of justification by works, which for liberal Protestants was the essence of the social gospel. For Mrs Macpherson the shared goal of theosophy and nationalism was the transformation of selfish, individualistic capitalism into a co-operative commonwealth wherein men would act according to their best instincts, freeing themselves from 'evil karma' and preparing for a higher life. 'Believe ye all in the Brotherhood of Man' was the essence of both theosophy and nationalism.[23]

This was a view which Phillips Thompson came fully to accept. In 1891 he took out membership in the Theosophical Society. Neither Christianity nor rationalism had provided a satisfactory philosophy for socialism. Secularism, he believed, failed to take into account the spiritual needs of man's nature, leaving man with nothing to hope for but the materialistic rewards of this world. 'If this life is everything, where is the incentive?' he asked, as Goldwin Smith had asked. 'Who is going to concern himself with whether a drove of boys have more or less swill? Not I, for one.' Socialists had to accept man's need for 'all round development,' including that development which evolution demonstrated continued after death. Both J.S. Woodsworth and W.L.M. King would have agreed with much of Thompson's explanation of the relationship between social betterment and religious belief. 'If the orthodox view of man's nature and destiny is debasing and degrading,' he wrote, 'the materialist view is no less so. Instead of groveling as "worms in the dust" for mercy at the hands of an arbitrary personal God, or seeking salvation through the blood of Christ, men should strive to develop the divine element within themselves and to realize that the only salvation possible or necessary is the upbuilding of character. The greatest obstacle to soul growth is depressing social conditions, which prevent the development of man's higher facilities, and stifle his better aspirations in the ignoble struggle for gold or for bread as the case may be.'[24]

Neither the class struggle nor historical materialism but only the law of karma could explain existing social inequalities and point to a more just future. When attacked for his failure to recognize the laws of materialism by a 'scientific socialist,' Thompson replied with his accustomed self-assurance, 'I am a class conscious socialist from the ground up, and I claim that my socialism is reinforced by ... in fact, I might go further and say, based upon the truths of Theosophy. Our present villainous social system is mainly due to the wrong and misleading theological ideas which are reflected in existing political and social institutions and we cannot expect much change for the better until we substitute more ennobling and correct views of man's relationship to the unseen world, his ultimate destiny and his relation to his fellows. The one essential truth which all Theosophists must accept is the principle of human brotherhood.' That was the essential principle of the social gospel in its most fully developed formulation.[25]

Like his frequent antagonist Goldwin Smith, Thompson was an idealist who was convinced that man's ideas – his theology – governed social relations. Where Smith worried that theological uncertainty would lead to social chaos, Thompson was convinced that a radical new religion was a prerequisite for a renovated social order. That idealism was the theme of one of the many ditties contributed by Thompson to *The Labor Reform Songster*. Entitled 'The Power of Thought' and set to the score of 'Comin' through the Rye,' one stanza went:

> Not by cannon nor by sabre,
>   Not by flags unfurled,
> Shall we win the rights of labor,
>   Shall we free the world.
> Thought is stronger far than weapons,
>   Who shall stay its course?
> It spreads in onward-circling waves
>   And ever gathers force.[26]

For Thompson, as for his contemporaries B.F. Austin and Flora Denison and his successors J.S. Woodsworth and Mackenzie King, social reform and religious liberalism went hand in hand. In this and in many other ways, social reform in Canada, as in Great Britain and the United States, was rooted in a search for a new interpretation of religion or an alternative to the old religion. Once men freed themselves from the religious beliefs that sanctified the status quo and postponed their happiness until the afterlife, they would develop a religion of more immediate gratification, one that promised bliss in this world.

Thompson began to design his blueprint for a socialist society before he read Edward Bellamy and before he joined the theosophical movement, but those two influences gave his thought shape. Many of the ideas he presented in *The Politics of Labor* had already been worked out in the

Phillips Thompson

columns he wrote as 'Enjolras' in *The Palladium of Labor*. Those same ideas enlivened the pages of his *Labor Advocate*, *Grip*, and other publications. Though he accepted much of Henry George's analysis of the evolution of industrial society, including the labour theory of value and the need to tax unearned increment, he moved well beyond the single-tax solution. Though George was instrumental in finding a publisher for *The Politics of Labor* in 1887, a distinct gulf had opened up between him and Thompson, as George pointed out. Privately, at least, Thompson had concluded that though a good propagandist for reform, George was 'a bourgeois reformer who opposes landlordism in the interests of the shop-keeping and capitalist classes,' a view shared by Karl Marx. In Thompson's analysis landlordism was not even the 'most oppressive and insidious monopoly' that existed in capitalist society. He defined the problem as 'monopoly above and competition below – monopoly of resources, of means of employment in the hands of the few, and competition among those dependent upon them for liberty to labor.' Instead of recognizing that labour was the source of all value, modern society treated it, along with land and capital, as a commodity to be bought and sold according to market forces. The time had arrived, Thompson maintained, 'when political economy needs to be rewritten from the standpoint of the Sermon on the Mount and the Declaration of Independence.' Traditional political economy had to be demystified: it was not a science but rather a rationalization for the injustices and inequalities of capitalist society.[27]

What would be the tenets of the new political economy? First, it had to be accepted that society and social relations were not static but constantly evolving. Though Thompson rejected that interpretation of evolution which justified laissez-faire as a naturally ordained struggle for survival, he nevertheless was deeply influenced by reform social Darwinism – progressive evolution. 'Bearing in mind the great truth that all human institutions, including government in all its forms and phases, and the entire industrial system, are the product of evolution; that they have not been imposed upon mankind, but have slowly developed in accordance with the necessities of the case, we must look to the same process of gradual change for the improvement of present conditions.'[28] This was not, however, a recipe for sitting back and waiting for change; for the direction of evolution could be altered by modifying the conditions in which the process worked. The existing direction of social evolution was toward the increasing monopolization of economic power in the hands of a plutocracy. That had its dangers, but it also had its advantages. Thompson cautioned against a nostalgic wish for a return to an agrarian Arcadia or even to an age of individualism and economic enterprise. Monopoly was a triumph of natural forces and should be accepted. That was one of the lessons taught by Edward Bellamy. And there were others.

While the growth of monopoly threatened democracy because it degraded citizens to the level of wage slaves, it also immensely simplified the solution to that very problem. 'It had created a system which was well-nigh perfect in its details so far as regards the organization of industry and the mechanism of exchange. For the crude and cumbrous methods of our ancestors it has substituted the nicely adjusted and smoothly working organization of forces by which the advantages of division of labor are realized, and the productive capacity of all forms of industry is marvelously increased.' That wonderfully efficient machine should not be tampered with. Instead, it should be made to work to the benefit of the community rather than for the profit of a few monopolists. The growth of private monopoly made socialism easier to attain: private monopolies would simply be transferred to the community. Monopoly capitalism was thus a stage on the road to socialism. 'It is easier to perfect a one-sided socialism than to build from the foundation.' From Henry George Thompson had adopted the idea of the progressive character of modern machine civilization. From Edward Bellamy he learned that monopoly was natural and that it should be transferred to community ownership. 'Capitalism,' Thompson believed, 'is cutting its own throat in a highly satisfactory manner.'[29]

For Thompson socialism was not a utopian dream that would material-ize overnight or even after the 113 years of Julian West's slumbers. It could only be achieved gradually through step-by-step evolution. It had to begin with the extension of public ownership into those areas where capitalist ownership was most obviously oppressive and where popular support was strongest. 'In place of the capitalist rule, which in the true sense now governs the people by prescribing whether they shall work or not, and how they shall receive, let us have a representative, popular, recognized government, conducted on business principles, doing the same thing, not for the profit of the few, but in the interests of all.' Railways, telephones, telegraphs, banks, and insurance companies, already the creatures of public statutes, provided the place to start. Once the process was begun there would be no logical place to stop before complete collectivization had been achieved. 'The final extinction of the capitalist,' Thompson announced, 'is the logical end and aim of the movement to extend the powers of government, whether those who agitate for it know it or not.'[30] That the same argument was used by the opponents of public ownership apparently did not worry the editor of the *Labor Advocate*.

Just as Thompson believed in progressive social evolution, so he was also convinced that individuals were evolving toward perfection. Once again, alterations in the environment would ensure that human nature would shed its selfish characteristics and multiply its humanistic instincts. Human history, he believed, demonstrated that 'human nature is progressive, and susceptible of improvement. Were it otherwise we should never have emerged from savagery.' That belief in progressive evolution, which he shared with Dr Maurice Bucke (whose 'cosmic consciousness' was strikingly similar to theosophy), led Thompson to a vision of a perfect society. That vision was infused with a religious millenarianism that might with a few changes have been heard at a Methodist camp meeting earlier in the nineteenth century or at a meeting of the Labor Church in Winnipeg at the end of the Great War. Thompson rhapsodized: 'Labor, in working out its own emancipation, will regen-erate the world. In solving the labor problem, the other vexed questions which have so long pressed for solution will be settled. All the various forms of social and moral evil which inflict humanity are traceable to caste rule and the spoliation of the labouring class. War, intemperance, prostitution, and crime are due either to the greed begotten of capitalism, the selfishness, arrogance and luxury of the monied and influential class, or the abject necessity, ignorance and debasement of the disinherited. With social and political equality established, and every man and woman secured in the enjoyment of the full earnings of their labor, the motives which prompt and the conditions which foster these evils would largely cease.'[31]

No single word more accurately caught the spirit of the developing reform movement of late nineteenth-century English Canada than 'regeneration.' It was, of course, a religious concept meaning to be born again. Once applied to individuals, it was increasingly used to describe social rebirth. For Thompson, as for many contemporary social critics whom he admired and read – Henry George, Edward Bellamy, William Morris, H.M. Hyndman, Edward Carpenter – socialism was, if not a new religion, then the philosophy of a 'new life' similar in its regenerative function to traditional Christianity. Its aim was not born-again individuals but born-again societies, where men and women would love one another in perfection. Thompson, like Dr Bucke, Flora Denison, and J.W. Bengough, often found the spirit of that 'new life' best expressed in Walt Whitman's *Leaves of Grass*. *The Politics of Labor* opened with the American poet's affirmation of this social utopia:

> I dreamed in a dream, I saw a city invincible to the attacks of
>   the whole of the rest of the earth,
> I dreamed that was the new City of Friends,
> Nothing was greater there than the quality of robust love –
>   it led the rest,
> It was seen every hour in the actions of the men of that city,
>   And in all their looks and words.[32]

It is hardly surprising that one reader of Thompson's *Labor Advocate* should respond to Thompson's teachings in a paragraph that anticipated by thirty years the essential message of Salem Bland's *The New Christianity*. That correspondent wrote: 'The present industrial movement, looking toward a higher social and cultural life for the masses of humanity, is emphatically the great moral and religious movement of that age. We can only serve God by serving humanity.'[33] That was certainly an accurate rendering of the message of Phillips Thompson's theosophical socialism.

10

'Was Christ, After All, a Social Reformer?'

In the depths of his 'crisis of faith,' Ryerson Embury, Albert Carman Jr's fictional hero, finally experienced the conversion for which he had previously struggled unavailingly. But the author of that conversion was neither an emotional revivalist preacher nor a modernist minister explaining difficult scriptural passages in symbolic terms. Rather, it was Henry George, the author of *Progress and Poverty*, a work combining Christian moralism and unorthodox economics. Reading that book led young Embury to answer what for him had become an increasingly urgent question: 'Was Christ, after all, a social reformer?'[1]

That was a question many Christians in late nineteenth-century English Canada were asking. Ryerson Embury's resounding affirmative had many echoes, even though the churches insisted upon 'preaching their dead Christ and leaving this plain work of God untouched.'[2] Christianity, in this view, simply had to be made more relevant to the social issues of the times if it was to remain a vital part of Canadian life. That this conclusion was pressed upon Protestants by the disparities of wealth and poverty and the harsh conditions of modern industrialism, was undoubtedly true. 'The class distinction on the continent of North America has developed further than we have realized,' Wilfred Campbell wrote in the Toronto *Globe* in 1892. 'The concentration of wealth in the control of a few, and the gradually growing poverty of the working classes, is becoming more apparent every day.' In his view, that demanded a religion infused with more humanity.[3] But it was not just material conditions, harrowing as they were, that forced this conclusion; it also developed out of the theological and philosophical controversies of the previous quarter-century. What came to be called the social gospel was not merely a response to a perceived social crisis. It was also, perhaps principally, a reaction to a profound intellectual crisis, and as part of that a questioning of the role of the clergy and the church in modern society. For many, science and historical criticism weakened the traditional basis of Christian belief and therefore raised doubts about the function of the church; the social gospel purported to provide a new rationale for Christianity and a new mission for the church.

Ironically, but not illogically, that new social message was remarkably similar to the one advocated by those free thinkers and social reformers who had completely rejected Christian doctrine. Ryerson Embury was more than a symbol: prefiguring the careers of Mackenzie King, J.S. Woodsworth, and A.E. Smith, he chose to practise his new belief in a secular role. That role represented the union of the sacred and the secular which was the essence of the modernist liberal impulse in Protestantism.[4] That drift in Protestant thought was accurately captured by a Presbyterian layman who, in congratulating Principal Grant on his recent plea for a more socially conscious Christianity, wrote, 'The world appears to me to be in a great tangle in which classes & masses, Capital & Labour must someday be extricated and not very far distant either. The world is full of situations which require the attention of the keenest, loftiest & most unselfish minds, and there is not time to defend old infallibles that won't stay defended. The Christian ministry has an immediate field yet scarcely entered upon ... The religion & Christianity that floats around in generalities and airy nothingness will pass away as the mist & only the Christianity that gets down & dwells on the earth weekdays & all week will accomplish what this age requires ... The value of the Christian ministry in the coming time will be seen more in its knowledge of *this* world than in that of the next.'[5] Few theologians could have improved upon that layman's definition of liberal theology.

I

The social and political implications of Christian teaching have been matters of debate almost since the first days of Christianity's history. The concepts of 'redemption' and 'reform' were central to the Christian mission in the world even though the precise meaning of these terms, like that of other theological concepts, was subject to almost permanent dispute.[6] By the late nineteenth century, in Canada as elsewhere, that debate again raged. Out of it emerged a 'social gospel' which in its most fully developed version insisted that the principal, perhaps the only, goal of Christianity was the reform of society, the building of the kingdom of

God on earth. It is important to emphasize that the social gospel was something much more radical in its religious implications than merely a social reform movement inspired by religious ideals. Most Christians had long believed that social action was a religious duty. They would also have insisted, as orthodox Christians always had, that individual salvation would have to precede social regeneration. Professor John Clark Murray, a McGill philosopher and one of the first systematic advocates of social reform in Canada, put the point explicitly in his *Handbook of Christian Ethics*. 'In regard to the bearing of Christian ethics on industrial problems,' he argued, 'it is essential to remember again that the aim of Jesus was not primarily any external reconstruction of the social order. His teaching, indeed, must affect the organization of industry, as well as other features of the structure of society. But ... his aim was primarily a moral regeneration of man.' This Presbyterian professor insisted that there could be no Christian morality without Christian belief and Christian doctrine; only the intellectually confused could talk of 'a creedless morality.'[7]

In the 1880s *The Week* could confidently assert that the distinction between Christianity and social reform was self-evident. 'Between Christianity and the socialist method,' the orthodox editor wrote, 'there seems to us to be a fundamental opposition. Christianity begins reform from within, socialism from without. Christianity teaches that happiness is not to be attained without self improvement; socialism leads you to believe that it can be gained by altering your social environment ... It is assumed [by socialists] that the existing structure of society alone stands in the way of universal bliss, and that if it can only be torn down all will be well. But Christianity can assume nothing of the kind.'[8] In the next twenty years what seemed self-evident was sharply challenged by a social gospel that threatened to reverse the order of regeneration: society rather than the individual became the object of salvation.

The nature of traditional Christian social reform thought is exemplified in the career of a prominent Methodist leader, Alexander Sutherland. Born on a farm near Guelph in 1833, Sutherland began his working life as a printer's apprentice. At nineteen he was converted to Methodism, and by the late 1850s he had preached on the circuit, graduated in theology from Victoria College in Cobourg, and entered upon a career that would lead him into some of the most important Methodist pulpits in Quebec and Ontario. He also began to assume a large burden of responsibility for general church work, especially temperance advocacy, missionary activity, and religious journalism. In 1881 J.C. Dent described him as 'a man of great energy and versatility. Had he not been a minister he might have been a successful journalist, politician, or man of business ... His early interest in the temperance question never flagged.'[9]

Dr Sutherland – Victoria awarded him a doctor of divinity degree in 1879 – saw no reason for any fine distinction between religion and politics. When the temperance cause seemed to be going nowhere in the late 1880s, Sutherland urged the Dominion Alliance, the leading 'dry' organization, to reject the established parties and found one of its own. Rewarding friends and punishing enemies had not worked for the prohibitionists. He split the Alliance convention after persuading a small majority of delegates that 'there is no distinct issue of principle between the existing parties which renders their continued existence either necessary or important.' A third party was to be created. The majority then caucused to draw up a platform which began by calling for 'Righteousness and Truth' in public affairs as well as in private business, and no compromise with wrong. It advocated support for 'equal rights' (an attack on Roman Catholics), a national sentiment and a national literature, absolute prohibition, retrenchment in government expenditures, an elected Senate, civil service reform, and votes for women.[10]

The platform provoked further controversy, for not everyone could accept all of its demands. Dr Sutherland, who apparently believed that he was the best judge of righteousness and truth, insisted that members of 'Canada's Third Party' should be required to subscribe to the entire platform without further discussion. The splinter party splintered further; as *The Templar* explained, for all his sincerity and talent Sutherland displayed a disposition 'to flagellate every critic of the party.' Sutherland's unwillingness to compromise, and the conviction of other temperance leaders that the quickest route to righteousness still lay through the existing parties, ensured that the Third Party came to almost nothing. But Sutherland's advocacy of direct political action to achieve moral reforms revealed that for him, as for many traditional Protestants, a Christianized social order was a natural Christian objective. Though Roman Catholic bishops and priests were roundly denounced for meddling in politics, Protestants like Alexander Sutherland and their supporters in the Dominion Alliance and the Women's Christian Temperance Union were no less convinced than Bishop Bourget and the Quebec ultramontanes of the need for social reorganization on Christian precepts. Sutherland's 'Third Party' was cut from the same cloth as the ultramontanes' 'Programme catholique.'[12]

Sutherland sketched the foundations and something of the structure of his Christian society in a series of lectures delivered at Vanderbilt University near the end of the century. Entitled *The Kingdom of God and the Problems of Today*, these lectures nicely distill the views of a Christian social reformer for whom the story of Adam and Eve, not materialistic Darwinism, explained man's historic beginnings, and whose biblical understanding owed little, if anything, to the higher critics. Nevertheless, Sutherland was convinced that 'the Kingdom of God is first and chiefly in this world.' Therefore Christian teaching should be expected to present specific principles to govern social organization and human relations. But first and foremost, Sutherland insisted, the reconstruction of society had to begin with the redemption of man: 'the highest good of society can be secured only by regenerating and saving the individual, so that in turn he may contribute to the regeneration of society.' Reforms that concentrated on society first were worthy only of scorn: 'it may be that when tariff millenniums and socialistic millenniums, and looking backward millenniums shall have vanished like the mirage of the desert, the disappointed and sorrowing hearts of men may return wistfully towards that real millennium, foreshadowed in prophecy and the gospel, and society shall be reconstructed because its units have been regenerated, and social conditions shall be equalized because human hearts have been renewed, and righteousness shall reign because Christ is enthroned.' Sutherland spoke for those traditional Christians who believed that social reform built on anything other than individual conversion would be ephemeral, 'more Utopian than Utopia itself.' Christ, unlike 'all other social reformers begins at the centre instead of the circumference.' For that reason Sutherland, referring to a host of contemporary reformers, maintained that those who claimed Christ's authority 'for every new fad and crude theory in social economics' were merely 'stealing the livery of heaven in which to serve the devil.'[13]

Having marked out this conservative position in black and white, Sutherland then advanced a restricted set of reform proposals. Heading the list was suppression of the liquor trade. Since Sutherland attributed virtually every social ill to alcohol – poverty, crime, corruption, insanity, inequality, low productivity, and waste of resources – it is hardly astonishing that prohibition was his omnibus panacea. 'The liquor traffic,' he exclaimed, 'is an unrelenting foe of the Kingdom of God – one of the most dangerous and deadly of them all.' Beyond that, Sutherland advocated a general set of social goals aimed at guaranteeing rough equality of opportunity, where all who worked could expect 'at the very least decent food, clothing and shelter.' With respect to the problem of class conflict in industrial society and the estrangement of the working class from the church, Sutherland gave his approval to an idea that enjoyed a considerable vogue among late nineteenth-century Christian reformers, namely, profit-sharing. He offered no very clear blueprint, but it is significant that he saw this solution as one founded upon Christian ethics rather than the 'selfish maxim of the *laissez-faire* school of economists.' Thus, for even so restrained a social reformer as Alexander Sutherland there could be no doubt that capitalist industrial society was a far cry from the kingdom of God. He admitted that Christians and socialists had much in common, though on one fundamental belief they parted company abruptly: 'While socialism and the Kingdom of God rest upon widely different foundations, and pursue their ends by different means, the results aimed at are, to some extent at least, the same – namely, an era of universal brotherhood, the improvement of social conditions, the reign of social justice and good will; in a word, they both aim – professedly at least – at the bringing about of an ideal condition of society in which oppression and injustice, and the poverty which causes suffering, shall cease to be. But Christianity proposes something which finds no place in the programme of socialism, but which is an essential factor in securing the results aimed at, namely, the regeneration of the individual. Socialism seeks certain results of Christianity, but repudiates its process.'[14]

In some important respects Sutherland's orthodoxy had already been subjected to serious questioning by the time he delivered these lectures. Certainly he stopped far short of what other reformers had been advocating for more than a decade, and associating those reforms with Christian teachings. But it is important to pay serious attention to Sutherland, not merely because he expressed a position widely accepted among middle-class Christians,[15] but also because that viewpoint could be developed beyond the stopping-point that Sutherland marked out. The very idea that Christians and socialists shared similar objectives had startling implications – implications that were almost certain to be drawn by a younger generation of Protestant activists.

II

If Alexander Sutherland's conservative Methodism made him only a cautious social reformer, John Clark Murray's liberal Presbyterianism took him somewhat further along the road to a full program of social regeneration. And Murray's views, fully worked out in the 1880s, indicate that Sutherland's position had already become rather outmoded. For Murray, issues such as temperance and the enforcement of Sunday observance laws, so central to men like Sutherland, really skirted the essential question: how could justice and equality of opportunity be established in an industrial society?

Murray was a Scottish-born philosopher and theologian, educated in the school of commonsense realism.[16] In 1862, at the age of twenty-six, he accepted an appointment as professor of moral and mental philosophy at Queen's University. He moved to McGill ten years later where he remained until his death in 1917. In some ways he might have been happier had he remained at Queen's, where his increasingly liberal views might have won a more sympathetic hearing from Principal Grant than they did from the McGill principal. Almost as soon as he arrived at McGill he began what turned into a bitter feud with Dawson over the issue of admitting women to the university, particularly over the matter of separate or integrated classes.[17] In an 1872 speech Murray announced that 'there are two great social problems of which our time is called to attempt a solution: the one refers to the question of capital and labour, the other to the position of women in society.' A significant part of his professional life was devoted to thinking, writing, and speaking about those two subjects, ones Murray knew were closely related. His social philosophy evolved within a specifically Christian frame of reference which provided the principles for a just society. This is clear from the basic premise which he advanced in his discussion of the 'woman question.' 'The spirit of Christianity,' he maintained, 'requires that our social institutions shall draw no invidious distinctions between the one sex and the other – that while neither exists for itself alone, women shall not be treated as if they had no function in society but to subserve the purposes of man, any more than men are treated as if they had no function but to subserve the interest of women.'[18] Like the secularist W.D. LeSueur and the liberal Methodist B.F. Austin, Murray was convinced earlier than the great majority of Canadian males – and females, for that matter – that women must be given equal access to higher education and to skills that would allow them the independence of freedom of choice rather than making them 'the slave of man.'[19]

By the 1880s, with women's educational rights still being heatedly debated, especially at McGill, Murray turned his attention to the other great social question: capital and labour. In a substantial manuscript, never completely published until long after his death, and in a series of articles which appeared in The Week, The Open Court (an American agnostic publication edited by B.F. Underwood and later Paul Carus),[20] and *The Monist*, Murray set out his social philosophy with great clarity.

At the outset of his *Industrial Kingdom of God*, the title he gave to his unpublished manuscript, Murray was at great pains to explain, as one might expect in a book with that title, that his aim was to elucidate the application of Christian ethics to industrial society. For him Christian doctrine and social action were utterly inseparable. 'It is impossible to explain the practical life of the Christian except by reference to those spiritual truths or "doctrines" from which it draws its inspiration,' he observed; 'while on the other hand, those spiritual truths find their proper significance in their ethical aspect, that is, by their realization in the life of the Christian.' That, for Murray, was the essence of all religion, but it made Christianity 'the true religion'; for the 'incarnation of God in the person of Christ' was the ultimate expression of the unity of theology and ethics.[21]

Murray, carefully trained Presbyterian that he was, insisted that ethics depended completely on the truth of Christian doctrine. He could not accept the validity of the humanism of a LeSueur or an Allen Pringle or a Captain Adams. Lacking doctrinal underpinning, Christian ethics lost their sanction. 'Christianity,' Murray wrote, 'can attach but little value to any scheme for the social amelioration of mankind which is not based on the spiritual regeneration of man.'[22] Here he was in complete agreement with Sutherland, though his orthodoxy was much more effectively expounded and his understanding of the social problems he sought to resolve much more sophisticated.

From theological orthodoxy Murray moved to a somewhat unorthodox political economy. If the Christian ethical system was founded on divine law, political economy could claim no such sure foundation, Goldwin Smith notwithstanding. The laws of political economy, in Murray's views, were not immutable physical laws, but rather were closer to moral laws, concerned not only with the explanation of existing social relations but also with defining what *ought* to exist. 'This implies,' he contended, '... that we are not helpless spectators of the pitiless operation of a natural law which dooms the mass of mankind to irremediable poverty, and accumulates the wealth of the world in the hands of the few; for if there is anything that we *ought* to do, it follows that we *can* do something to modify the existing condition of things.'[23] This un-Presbyterian commitment to free will led Murray to a position closer to the followers of Henry George than to the exponents of classical political economy.

Unlike Sutherland, whose views were the product of a simpler, pre-industrial era, Murray recognized that the Canadian economy had entered a new phase in which concentrated economic power had replaced the individualism of an earlier age. 'The disappearance of the small master workman,' he wrote in 1894, echoing the observations of the Royal Commission on the Relations of Labour and Capital (which had reported a few years earlier), 'the displacement of small industries carried on with the limited capital of individuals by vast enterprises requiring the united capital of joint stock companies, the aggregation even of such companies in combinations vaster still:–these are perhaps the most striking features of the industrial era in which we live; and they are evidence of the growing conviction among the industrial workers of the world, that their work can no longer be carried on effectively except by concerted action taking the place of unrestricted competition.'[24]

Turning to the rights of workers in the impersonal, monopoly-capitalist society he saw emerging, Murray argued that both religious and philosophical imperatives demanded that men and women always be treated as persons and never as things. 'This fundamental right,' he observed, 'is incompatible with any industrial system which reduces the labourer to the condition of the slave.' Given that principle, labour could never be treated as a mere commodity, but must rather be recognized as a co-partner with capital in the industrial system. In contrast to Georgeites and labour reformers like Phillips Thompson, Murray did not accept a full-blown version of the labour theory of value. Rather, he argued that in the co-partnership of capital and labour each partner was 'entitled to a share of the product equal to his contribution as a whole.'[25]

That was what *ought* to be. But the most obvious fact about the emerging industrial order was that labour failed to receive anything close to a fair share of the wealth it helped to create. As the rich grew more affluent, the working people found themselves mired deeper and deeper in poverty: wretched housing, inadequate diet, lack of leisure time and, perhaps worst of all, labour's lack of power in a market that forced workers to sell their talents at the lowest rates. 'The raw materials of labour being in the hands of private persons, and labour being an impossibility without materials to labour upon, the labourers of the world are placed at an immense disadvantage in offering their labour for sale, because the commodity they have to sell becomes of value only when it is accepted by the buyer.' That condition ensured that workers were incapable of winning a fair share of the product of their labour. The lack of a just wage formed the central problem posed by modern industrial society. 'The process of producing wealth, and the laws by which the process is governed, are fairly well understood. That is not the part of economical science which troubles the thoughtful mind. But how to distribute the wealth, so as to avoid the appalling inequalities of the present system – the answer to this question will form the crowning achievement of Christian philanthropy and of social philosophy.'[26]

The first step toward an adequate answer to that question, Murray maintained, consisted in rejecting the notion that existing property relations and the theory of competition were sanctioned by natural law. An economic system based on private ownership of property could only be justified if the owners accepted the obligations inherent in possession. Those obligations included recognition that the rights of the community took precedence over property rights. That obligation, Murray recognized, was all too rarely accepted by the powerful. 'The great capitalistic conspirators of our day are in fact simply a survival, under altered conditions, of the great predatory chiefs of a ruder social state, who levied blackmail on all who accepted their rough and uncertain protection, while they plundered unrelentingly all who refused to submit to this capricious and oppressive tax.'[27] Surely as precise a definition of a 'robber baron' as was ever attempted!

Second, Murray contended, property owners owed a specific obligation to their employees – an obligation to remove the conditions of poverty in which so many working people found themselves. Since individual action would be inadequate to deal with these social conditions, Murray called upon the state 'to work out a scheme that is essential to the welfare of society.' Beyond this rather tentative commitment to a welfare system that would ensure adequate housing, nourishment, and recreation, Murray's prescription for social reconstruction involved the establishment of fair wages, a scheme of profit-sharing, and the formation of co-operatives. In the final analysis Murray believed that social regeneration could only be achieved by Christian businessmen acting in accordance with Christian moral precepts. Brotherhood, the characteristic idea of the social gospel, would then replace class conflict. 'It may be,' he wrote in 1894, '... that the evolution of society, instead of introducing a forcible, external, legal communism, will rather inspire the old concept of property with a new ideal, and that the feverish eagerness with which property is sought under the present system will disappear when large property, like every superiority over others, will intrude upon the moral consciousness of its owner, not so much the idea of right, as rather that of an obligation – not so much a claim to be ministered unto, but an obligation to place his property and even his life, if necessary, at the service of his fellow man.'[28]

That optimistic message, one which displayed a preference for Andrew Carnegie's *Gospel of Wealth* over Henry George's *Progress and Poverty* or Karl Marx's *Capital*, fell considerably short of the radicalism of, for example, a Phillips Thompson. Founded as it was on the orthodox Protestant conviction that individual regeneration must precede effective reorganization, Murray's social philosophy advocated little of a specific nature that should have seriously disturbed the wealthy patrons of McGill University. Yet his importance should not be underestimated. By maintaining that classical economics and utilitarianism were inadequate guides for a society that sought social justice he gave systematic expression to a conviction that motivated virtually every moral and social reformer of the late nineteenth century. The claim that ethics and economics were inseparable was certainly the starting-point for those who would eventually call themselves social gospellers. Murray, after all, had identified the central problem: how could wealth in a capitalist society be equitably distributed? That, he insisted, was a religious question.

III

By the 1890s theological liberalism had made a noticeable impact on Protestant thinking in English Canada. Nowhere was that impact more obvious than in the Presbyterian Church, and most markedly in that branch represented and influenced by Queen's University. There the influence of such men as Principal Grant, the philosophcal idealist John Watson, and, later, the political economist Adam Shortt all led to a conception of Christianity that emphasized the ethical over the theological. Shortt could have been describing the theological outlook of a growing number of Protestant clergymen when he wrote of the Reverend James Alexander Macdonald, who had moved from the editor's chair at *The Westminister* to a similar post at the Toronto *Globe*, that for him 'the essential function of religion was to redeem from gross materialism and sordid selfishness the living practical interests of men – their business, their politics and their social life.'[29]

Macdonald was not a Queen's man; he had been educated at Edinburgh University and at Knox College in Toronto, from which he graduated in 1887. During his student days at Knox and in subsequent years the *Knox College Monthly* frequently published discussions of social and economic problems and offered critiques of the single tax, Bellamyite socialism, and other nostrums of the day.[30] Among the contributors were Adam Shortt and J.G. Hume of the University of Toronto, a Canadian disciple of the

American social gospel political economist Richard T. Ely. Macdonald's own contributions were among the most advanced in their expressions of liberalism and their appeal for a more socially oriented Christianity. A visit to that Mecca of late nineteenth-century Christian social reform, Toynbee Hall in East London, led him to condemn the churches for offering 'a ghostly, otherworldly substitute' to the poor instead of the true Christ. In a second article in 1889 he urged his fellow Presbyterians to read Edward Bellamy's *Looking Backward*. 'Christianity must vindicate her claim to Divine origin and her right to continued support not by appeals to historic records or documents or creeds or confessions but by showing her adaptability to present-day human problems. And when ministers of religion in increasing numbers become impressed with this truth, and turn again to their textbook – the Bible – they will find the true principles of political economy enunciated more clearly by Moses and by Christ than by Malthus or Spencer or Mill or Rogers or Cairns or Ashley.'[31]

By the 1890s those sentiments were expressed with growing frequency in Presbyterian circles, most notably at the theological alumni conferences Principal Grant inaugurated in 1893. There during the next decade Presbyterian ministers, and a few like the young Methodist Salem Bland, heard carefully prepared papers on philosophical idealism, the higher criticism, poverty, socialism, the single tax, modern literature, and ethics.[32] The underlying liberal assumption of those meetings was described by Grant in 1886. 'The work of the church in our day,' he told Sir Sandford Fleming, 'is to reconcile itself to all that is best in modern thought. There is no institution where that can be done so as to reach the whole church but Queen's.'[33] For Grant, Christianity and modern, progressive western civilization were closely identified. 'The content of Christianity becomes richer as the evolution of humanity proceeds,' he wrote in *The Religions of the World*. 'The high capacity for good, which according to the insight of Jesus, pertained to humanity, is being realized. Civilization is Christian; the root of life of every Christian people is Christ; and the non-Christian nations have to assume the methods and instruments of Christian civilization in order to succeed.'[34]

Still, Grant's liberalism did not lead him to reject the whole of traditional Protestant teaching. Sin, 'the rebellion of the free will,' still stood as 'the obstacle to human progress.' Social reformers who failed 'to go down to the basis of character' would meet only disappointment. That was the 'meaning of the Cross of Christ.'[35] That admitted, Grant still contended that Christianity, intimately tied to human culture, bore the responsibility for the moral quality of social life. There could be no separation between the sacred and the secular, the natural and the supernatural. That was essentially the message of his moderator's sermon preached before the general assembly in June 1892. Grant warned the gathered commissioners, 'Everywhere the masses are in a condition of unrest. The wage relationship between man and man is felt to be inadequate. It is better than slavery, better than feudalism, but it is not up to the ideal of Christianity. It is not what the Fatherhood of God or the Brotherhood of Man demands and implies. Has the Church no message but one of future blessing to the millions who toil for daily bread, for a daily wage that may be taken from them at any moment? If so it will be no church for them.'[36]

Grant, like many others, toyed with ideas of profit-sharing, expressed sympathy for experiments in co-operative enterprise, and insisted on the application of ethics to economics. But he was an outspoken opponent of Henry George, the Anti-poverty Association, and the socialistic views advanced by Phillips Thompson's *Labor Advocate*. The failings of the Georgeites stemmed from their over-pessimistic assessment of the condition of modern society which, Grant insisted, was an improvement over past societies and was getting even better. 'The world is not getting worse,' he declared in an attack on the single-tax movement in 1891; 'it is getting better in consequence of the diffusion of education, the increase of producing and distributing forces, the invention of labour-saving machines, and the moral virtues which the management of such machines calls for.' Once man learned to love God and his brothers, 'social and economic evils would vanish even more speedily than even the dreamers of social Utopias hoped for.'[37] Grant, at his worst, was entirely capable of service-club inspirational preaching.

Among those who disagreed with Principal Grant's Panglossian assessment of progress and poverty in Canadian industrial society was a brilliant woman named Agnes Maule Machar. Her father, a Scottish Presbyterian clergyman, had been principal of Queen's in the 1850s, and had had the additional distinction of performing young John A. Macdonald's first marriage. Her older brother, John Maule Machar, was a Kingston lawyer who in the 1880s was a devoted follower of Henry George and a supporter of the Knights of Labor.[38] Agnes, despite the limited formal education available to her, became one of the most gifted intellectuals and social critics in late nineteenth-century Canada. She wrote fiction and poetry, displayed a wide knowledge of natural history and theology, and composed several respectable, if romantic, works of popular history. She demonstrated a multitude of interests in her numerous articles.

Though Agnes Machar stayed close to Kingston, her intellectual interests encompassed most of the English-speaking world. She read voraciously in many fields, and counted among her acquaintances the Kingston-born George Romanes, the celebrated associate of Charles Darwin and somewhat uneasy agnostic, and the Darwinian popularizer Grant Allen, to whom she was related by marriage. Perhaps it was through these associations that she came to know Alfred Russel Wallace, and probably discussed both natural selection and spiritualism with him at her summer house in the Thousand Islands. It was there that she entertained the American social gospel leader Dr Lyman Abbott. She held office in the Kingston Humane Society, helped found the Canadian Audubon Society, and devoted a great deal of energy to the National Council of Women of Canada. Included in the many causes she supported was the campaign to prohibit the use of birds' plumage in women's hats, and the promotion of wilderness parks. The Thousand Islands, she hoped, would be preserved in their natural state as a national park, for she foresaw what would happen if private ownership was permitted: 'The rich American wants, not to enjoy unadulterated nature, but to transplant the luxury and ostentation of his city life to the midst of the St. Lawrence, where he may go a-fishing with a steam launch and return at evening to the pretentious villa with its lawn and its house plants and its summer houses; and to accomplish this the island is completely transformed, and then in place of the wild, careless charm of nature draping tenderly tinted rocks and crags with luxuriant vines and fluttering of birch and maple, and cresting them greener with murmuring pines and hemlocks, while the sweet notes of the forest warblers ring unchecked through the bosky recesses, we have simply the very flat prose of a conventional suburban villa, with trees and lawn (artificially made) and gaily painted pavilions and boat houses.'39

What was most striking about Agnes Maule Machar's career was the breadth of her concerns. She was willing to defend her views against all comers, no matter how skilled in the arts of controversy – W.D. LeSueur, for example. What lay at the basis of her thought was her firm conviction that Christianity, once brought into line with contemporary intellectual developments, provided the surest method of both comprehending and reforming modern industrial society. Machar's Protestant liberalism, which bore a close resemblance to that of Principal Grant, was evident in her earliest forays into intellectual dispute. Her defence of the Christian belief in the efficacy of prayer against the positivist scepticism of W.D. LeSueur was based more on experience than on theological dogma. Her admiration for Charles Kingsley revealed her strong conviction that

Christian social action – 'earnest, active, practical' – was more important than the preaching of sound doctrine. Her liberalism was explicitly stated in an article entitled 'Creeds and Confessions,' in 1876 when she concluded that 'Christianity is no collection of rigid dogmas or abstract propositions, but the life and spirit of Christ translated into the life and spirit of every faithful believer.' Her extensive reading of theological writing led her to a willing acceptance of both the higher criticism and the modernist view that there was no conflict between Christianity and modern culture.[40]

This strong liberal tendency was Machar's fashion of defending what she believed to be Christianity's essence: its ethical teachings. That did not suggest any slippage toward agnosticism: for her, Christian morality depended upon Christian belief. She made a telling point when she wrote, with LeSueur and other secularists in mind, that 'when we find men talking, unconscious of how the Christianity they reject has moulded their thoughts and words, of the "moral resources of a true humanity" ... as separate from faith in, and love of God, we know they are only holding to the shadow of the substance they would throw away; and if they could throw it away they would find that the shadow had an inconvenient tendency to follow.'[41] Here she was in agreement with Goldwin Smith, though Machar was in doubt about the solution to the riddle of existence.

During the 1870s and early 1880s Machar developed a growing preoccupation with several social issues. Like many reformers (though here she differed from Principal Grant) she favoured the complete prohibition of the manufacture and sale of alcoholic beverages. Such prohibition, she argued, was not an attempt to legislate morality. That would be impossible. Rather, it was intended to remove alcohol from the reach of those who were its victims, to save them from themselves. Alcoholism to her appears to have been more a disease than a manifestation of moral weakness. Another issue that attracted her in the 1870s was women's place in society. Like John Clark Murray, she strongly favoured equality of educational opportunity and a wider field for women's employment. Not unexpectedly, since she remained single, she expressed a special concern that women who preferred to remain unmarried should obtain good liberal and professional educations. But she also contended that there was no need to worry that marriage and the family were in any way threatened by the expansion of woman's sphere.[42]

By the 1890s, with the economic depression making the limits of Canadian material progress painfully plain, Machar displayed an urgent concern for the condition of women for whom industrial labour rather than higher education was the immediate reality. Arguing that society was an organism with interacting parts, Machar insisted that it was the responsibility of middle-class women to take up the cause of their less fortunate sisters for whom wage labour was a necessity. Maternalistic as she sometimes sounded, Machar was nevertheless clear-eyed about the sources of women's special inequality in the industrial system. 'The answer lies in the hard necessities of poverty,' she emphasized, 'which compels them to take the work on the terms offered, and makes them so much afraid of dismissal that they will seldom ever complain of oppression.' Shorter hours without reduction of wages was the obvious answer.[43]

Machar's social concerns, evident in an 1879 article in which she maintained that unless the church took up the issue of poverty the lower classes would naturally succumb to atheistic communism, became her central preoccupation by the 1890s.[44] Repeatedly she returned to the theme that was to dominate her best novel, *Roland Graeme: Knight*: the need for a socially oriented Christianity. When Principal Grant criticized the Georgeite Episcopalian J.O.S. Huntington, who campaigned in Canada in 1891, Machar insisted that both Huntington and General Booth in England were on the correct course, the one charted by the Sermon on the Mount. 'Had this been kept in the foreground as the integral, human side of the Christian religion,' she wrote, 'had the Christian church been steadily faithful to this part of the message to "all sorts of conditions of men," should we have, today, the spectacle of capital endeavouring everywhere to screw down the receipts of a labourer to a minimum for which men otherwise starving can be induced to work? Should we have the complementary spectacle of labour everywhere striving to free from the reluctant grasp of capital a fairer share of its profits that labour toils to gain? Is there not everywhere the assumption that the employing classes have a prescriptive right to live in spacious and generally luxurious houses, to wear "purple and fine linen" and "to live sumptuously every day"; while the employed must consider themselves fortunate if they can "make both ends meet" in a bare subsistence; if their cramped bodies have a roof that will keep out the rain, walls that will afford some adequate protection from the winter's frost, and a floor not charged with hidden germs of disease; an idea by no means frequently realized even in this Canada of ours?' Here was an indictment of developing capitalism that would have warmed the cockles of Phillips Thompson's heart. He would even have approved Machar's vision of an alternative society as a step in the right direction. While postponing final

Agnes Maule Machar

judgment on the single-tax panacea and the details of General Booth's program to bring light to darkest England, Machar nevertheless felt that 'one thing ... in which all true friends of the working class will agree with him [Booth] and with Father Huntington is in the approval of the principal of co-operation and organization among workmen, as absolutely necessary to protect their rights in these days of "combines of capital."' And Machar believed that women had a special role to play in the coming struggle for social regeneration, a role exemplified by their part in the Salvation Army. '"Our Lady of the Slums" is wise as well as loving – often wiser than the cold political economist, sometimes wiser than the professional "divine."'[45]

These are the themes that Machar developed in *Roland Graeme: Knight*. The hero, perhaps modelled on Machar's brother, is both a Knight of Labor and a follower of Henry George. His views and actions are depicted as the natural application of social Christianity. But those beliefs are arrived at only after young Roland shakes off the simple religious beliefs of his childhood. At college, scientific knowledge contradicted much of what he had previously learned, and his social conscience revolted at the aridity of theological teachings. But Henry George's *Progress and Poverty* pointed in the direction which he saw practised by labour leaders, a socially oriented Protestant minister, and a young woman, inspired by new ideals of womanhood which drove her to work for the betterment of working women. Roland turned to radical journalism and founded a newspaper with a typical social gospel name, *Brotherhood*. Graeme's career and ideas bore a striking similarity to the program of an organization founded in 1892 by the leading American social gospel theologian, Walter Rauschenbusch. That organization, 'the Brotherhood of the Kingdom', was based on the conviction that the establishment of the kingdom of God on earth was 'the central thought of Jesus,' a message Rauschenbusch had preached to Canadian Baptists as early as 1889.[46]

In *Roland Graeme* the Reverend Alden, a Protestant clergyman, summed up those elements of the theological liberalism that underlay the social gospel which Agnes Machar and many other Canadians had come to believe represented true Christianity. He offered Roland a way out of agnosticism: 'to my mind,' he explained, 'religion is not a literary or historical question. Neither is it to be found, as some tell us, on the witness of the intellect ... neither as others tell us on emotion ... [but on] something deeper than either; on the sense of *righteousness*, the deepest, truest consciousness of humanity. Speaking for myself, *I want God* – want the Divine Perfection which is the same thing. I look for Him in Nature, but I cannot find him there, except in hints and hieroglyphs. Nor can I find in humanity the perfection I long for. I see imperfection and limitation in all, even the best. But what I want I find in Jesus of Nazareth, nothing else satisfies me; *that does*. If I cannot see God there, I can see him nowhere. I find in Him, as I see in the gospels, a moral beauty such as I could never of myself have imagined, but which the more I know of men – even the best – the more I must appreciate and adore. It sometimes seems to me that this age of ours is saying, like Pilate, and very much in his spirit, "Behold the Man!" Well, the more it learns to truly behold the *Man*, the more it will be compelled to recognize that Manhood as Divine.'[47] By emphasizing the humanity of Christ, the 'Jesus of History' rather than the 'Jesus of the Creeds,' and making ethical teaching the essence of Christianity, Machar gave expression to a viewpoint very similar to that of such American liberals as the Reverend Lyman Abbott, to whom she dedicated her novel.[48] In this manner the intellectual problems raised by the higher criticism and the new biology could be dismissed rather than answered, without reverting to a literalist defence of the Bible and Christian doctrine. With an emphasis on the practical, both agnosticism and ecclesiasticalism could be banished by a 'return to the simple gospel of faith and love, which "the Carpenter's Son of Nazareth" and his humble disciples taught with such living power to a world more antagonistic to it than is the world of today.'[49]

That social gospel which Machar had come to see as the heart of the

Christian message was drawn out more fully in a second novel that appeared at the end of the century. Like Machar, Albert Richardson Carman Jr, author of *The Preparation of Ryerson Embury*, had excellent clerical antecedents. His father, the Reverend Albert Carman, was the most powerful Methodist in Canada. A one-time bishop in the Methodist Episcopal church, he was the founding principal of Albert College in Belleville and a supporter of Alma Ladies' College in St Thomas. In 1883 he became the general superintendent of the Methodist church in Canada, a post he held for over three decades. His theological and biblical views were conservative; for him the Hegelian idealism that infused the 'new theology' was 'heathenism.'[50] But his social views were radical. Perhaps it was his biblical literalism that convinced him that it was no easier for a rich man to enter heaven than it was for a camel to pass through a needle's eye. In 1891 he preached a sermon entitled 'The Gospel of Justice' in which he espoused the doctrines of Henry George and denounced the preaching which he claimed was prevalent in Canadian churches where the rich convinced ministers of the need to trim and moderate Christ's ethical demands. His words were worthy of the early Marx: 'Should the suddenly rich, the monopolists, those who have filched the savings of the people, all who live by the labour of others, meet in secret council to frame a religion under which they would like the world to live; what better could they enact but that the oppressed would bear with Christian humility their oppression, and that the wronged would live with silent lips, looking for right only beyond the grave? And yet that is in practical effect the gospel heard today in many an upholstered pew – the gospel of charity on the part of the rich and humble gratitude on the part of the poor – of exhortation to the rich to give, that they may evidence their goodness, and of promises to the poor of a fairer distribution of God's mercies in the future life. And then we wonder, wonder, wonder at the awful perversity of the poor who will spend the Sabbath in God's sunlight, having taken us at our word that the Gospel has nothing particular for them until after death.'[51] Rev. J.S. Woodsworth never spoke harsher words about the church.

Albert Carman Jr was twenty-six years old when those thundering sentiments were preached, and he must have heard them often enough from his forthright father. After graduation from Albert College, having won the gold medal for science in 1883, he took up journalism, first with the Toronto *Globe* and later with the *Montreal Star* where he eventually became editor-in-chief.[52] Carman's first novel – he wrote two – gave expression to his father's social radicalism, but contained very little of traditional Methodist theological or biblical conservatism. In summary, the story of Ryerson Embury is an account of a brilliant young man – perhaps Carman himself – who, despite a careful religious upbringing, failed to experience conversion. That was a difficulty shared by many, including J.S. Woodsworth, who eventually followed the path to theological liberalism and the social gospel.[53] In search of answers, young Embury turned to such writers as Tom Paine, D.F. Strauss, and Robert Ingersoll, and became a member of the Free Thought Society. (An appearance by Allen Pringle would not have been out of place!) Neither biblical conservatism, undermined by the higher criticism, nor the evasive 'symbolic' interpretations of a liberal theologian could prevent his slide into agnosticism. Yet his growing scepticism was accompanied by an increasing sensitivity for the plight of the working people in his college town. Through his connection with local union leaders he discovered the hypocrisy of the rich religious élite of the town. He also discovered the writings of Henry George. Forced to choose between his position with a prominent law firm and the radical principles he has espoused, Embury not unexpectedly opts for virtue over wealth. He undergoes what is in effect a conversion that carries him into 'Christian work.'[54]

What is most significant about Embury's renewed faith is that it is discovered during a rational discussion with a leading free thinker and Georgeite. And the Christianity to which he returns is not the simple religion of his upbringing or, for that matter, of Albert Carman Sr. It is instead faith in an ethical system of brotherhood, the teachings of Jesus, 'the greatest of reformers,' not Christ crucified but the Jesus of the Gospels, a man who attacked privilege, fought for the poor, and insisted 'upon the equality of the human family,' the kingdom of God on earth. 'Take that part in the Sermon on the Mount in which he advises them to take no thought for what they shall eat or drink, or wherewithal they shall be clothed. "But seek ye first the Kingdom of God," He says, "and His Righteousness and all these things shall be added unto you." Now did that mean anything? ... Was Jesus in earnest? If so, it meant that if these people obtained the Kingdom of God they needed not to worry any more about food and raiment. And what interpretation of the phrase "Kingdom of God" will fit that except "a right social order."'[55]

By putting those words into the mouth of a free thinker, Carman perhaps intended irony. But intentionally or not they revealed Carman's acceptance of the essentially humanistic view of Christianity, a liberalism so capacious that 'Free Thinker' could be its spokesman. Neither W.D. LeSueur's gentle agnosticism nor Colonel Robert Adam's more doctrinaire secularism would have found anything very objectionable in this formulation of liberal Christianity. Even Allen Pringle, for all his anti-clericalism, would have lauded the conviction that 'every great religious leader has had but the one purpose of rescuing the suffering section of humanity. Look at Buddha, and Moses.'[56] Flora Denison and the Reverend B.F. Austin surely would have concurred, while Dr Bucke had long had these, and others, on his list of the cosmically conscious.

IV

By the end of the nineteenth century all of the elements of theological liberalism and the social gospel had found clear expression in English Canada. The influence of those views would expand in the new century when economic growth and prosperity brought materialism, public and private corruption, and harsh inequality. But the basis had been laid in the controversies over Darwinism, biblical criticism, and the social teachings of Protestantism. With the question of religious orthodoxy had come a parallel scepticism about economic and political orthodoxy. 'The lower *mechanical* laws of supply and demand,' a prominent Anglican clergyman wrote in 1894, 'must be regulated and supplemented by the higher *ethical* law which lies at the basis of socialism; the law that recognizes the mutual obligation of man to man above and beyond all calculation of interest and advantage.'[57]

To some clergymen the rediscovery of the church's social mission must itself have seemed something of a godsend at a time when intellectual confusion, the famous 'crisis of faith' that characterized the last years of Queen Victoria's reign, threatened to end in the triumph of secularism.[58] Now Christian clergymen had a new urgent calling and a new defensible justification. Old, intellectually difficult theological questions could be set aside.[59] All that was required was a relevant apologetic. And for some, at least, its general outlines were plain. The Reverend S.S. Craig, a Presbyterian minister, wrote with Calvinistic certainty (but with an un-Calvinistic attitude to theology), 'The only sufficient apology for the existence of the church today is that it gets God's will done on earth ... The desideratum to be arrived at in the new apologetic is not how to meet the infidelity of a few learned men, but how the inherent forces of Christianity may be made immediately effective in delivering the masses from industrial slavery, in the purification of politics, in the redemption of man socially, in the harmonizaiton of all true human interests, in the perfect correlation of all rights and duties, in the realization of the Kingdom of God on Earth.'[60]

James L. Hughes, Ontario's leading progressive educator, advanced a similar view for a Methodist audience when he wrote that 'men are beginning to understand the revelations of Christ in regard to the greatest ideal – community – and to believe that Christian principles are for everyday use; they are in fact the fundamental principles of all social evolution. The new theology and the new education are in perfect harmony in teaching that the greatest work a man has to do *is not the mere saving of his own soul*, but the fullest development of his soul or selfhood in order that he may do his best work for God in accomplishing the highest destiny of mankind as a unity. This ideal is making Christianity a vital force in the social and industrial organization of humanity and an essential element of a progressive civilization.'[61]

Protestants like Craig and Hughes believed that social ethics would succeed where theology, apparently, had failed: namely, in regenerating man and society. This union of the sacred and the secular, of Christianity and 'progressive civilization,' sanctified by theological liberalism, was destined eventually to give birth to the secular social science of sociology.[62] 'The perfect sociology, perfectly applied,' the Reverend Dwight Chown, Carman's successor as general superintendent of the Methodist church, maintained, 'will realize the Kingdom of God on Earth.'[63] If Christ was, after all, a social reformer, then the 'perfect sociology' was obviously the central concern of Christian thought.

11

The Modernist Pilgrim's Progress

If Jesus Christ was pre-eminently a social reformer, the task of interpreters was to expound not a theology but a sociology, a program for reform. By the beginning of the twentieth century there was general agreement among social reformers who took Christianity as their point of departure that the new industrial society failed to measure up to Christ's ethical teachings. Henry Harvey Stuart, a New Brunswick social critic, expressed this sentiment in 1912 in a fashion that would have won wide general consent. 'Our economic system and the religious ideas we have founded upon it are wrong,' he wrote. 'Only the spirit of brotherhood and co-operation dimly foreshadowed by the early prophets and fully taught by Jesus and His Disciples can save the world. The individualist theory of everyone for himself has failed and can never succeed. All for each and each for all is the better way. Not until the spirit of Jesus dominates society will the objects of social and moral reform be achieved – poverty abolished, crime and suffering reduced to a minimum and the Kingdom of God established upon Earth.'[1]

While these generous sentiments might receive wide acclaim from individuals and church groups and from such broadly based national organizations as the Social Service Council of Canada,[2] there was no real consensus about how to achieve the kingdom of God on earth, or even what it would look like. Perhaps nothing more graphically illustrates the problems of biblical exegesis than the Christian sociologies devised by three young reformers in early twentieth-century Canada. The Reverend A.E. Smith, the Reverend J.S. Woodsworth, and W.L.M. King were all devoted to the advancement of the kingdom, for each was a product of the intellectual and material changes that had fostered liberal Protestant social reform thought. Yet from that common heritage each modernist pilgrim devised sharply contrasting sociologies of salvation.

I

For William Lyon Mackenzie King the most consuming struggle of his youth centred on the choice of a career that would satisfy both his vocation and his ambition. He never doubted that greatness of some sort awaited him. Nor did he doubt that public service was his destiny, service in a form that would continue and complete the work of his grandfather, whose memory inspired and weighed heavily upon him. 'His mantle has fallen upon me, and it shall be taken up and worn,' King wrote in 1898. 'His voice, his words shall be heard in Canada again and the cause he so nobly fought shall be carried on.'[3]

If he was to walk in his grandfather's footsteps, a political career might have seemed obvious. But for the young King politics was only one of several possibilities. What he did know from an early age, and with certainty, was that whatever career he chose the ultimate goal would be the same: putting into practice the Christian ideals he had learned from his family, his regular Bible reading, and the hundreds of sermons and religious discussions he had listened to and engaged in by the time he obtained his PH D. Whether as a settlement-house worker, professor, civil servant, clergyman, or politician, King knew that his 'very double life' could only achieve oneness if he lived and applied his Christian beliefs. At the beginning of 1902, having only just settled into his duties as deputy minister of labour – a career which fell far short of fulfilling his worldly or religious ambitions – King confided to his diary: 'I felt that a silent voice was ever whispering to me that this work was but preparatory to something else; it may be work in the Church, the university or active politics. I am inclined to feel that it is more likely to be the first than the last. My desire is unquestionably to reach large audiences of men, to influence them in a direct personal way to better living and higher thinking, and firmer believing in the present realities of life. I believe God has endowed me with a power to do this, and that it is not ambition merely. If it is may I never have the opportunity of satisfying it. My aim in life is to be able to reveal the purpose of God in the Universe and in the lives of men, to this great master passion of my moral and spiritual nature all else is subservient and ever must be.'[4]

The most unambiguous aspect of King's Protestantism was this sense of vocation, of being one of God's chosen, and the ability to represent, even to himself, his own powerful ambition as a divine guidance. No wonder he idolized William Ewart Gladstone.[5] Beyond these sincere if obviously self-serving convictions, King's religious beliefs and ideas were a mélange of modernist platitudes that were more often sentimental than coherent.

In this as in many other ways King reflected the intellectual confusion of a society passing from Protestant orthodoxy through religious liberalism to a secular humanism founded on social science.

Mackenzie King was born into a Presbyterian family, and he remained a faithful, if unorthodox, member of that church all of his life. But it was family tradition much more than theological understanding that determined his denominational preference. While he was growing up he attended churches of various Protestant denominations and participated in interdenominational organizations. He read his Bible regularly but, though he read a great deal, he appears to have had no interest in theological works. Beyond political economy and history, which his academic studies required, he devoured works of moral uplift and social concern. Charles Kingsley 'saw men as they are.' Carlyle had 'the true conception of the dignity of labour,' while Matthew Arnold failed 'to bring out the concept'n of "love" as the essential of life, its place in Christ's teaching and the Universe.' Charles Dickens, almost predictably, was the 'most inspiring. I love him for his love of the poor, his strong human sympathies & his knowledge of the world.'[6] His taste in poetry was for the romantics, and especially for the rather sentimental verse of his friend Wilfred Campbell, whose religious views emphasized 'putting more of the humanities into religion.' Campbell was 'one of the greatest poets the continent has produced ... a mystic, a seer, a man of great force,' a man who might even be entrusted to write King's grandfather's biography. King and the poet agreed on such weighty matters as the 'need of insisting on the moral order & the presence of God in the Universe, eternal laws, etc.'[7]

Though King appears never to have had serious doubts about the validity of religious doctrines, no 'crisis of faith' comparable to that of J.S. Woodsworth, for example, he was certainly aware that recent scientific discoveries had created difficulties for believers. Early in his undergraduate career he read Darwin's *The Origin of Species* 'carefully & rather sceptically.'[8] While the work may have challenged the faith of his childhood, he soon turned evolution – apparently of the Spencerian rather than the Darwinian variety – into evidence supporting an ever-increasing optimism about Christian life. The doctrine of evolution, when applied to society by writers like the American sociologist Lester Ward, led King to conclude that science would lead to the reinforcement of Christian belief. 'The reformat'n in religion which the next century will witness,' he wrote in 1898, 'will be its establishment on a scientific basis – its greatest advance. The inevitability of law in the spiritual as in the material world will be shown. What is love but part of Infinite love, as well as force is part of universal force. There is a splendid field here for a great mind. I wish I were capable of beginning the task.' Those lines contained both the genesis of *Industry and Humanity* and a hint of King's later attraction to the 'science' of spiritualism. The following year King was both elated and a little disappointed to discover that Drummond's *Natural Law in the Spiritual World* (1883) made it unnecessary for him 'to make religion scientific or rather to show it to be such, and to show the teachings of Christ to have been a statement of law.'[9] For King, as for other Christians, Drummond appeared to make evolution and Christianity partners in progress.[10] Some years later, after reading Drummond's *The Ascent of Man* (1894), King mused, 'This large subject of evolution affords food for the larger vision in thought, is stimulating to the imagination, appeals to reason, and uplifts the soul.' For King, as for Dr Bucke, whose *Cosmic Consciousness* he acquired only in later life, progressive evolution provided the key to the scientific understanding of religion and society.[11]

King concluded that man and society were governed by Christian laws of spiritual evolution. Once man accepted God's omnipresence, the divine influence would be 'ever towards perfection in our natures.' He recognized that his doctrines were somewhat unorthodox. Summing up, he affirmed his belief 'in God who controls the universe, Christ Divine, but differing from us in degree rather than kind. We ourselves have divine natures. There is a reasonableness about Christ's teachings.' Emerson had brought him this far toward Unitarianism, but 'early training and traditions' kept him within the Presbyterian fold;[12] similar beliefs almost drove J.S. Woodsworth from the Methodist ministry.

King, in these early years, had developed a thoroughly liberal version of Christianity. After attending a prayer meeting in 1900 he wrote, 'I feel I cannot stand by the old fashioned, orthodox way of doing – religion and life are inseparable.' A few years later he told Dr Herridge, his minister at St Andrew's Presbyterian Church in Ottawa, that 'settlement work was more in accord with the spirit of Christ than Sunday school work.' Evidently he had fully absorbed the essentials of the social gospel. While reading *The Story of Jesus Christ*, by the American social gospel novelist and writer Elizabeth Stuart Phelps, he confided to his diary, 'I admire Christ more than any man in history & my aim is to become like him ... The work I hope to give my life to is very great. The solving of social & industrial & political problems and the spreading of the light of truth upon these & the voice of right concerning them. I know I have exceptional powers given me for this service if I can train myself to it ... In this Life of Christ I do not care much about miracles & I think the wonder working power was by him little thought of. The Sermon on the Mount reveals the Christ better than anything else.'[13] It was in the life of this liberal Christ that more than a decade later King found the secret of heroism – the title of the memoir he wrote about his alter ego, Bert Harper, who had drowned in a skating accident on the Ottawa river.[14]

Despite the fullness of his religious liberalism, King retained at least a skeleton of traditional Christian doctrines. That in part explains the moderation of his prescription for social regeneration. The doctrines of immortality and sin, modified and modernized, remained part of his theology. The doctrine of life after death had been rejected or at least cast into serious doubt by nineteenth-century rationalists and agnostics. Yet the power of the idea retained a strong grip on even the most unorthodox – those like Phillips Thompson and Flora Denison, who turned to spiritualism and theosophy. Goldwin Smith, a friend of the King family, presented young Willie with an inscribed copy of his 1898 edition of his *Guesses at the Riddle of Existence*, which King read with great care.[15] But he evidently found Smith's scepticism unattractive, whereas William James's untheological case for immortality, which he read a few years later, made a strong impression on him. 'I liked greatly James' interpretation of the truth that every man has a soul within him bursting for immortal life.' And he continued his thought, somewhat unexpectedly: 'this is the basic principle of the whole Labour Movement.'[16] While that might have surprised Samuel Gompers or Alf Jury, what King meant, apparently, was that the labour movement should be concerned about its members' spiritual as well as material well-being.

If a continued belief in the reality of the afterlife tempered King's zeal for building the kingdom of God on earth, his definition of 'sin' as an individual rather than a 'social' fact had a similar effect. Social reform panaceas that concentrated on institutional changes rather than on altering individual attitudes always seemed dubious to King. In his view every man led a 'double life,' and it was only rarely that his 'better self' prevailed. The chief function of religion, then, was to nurture man's divinity so as to make perfection possible. That was what he meant when he explained to Dr Herridge that 'in the last analysis character will be the only salvation & in the making of character the church has its real patriotic service to perform.' He went on to make a remark about the church and religion which, unintentionally, revealed his own basic attitude to social reform. 'It seems to me,' he said, 'that institutions & ordinances are quite a secondary part of Christ's teachings. His emphasis was on life, on daily conduct, motive, action.'[17]

King wrote those lines on his thirtieth birthday. By that time the religious beliefs that were the basis of his thought and action had acquired an overlay of social science. But his academic education supplemented rather than supplanted the convictions and values which liberal Christianity had taught him, for King 'never dissociated his liberalism from his religion.'[18] As a student King was a practical-minded young man anxious to settle on a career. Perhaps it was his practical nature which, despite the obvious attractions of the church, drew him toward the social sciences. Yet he never saw his study of political economy as contradicting his sense of religious calling: he studied political economy so that he could learn the most effective technique of Christianizing society. Even when drawn toward a political career, as he was after hearing Wilfrid Laurier speak at Massey Hall in 1895, he resolved 'to have first a solid Christian basis.'[19]

Having chosen political economy, King obtained an excellent introduction to the main currents of his discipline in the 1890s. The University of Toronto's department of political economy had been founded by W.J. Ashley, a proponent of the historical approach to economics. When King arrived the department was headed by James Mavor, who introduced his students to ideas that raised important doubts about the universality of the laws of laissez-faire economics.[20] King read the classics, Adam Smith and Thomas Malthus, and minor writers like Goldwin Smith, dutifully but without much enthusiasm. (Of Adam Smith he complained that 'he takes a long time to say very little.'[21]) It was during the summer vacation of 1894 that King found an economist who excited him intellectually. This was the Christian social reformer and economic historian Arnold Toynbee, author of *Lectures on the Industrial Revolution* (1884). In the cheap edition of the book that King purchased in the fall of 1895 he heavily underlined Toynbee's essential thesis: 'The historical method has revolutionized Political Economy, *not by showing its laws to be false, but by proving that they are relative for the most part to a particular stage of civilization. This destroys their character as eternal laws and strips them of all of their force and all of their sanctity.*' Toynbee went on to describe the inequalities and conflicts of industrial society; he stressed the importance of trade unions in defending workers' rights and thus preventing revolution. For Toynbee industrial civilization was only acceptable if it was Christianized, which did not mean radically altered structurally but rather operated according to the principles of charity, equity, and justice. An example of what that meant in concrete terms was his suggestion that boards of conciliation should be established in industry to settle management–labour conflicts, thus institutionalizing 'a higher gospel than the gospel of rights – the gospel of duty.'[22]

After his first contact with Toynbee's work King wrote excitedly, 'I was simply enraptured by his writings and believe I have at last found a model for my future work.' Just a little more than a year later King appeared before the Toronto Socialist Labour party to lecture on 'Arnold Toynbee and the Indust'l Revol'n in England.' He recalled, 'I tried to speak earnestly & to close with an appeal on behalf of religion, quoting it as giving the secret to Toynbee's work.'[23] That meeting revealed a lot about the youthful King, his religious outlook, Toynbee's influence, the appeal of the public platform, and his growing contacts with life outside the university. Perhaps the most underestimated aspect of King's education in these years took place in the university of the streets: open-air meetings with Phillips Thompson's socialists, W.A. Douglas's Single Taxers, and Alf Jury's trade unionists. He attended church- and YMCA-sponsored conferences on social problems and, as has become notorious, carried on missionary work among prostitutes, work which may on occasion have satisfied his sexual as much as his spiritual desires. He also experimented with mesmerism and phrenology.[24]

In his contacts with working people and radicals King was intent upon achieving at least two goals. One was certainly to learn about working-class life, an interest that later led to his investigations of 'sweating' in industry. His second concern was to play the role of reformer, stressing the importance of Christian beliefs and values. Evidence of agnosticism and free thought among workers surprised and disturbed him. A typical diary entry of October 1895 read: 'This afternoon I went to a meeting of the Socialist Labour Party at which Rev. Mr. Bliss of Boston spoke. I also addressed the meeting briefly pointing out that it was not so much Socialism, Single Tax etc. that we were to argue about but rather consider the question of more immediate reforms.'[25] This gradualist approach to reform would become King's hallmark.

The Reverend W.D.P. Bliss, a prominent American Christian socialist, was only one of a number of visiting and local social gospellers whose acquaintance King made. From his socialist friend Andrew Tweedie, King obtained a copy of W.T. Stead's *If Christ Came to Chicago* (1894). Though he found its style too sensational, he thought that it contained 'much valuable information.' Some Toronto clergymen impressed him, notably the Reverend Charles Shortt, but others seems uninformed or worse. At a theological conference at Victoria College in 1895 he heard S.D. Chown deliver a paper that was 'word for word from Toynbee,' while most of the other clergymen 'know little of practical and economic conditions especially of labour.'[26] At twenty-one he already thought of himself as an expert.

The social reformer who made the most profound impression on King was Jane Addams. The founder of Hull House in Chicago addressed the Pan-American Congress of Education and Religion in Toronto in July 1895. King immediately made her acquaintance; he was never shy about presenting himself to people of importance. After meeting Addams at St Andrew's Institute, which liberal Presbyterian Rev. D.J. Macdonnell had founded to bring the church closer to the working people, King dined with her and fell totally under her spell. On hearing a speech she delivered on Toynbee's contribution to the settlement-house movement, King gushed: 'I love Toynbee & I love Miss Addams.' Two years later at a conference where King met Agnes Machar, he was again overwhelmed by Jane Addams. 'I pray earnestly to become a better man more like Miss Addams,' he recorded; 'to me she is Christ-like.' King took away from all of these meetings a heightened interest in social reform and a renewed conviction that Christianity provided the prescription for change. After hearing numerous lectures on Henry George, Bellamyite socialism, Tolstoi, and other themes, his response was almost automatic. 'Tonight I went to hear Rev. Dr. [Washington] Gladden on "True Socialism". It was not very different than the teachings of Christ. All men will have to come back to Christ again.'[27]

As an undergraduate King had been drawn strongly to a career in the church, but on graduation he chose to continue his studies in political economy. First at Chicago and later at Harvard he made contact with some of the most prominent academic economists and social thinkers in the United States. He read widely and extended his social contacts (including young John Rockefeller at Harvard, whom he liked, and the family of Elbridge T. Gerry, whose summer home reminded him of the 'rottenness of Sodom.') Outside the university he listened to Eugene Debs, whom he pronounced confused, and the free thinker Robert Ingersoll, who 'disgusted' him. 'He strengthened rather than weakened my old conviction,' King recorded.[28]

In Chicago King renewed his acquaintance with Jane Addams, visited Hull House, and informed the Presbyterian readers of The Westminster of 'the crying evils direct and indirect of the sweating system.' At the University of Chicago he worked with Thorstein Veblen, the iconoclastic social theorist whose course on socialism introduced King to such radical writers as Henry George and Karl Marx. As an economist George did not measure up; Marx was 'very abstract & not always clear' and 'does not seem to me at all convincing.' But Veblen made a very positive impression – the best teacher King had ever worked with – and he worked hard. Veblen's prestigious Journal of Political Economy published the results of

King's research on the International Typographical Union, a straightforward historical analysis. The course on socialism greatly stimulated King. 'I believe that socialist tendencies are coming to be the prevalent ones,' he wrote at the end of the course. Though Veblen was not a socialist, he had introduced King to radical ideas in a much more sympathetic fashion than had been the case at Toronto. In the autumn of 1897 King summarized his now more open-minded attitude after reading Engels' *Socialism: Utopia to Science*. 'There is something about socialism which interests me deeply,' he mused. 'There is truth in it – it is full of truth. Yet there is much that is strange and obscure.'[29]

If at the end of his Chicago years King was moving slightly leftward, the Harvard experience put him back on track. The call to Harvard came just as he was preparing his own course on socialism to be taught in Chicago's extension program. Harvard awarded him a scholarship (Toronto had turned him down). God had rewarded him as he would doubtless punish his old teacher, Professor Mavor. And King never lost his resentment. The University of Toronto remained a 'whited sepulchre' where 'there are many dead bones within, men of narrow views & some scant scholarship, some uncouth in manners, some anything but gentlemen and scholars.' Harvard proved to be everything that Toronto was not. Armed with a letter of introduction from Goldwin Smith, King moved quickly into such gentlemanly, if reactionary, circles as that which gathered at the Shady Hill home of Professor Charles Eliot Norton.[30]

Academically, King fell under two principal influences at Harvard. One was Frank Taussig, who, while open to new ideas, remained 'first to last a follower of the classical tradition of Ricardo and John Stuart Mill.' He was an excellent teacher, a strong personality, and extremely sympathetic to his students. His special interest was the wages fund theory, which argued that wages could never exceed the amount available in the 'fund.' King was convinced: 'In the light of what Taussig has said, I see much that Toynbee has missed.' He was also impressed with the Harvard professor's defence of capitalist accumulation and private property against single-tax and socialist critics.[31]

Yet if Taussig's orthodoxy appealed to King, another teacher who visited Harvard during his second year reinforced King's Christian social reformism. This was Dr William Cunningham, a Christian reformer and economic historian from Cambridge, who belonged to the school of Arnold Toynbee and W.J. Ashley, so-called socialists of the chair. Cunningham, like Toynbee and Jane Addams, spoke and wrote in a rhetoric of Christian morality and spirituality that instantly touched King.

Interested as King was in questions of technical economics and social science, his overriding preoccupation was always religious and moralistic, less intellectual than sentimental. That was especially clear from his enthusiastic response to Cunningham, whose *Modern Aspects* 'speaks of the need of high ideals and self-discipline as the great factors in individual progress. He is right. This man is having a great influence on me. He is the sort of personality I have sought most & I meet him now at the end of my course. A Christian Economist. The Harvard men present the Utilitarian point of view most strongly. Taussig is a strong utilitarian. It is well that Cunningham asserts so strongly the Christian point of view, it goes to show the completeness in life which would be wanting but for religion.' By the end of the term the British professor and the Canadian graduate student had become fast friends and King's commitment was complete. 'It seemed to me like Arnold Toynbee's influence sent through him to bid me on again! ... I will go ahead and be a man, a good man, and shew the world the power of Christ, even as Dr. Cunningham is shewing it,' he resolved.[32]

Cunningham's influence, like that of Toynbee and others, did not really contradict any specific tenet of King's social philosophy. For one reason, those tenets were far from specific: Christian goodwill and a general sympathy for the working class was close to the sum total. Whatever drifting in the direction of socialism King had experienced at Chicago was halted and reversed at Harvard. Taussig played a role, but King's general reading may have been even more significant. In the spring of 1899 he began reading the works of two French social theorists, both of whom buttressed King's belief in individualism and in the need for a reform program that concentrated on character as the root of social injustice. Gustav Le Bon's study *The Psychology of People* argued that there was a natural division of labour in society and among 'races' which required, as King noted, 'that each do that for which he is best fitted with a consciousness of individual responsibility to God for the use of his time & talents.'[33]

The second writer was Edmond Demolins, a Christian sociologist of the Frederic Le Play school. King read his *Anglo-Saxon Superiority: To What Is It Due?* very attentively. 'Social salvation ... is like eternal salvation,' Demolins wrote and King underscored, 'an essentially personal affair; everyone must shift for himself.' That was what the Anglo-Saxons understood, as compared with the communitarianism of the French. 'Nations, which by all sorts of convenient combinations, manage to escape the law of intense personal labour, are bound to moral depression and inferiority. Thus the Red-skin compared with the European; thus the

Oriental compared with the same European; thus the Latin and German races compared with the Anglo-Saxon.'[34] King recognized that Demolins was more polemical than scholarly, but the polemic rang true. 'The emphasis put upon indiv'l enterprise & initiative, self-reliance etc. as against state aid etc. is the underlying thesis of this book. Here is an element of character and conduct & is rightly, I believe, at the bottom of the great social questions. Indivil'ism vs Socialism considered from this point of view seems to give everything to the individualistic point of view. This sort of reasoning has won me over to the individualistic from the socialistic camp.'[35]

The reinvigoration of King's individualism was further strengthened by a reading of a British social Darwinist, W.H. Mallock. In *Aristocracy and Evolution* (1898) he argued that unfettered social evolution ensured that talent reached the top, while socialism and even democracy threatened the survival of the fittest. 'Just as there is no tendency toward equality in capacity,' Mallock wrote, 'so ... there is no tendency toward equality in social conditions.'[36] King swallowed the message whole; he was so impressed that he read a good deal of Mallock aloud to his mother and his brother Max. When he finished he drew his own conclusion. 'I found it a most profitable book, the point of view essentially the opposite of the Socialists. It is a justification of things as they are and to my mind there is a great deal of truth in what the writer says. He maintains that there are innate differences in the wealth and social well being. That the many must always be led by the few if there is to be true progress and that progress will be & has always been the work of the few ... I find that I have come round strongly to the individualist point of view ... Under the regime of social[ism] the secret of present indust'l greatness wd. be taken away – viz private property as a stimulus to exertion & the socialist alleged motives cld. avail little with man as he is now – & man does not change in a day.' King recognized exactly what was happening to him: he was moving to 'maturity,' becoming 'more conservative & less a believer in radicalism.'[37]

It is worth emphasizing that although King was trained as a political economist his social outlook was little affected by detailed arguments of technical economics or abstract considerations of political philosophy. He found writers like Adam Smith and Karl Marx indigestible. The Toynbees, Veblens, Demolins, and Mallocks, with their sweeping generalizations and moralistic conclusions, were the thinkers who caught King's fancy. Their ideas fitted into his own moralistic mentality, and they seemed more useful to a young man who despite his intelligence was not an intellectual. Application, not speculation, attracted King. And he was not always willing to distinguish rhetoric from analysis.

His work at Harvard finished, King set out on a research trip to Great Britain. There he established contacts with leading labour reform figures and examined social conditions. With the ideas of Demolins and Mallock dancing through his head, it was not surprising that he found the Fabians little to his liking: 'Two of the women smoked, some of the men stayed near the wine & whiskey, others talked.' The leaders of the co-operative movement impressed him a good deal more favourably. 'Co-operat'n has in it all the virtues claimed for Socialism, without its defects, it is individualistic, all self-help, self-initiative, & self-dependence, no govt protection.' Naturally, he approved of the work of Toynbee Hall and other settlement houses. When asked to present a series of lectures on social problems he chose to conclude with one entitled 'Christianity & Labour' based on Dr Cunningham's writing. His message summed up the main points of his social philosophy and prefigured *Industry and Humanity*. 'I began reviewing the course & linking this lecture to the last by pointing out end of State & means of reform by Social Philosophies such as Socialism, Anarchism etc & contrasting these with the ends of Xianity – Perfection of Mind and immortal soul, and means of achieving that. Pointed out that former looked to change in external condit'ns, that Xianity regarded these as due to individ sin & only permanent good by removing sources of this, human heart & motive. In diagnosis of world, Christianity saw the greatest law broken. The unhappiness etc were evidences of this – they showed a want of harmony with the purpose of the world, which was love – as remedy it looked not to a change in conditions, but in causes wh. brought them about, heart of man and fulfillment of law of love. Pointed out how social changes without this wd. fail, with this social conditions wd. soon adjust themselves. Then spoke of Xianity as motive power in social reform.'[38]

For King, then, social reform was religious in a rather traditional sense: regeneration of man had to precede social regeneration. He was a moralist much more than a social critic. That perhaps explains why his closest academic advisers – Taussig and Cunningham in particular – urged him to enter the civil service rather than take up an academic career. He had worked hard at his academic studies and he had learned a great deal. But what he learned he fitted into a set of social principles based on his liberal Protestantism, which altered very little during his university years – or later, for that matter. So he moved from academic life to practice, first as deputy minister of labour, then as minister. He believed that this new work would allow him to implement the Christian sociology he had developed, a sociology that involved applying the laws of God to society. Looking forward to graduate work in 1895, he had

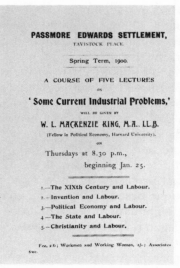

PASSMORE EDWARDS SETTLEMENT,
TAVISTOCK PLACE

Spring Term, 1900.

A COURSE OF FIVE LECTURES
ON
'Some Current Industrial Problems,'
WILL BE GIVEN BY
W. L. MACKENZIE KING, M.A., LL.B.
(Fellow in Political Economy, Harvard University).
ON
Thursdays at 8.30 p.m.,
beginning Jan. 25.

1.—The XIXth Century and Labour.
2.—Invention and Labour.
3.—Political Economy and Labour.
4.—The State and Labour.
5.—Christianity and Labour.

Fee, 2/6; Workmen and Working Women, 1/-; Associates free.

written, 'I believe a sound theoretical base is what I need, I am strongly inclined practically. I need a solid base. I believe in conservative as opposed to radical measures of reform.'[39] Nearly twenty years later, when he published the fruits of his theoretical and practical knowledge in *Industry and Humanity*, he might have used those last words as an epigraph.

Industry and Humanity is best read as a sermon preached by a socially conscious, but certainly not radical, liberal Presbyterian. (One reviewer remarked that King, like 'some economists at times and most college professors all the time is primarily a preacher.'[40]) In summary, it said little more in 529 pages than the following paragraph from a book prepared in 1910 for Presbyterians concerned about the social application of Christianity: 'Jesus demands a return to the spirit of brotherly love, to the exaltation of the spiritual above the material, and to sacrifice as the law of service. Already something has been done. Arbitration and conciliation have accomplished much. The same spirit of brotherly co-operation can complete the task. The church can educate both parties and all parties in the principles of the Kingdom of God.' That was the tradition to which King's thought belonged. It was based upon the proposition advanced by the Reverend J.G. Shearer, a leading Presbyterian advocate of social Christianity: 'It is not enough to change the environment; it is not enough to transform social life. This is necessary but not sufficient. It is essential that the heart be regenerated, that the people should be saved, that the character should be transformed.'[41] These ideas – arbitration, concilia-tion, co-operation – were commonplaces which echoed John Murray's writings in the 1880s, Agnes Machar's proposals in the 1890s, and a flood of speeches and articles by church and secular reformers. King merely dressed them up in the language of social science and presented them as a new plan for social regeneration.[42]

King expressed no doubt about the fundamentally sound character of capitalism from an economic and material perspective. Of all systems it worked best and produced most. That judgment, however, did not 'touch ethical side which treats of responsibilities & duties they entail.' There-fore, social relations within the capitalist order had to be Christianized, which for King meant giving precedence to the 'spiritual' over the 'material.' While writing *Industry and Humanity* in 1915 he explained that he was 'working up the spiritual interpretation of the universe as against the material. I am sure that in a failure to recognize this lies the fundamental cause of error in much of the effort at social reform and that it is also at the bottom of conflict. If I can make this clear and broadly reveal the practical application of Christian principles to industry I will have helped to make a real contribution.' To achieve that end, he believed it was necessary to devise scientific laws of ethics paralleling the scientific laws that governed material development. 'The *Law of Survival of the Fittest*' had to be replaced by the '*Law of Christian Service.*' The science of ethical law was expressed in this manner: 'The problem of the nature of the universe is necessarily bound up with the parallel problem of human personality. Abundance of life is to be attained, not through any brute struggle on the part of men or nations in accord with some biological law of survival of the fittest, but through mutual service in accord with the principles of a higher law, the law of human brotherhood which finds its sublime expression in Christian sacrifice and love.'[43] Like Bucke and many other late nineteenth-century thinkers, King was attempting to think 'cosmically,' to formulate a science of society that accepted evolutionary theory. And like other 'reform' social Darwinists, King rejected, at least in its unadulterated form, the mechanism of natural selection.[44]

King had always believed that reform had to begin with man, with 'human personality.' 'To talk of the "solution" to the Labour problem, apart from the "solution" of "restoring humanity" is to speak of an impossible thing,' he had written in 1903. Of course, some obvious injustices in society could be removed or ameliorated, but that was secondary. 'Machinery is nothing,' he insisted. 'Personality is everything.'[45] But what was the problem of individual 'personality' that needed to be tackled? Here King's modernism becomes plain: he belonged to a generation for whom the traditional Christian conception of sin as alienation from God had lost its meaning. He believed that man's 'sin' – his limitations – was largely a matter of anti-social attitudes. 'Fear,' he contended, had to be replaced by 'faith'; that would remove virtually every obstacle to the smooth and just functioning of society.[46] 'A belief in our fellow man equal to that which we have in ourselves is all that is necessary to remove the *human blindness* which has so long made us strangers to one another, and oftimes enemies as well.'[47] Such a naïve faith in the power of positive thinking revealed how far King had wandered from the disciplined Calvinist heritage of his church. Nor, evidently, had his long years as a student of political economy provided him with any adequate alternative understanding of human social behaviour. Lacking either a systematic theology or a systematic social theory, King was left with little more than Arnold Toynbee's general admonition that 'morality must be united with economics as a practical science.'[48] King's belief that a science of society that was as 'valid as the science of nature'[49] led him to camouflage his intellectual deficiencies behind a barrage of pseudo-scientific banalities – 'The Law of Peace, Work and Health,' 'The Law of Blood and Death,' and so on. But these 'laws' were little more than King's attempt to demonstrate that his own deeply felt but nevertheless almost childlike conceptions of good and bad and right and wrong existed as objective, scientifically verifiable truths.

As he appealed to 'science' as the sanction for his social ethic so too he appealed to the authority of Christ's teachings to support the proposals he advanced as the social reforms necessary to establish justice. These proposals included profit-sharing, co-partnership in industry, consumers' co-operatives, and the removal of the insecurities that plagued working people. The last was to be accomplished by the establishment of a 'National Minimum' standard of life and health. Finally, there was conciliation as the Christian means of resolving industrial disputes – an idea he learned from Toynbee and W.J. Ashley and which he had practised as minister of labour.[50] For King conciliation was no mere industrial-relations technique. It was quite simply an attempt to translate literally Christ's teachings as found in the Gospel according to St Matthew, chapter 18, verses 15–17.

V.15: 'If thy brother shall trespass against thee, go and tell him his fault between thee and him alone: if he hear thee, thou hast gained thy brother.'

That is the method of Conciliation and Mediation.

V.16 'But if he will not hear thee, then take with thee one or two more, that in the mouth of two or three witnesses every word may be established.'

That is the method of Investigation and Arbitration.

V.17 'And if he shall neglect to hear them, tell it unto the Church: but if he neglect to hear the Church, let him be unto thee as an heathen man and a publican.'

That is the method of reliance upon an informed Public Opinion, and upon the power of the Community to ostracize where a wrong is done its sense of justice.[51]

Here was King, the modern liberal preacher, giving a relevant interpretation to biblical texts. What he failed to acknowledge in *Industry and Humanity* was that he had borrowed the interpretation from a Baltimore clergyman and former miner who worked for the YMCA.[52]

The implementation of these few simple reforms would, in King's view, lead to the establishment of God's kingdom on earth. He concluded his sermon in the rhetoric of the New Jerusalem, revealing the liberal Protestant social Darwinism that had been the essence of his upbringing and his education: 'It is not alone a new dawn Labor and Capital may summon forth; they can create a wholly new civilization. Let Labor and Capital unite under the inspiration of a common ideal, and human society itself will become transformed. Such is the method of creative evolution ... Is it too much to believe that having witnessed Humanity pass through its Gethsemane, having seen its agony in the Garden of Fears, having beheld its Crucifixion upon the Cross of Militarism, Labor and Capital will yet bring to a disconsolate and broken-hearted world the one hope it is theirs to bring; and that, in the acceptance of principles which hold deliverance from the scourges that beset Mankind, they will roll back the stone from the door of the world's sepulchre to-day, and give to Humanity the promise of its resurrection to a more abundant life?'[53]

Thus, *Industry and Humanity* ended where it began. It was little more than an old-fashioned appeal for moral regeneration as the foundation of social progress which King had once described, after reading Benjamin Kidd's *Social Evolution*, as 'ever unfolding upward toward God.'[54] But it cannot be stressed too firmly that King, like his mentors Toynbee, Cunningham, Demolins, and Mallock, believed that the regeneration of society had to begin with the regeneration of man. Given that belief, the modesty of his reform proposals is understandable. But it might be legitimate to wonder if King had not, in the end, chosen the wrong career. If the cure of souls took precedence over the cure of societies, should he not have chosen the pulpit over parliament? His own answer, the way he

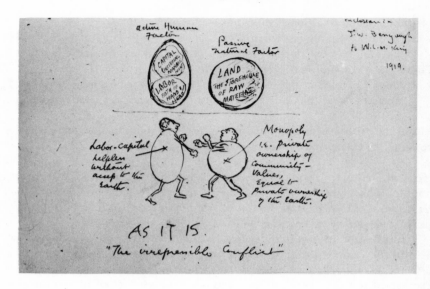

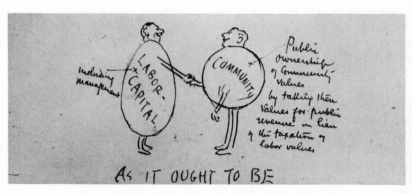

J.W. Bengough's summary of *Industry and Humanity*

resolved the conflicting ambitions of his youth, was to unite the sacred and the secular in his conception of political leadership. Just a year before Sir Wilfrid Laurier's death, King had a dream that Dr Bucke might have interpreted as a liberal Protestant version of cosmic consciousness. 'When I awoke at daybreak,' he recorded, 'I was dreaming very vividly. I saw Sir Wilfrid Laurier in Bishop's robes, high in a pulpit, speaking as Prime Minister of this country. A flood of tears rushed to my eyes in joy at beholding the very apocalypse of my aspirations so embodied. A political leader who will be a true servant of God, helping to make the Kingdom of Heaven prevail on Earth. That is what I love politics for.'[55]

A little more than a year later, in August 1919, King's unremitting quest for a Christlike role was answered when the Liberal party (God being on the side of Ernest Lapointe's big Quebec battalions), elected him as its new leader. King was doubtless in a minority in believing that the New Jerusalem was at hand. But at least those who had taken the trouble to thumb through *Industry and Humanity* should have realized that the party was now in the hands of a Christian sociologist. They might also have agreed with the student diarist who had remarked in 1898 that 'there is something about sociology which is loose and flabby. Big words & commonplace ideas.'[56]

II

If Mackenzie King was certain of his vocation but uncertain about a career, his contemporary, James Shaver Woodsworth, had the opposite problem. His career choice was almost inevitable, but he had serious doubts about his vocation. As with King, the ministry, a teaching post, and politics were all possibilities, with politics, perhaps as third best, the final destination. If their points of departure were similar, the roads they followed diverged, leading to opposite sides of the Canadian House of Commons.

Entry into the Methodist ministry was a natural step for young Woodsworth. His father was a leading Methodist and his parents expected that James would be ordained. 'With me,' he wrote in 1907, 'it was not a case of entering the church. I was born and brought up in the Methodist Church and easily found my way into its Ministry.'[57] But uneasiness in the ministry and doubts about the Methodist discipline and doctrine plagued him almost from the outset. He was far less clear about his calling, and God's sanctification of it, than Mackenzie King. He had never experienced 'conversion' as a good Methodist traditionally was expected to. His education at Wesley College in Winnipeg and later at Victoria in Toronto encouraged doubts about the validity of orthodox teachings which he never succeeded in completely quelling.[58] For the first decade of his ministry he was frequently preoccupied, sometimes almost to the point of paralysis, with questions about his orthodoxy. What kept him in the ministry, apart from an understandable desire not to hurt his parents, was an unshakeable certainty about the ethical, as distinct from the theological, teachings of Christianity. Once he had concluded, as he did in 1918, that the church had lost its determination to fulfil that mission, he left in search of some other institution that would take up the cause. He thought he had found the alternative in a variety of places – the trade union movement, the farmers' movement, the Labor Church, the Independent Labour Party, and finally in the Cooperative Commonwealth Federation. His evolution, even more clearly than that of Mackenzie King, revealed much about what was happening to Protestant Christianity in what one Methodist leader called 'the sociological era of the world.'[59]

Perhaps even before he left college Woodsworth had developed doubts about his ability to function as a traditional clergyman. A teaching career appealed to him, but he knew that he had to serve first on a mission field. So, like so many other young men in the early twentieth century, he went west. But he was not long there before he found himself in a profound crisis of faith. In 1902 he confessed a 'rationalistic tendency' that led him to doubt 'some of the most fundamental doctrines of the church.' He needed an authority to settle his questions. But he knew that a Protestant could appeal neither to a pope nor a church council for final certainty. And the Bible, once the Protestant's rock, could no longer be accepted, for its interpretation varied according to the interpreter and its 'historical accuracy cannot be maintained in the light of modern criticism.' There was only one remaining alternative: 'For each individual then the final authority is his own religious consciousness (whether called reason, conscience or common sense.)' His rationalism had also led him to doubt Christ's divinity, though he claimed his 'faith in God and his personal guidance' remained firm. But was that enough to remain in the Methodist ministry?[60] he asked Nathanael Burwash, a liberal who had taught him at Victoria. Theological doubts were accompanied by a concern that his ministry was ineffectual, for he felt an 'artificial and unnatural' separation between himself and his congregation. 'My world is different from theirs from which I am almost excluded,' he told a close friend. The more he came into contact with the condition of life outside of his world – in 1903 he prayed with a prostitute, 'helping one who is generally despised' – the more troubled he became.[61] Somehow the world and the church, the profane and the sacred, had to be brought closer together.

A trip abroad, including a visit to the Holy Land, a move to Winnipeg, greater involvement in social action, and more reading did nothing to quiet his restless spirit. He badly wanted out of regular parish work. College teaching strongly appealed to him, but positions were few. In 1906 he offered to go to the foreign mission field, to Japan or China.

He wanted to leave Winnipeg: the winter was harmful to his health, he complained.[62] Nothing came of these initiatives taken in 1906 and within a year, his religious doubts reached a new crescendo. His conscience demanded that he leave the Methodist ministry.

The events connected with what proved to be an abortive attempt to resign from the clergy in 1907 must be among the most extraordinary – and revealing – in Canadian church history. In a lengthy letter of resignation Woodsworth confessed that in effect he had rejected a major part of the Methodist discipline, and entertained profound doubts about all of the principal doctrines of orthodox Protestant Christianity: original sin, Christ's divinity, the atonement, salvation by faith, and much more. 'Many of the doctrines, of course, I believe,' he stated, without identifying them; 'but there are some that rest upon historical evidence which, for me, is not conclusive. Some are founded on psychological conceptions and metaphysical theories quite foreign to modern thought and are, for me, meaningless. Some deal with matters upon which it seems to me, it is impossible to dogmatize. Upon some I suspend judgment. Some I cannot accept in the form they are stated. Some I cannot accept at all.'[63]

Given that catalogue of doubts and reservations, it seemed obvious to Woodsworth that he no longer had a place in a profession which required that he preach those doctrines and demand that his congregation accept them. What was obvious to Woodsworth was not at all obvious to his peers, including some of the most influential Methodists in western Canada. The Manitoba Conference after a committee discussed Woodsworth's letter with him, refused to let him go. 'There is nothing in his doctrinal beliefs and adhesion,' the Conference resolved, 'to warrant his separation from the ministry.'[64] That outcome was truly astonishing – a theological position, Unitarian if not agnostic, apparently conformed to the standards of modern Methodism. The Reverend B.F. Austin, the 'spiritualist,' the Reverend Ralph Cecil Horner, the 'holiness' preacher, and Professor G.C. Workman, the higher critic, had all been punished for less serious heresies a decade earlier. Perhaps being a Woodsworth helped. But there was more to it than that. By 1907 theological liberalism had made such substantial inroads into Canadian Methodism and Presbyterianism[65] that traditional Protestant doctrines were in almost total disarray. Woodsworth, surprised at his unexpected fate, recognized the true state of affairs when he confided to his friend Charlie Sissons that he could not agree with the Conference's interpretation of the church's doctrines.[66] As he told his wife, with a sigh of puzzled relief, 'Certainly the Church is broad and generous and sympathetic, whatever the standards are.'[67]

Woodsworth now considered himself a free, if marked, man. He could work to alter the doctrines of the Methodist church. More appealing, he could throw himself into social action by taking charge of All Peoples' Mission in the immigrant quarter of North Winnipeg, 'practical work that I like, and no end of scope.' Here his social gospel, which combined Christianizing and Canadianizing immigrants with a developing critique of materialism, competition, inequality and political corruption in Laurier's booming Canada, would rapidly develop. And gradually he would realize that though social settlement work was important, it was limited – a palliative rather than a remedy. He began to wonder if, in concentrating on settlement work, the church might not be avoiding the real challenge. 'We can hardly be accused of underestimating the value of social settlements, institutional churches and city missions,' he wrote in *My Neighbor* in 1911, 'but more and more we are convinced that such agencies will never meet the great social needs of the city. They serve a present need; they bring us face to face with our problem; they point out the line of advance. Then by all means let us multiply them and extend the scope of their work. But the need will remain until the community at large is dominated by the social ideal. This is surely the mission of the Church, and yet the Church itself is hardly awake to the situation, much less fitted to meet it. Will the Church retain – perhaps we should say regain – her social leadership?'[68]

Woodsworth was obviously moving to a realization, shared with many social settlement workers in the United States, that only broad social reforms could resolve the problems that the very existence of social settlements epitomized: poverty, slums, and inadequate medical, educational, and recreational facilities.[69] Spreading the 'social ideal' and preaching social redemption – these were the proper tasks of the church in modern society. But was the church or its ministry adequate to the task? These questions pressed themselves more urgently on Woodsworth in the last days before the outbreak of the Great War.

Certainly the work at All Peoples' Mission, satisfying as it was, did nothing to remove Woodsworth's doctrinal difficulties. And he was not the sort of man who could forget them. As he moved toward the position that the church's mission was social redemption and that the clergyman should be a sociologist or social reformer, his own definition of religious doctrine clarified, though not in the direction of orthodoxy. Early in 1913 he contributed a short article to *Acta Victoriana* entitled 'Heterodoxy or Hypocrisy – A Minister's Dilemma,' in which he contended that the majority of young ministers no longer accepted the standard statements of belief. He therefore urged that the hypocrisy involved in accepting

All Peoples' Mission, Winnipeg

those doctrines with 'mental reservations' should be replaced by the recognition of the legitimacy of heterodoxy. 'Is not sincerity of greater importance than orthodoxy?' he asked rhetorically.[70] What the article left unsaid was brought out in a reply Woodsworth made to a challenge from James Mills, a distinguished Victoria graduate who had read his article. What, concretely, would Woodsworth put in the place of the traditional creeds? Mills asked. Woodsworth was ready with a revealing reply, beginning with a definition of religion. 'Religion,' he wrote, 'is essentially a life – not a dogma. Psychology recognizes personality as manifesting itself in knowing in feeling and in willing. Religious manifestations correspond more or less to this classification. In the experience of some individuals the manifestation is largely intellectual, in others emotional, in others practical. So certain churches have laid emphasis on belief, others on experience, others on "practical Christianity."'

For Woodsworth, obviously, it was 'practical Christianity' that was most appealing. He felt that Jesus himself had pointed to that manner of religious expression: 'Not everyone that saith unto me, Lord, Lord, shall enter into the Kingdom of Heaven; but he that doeth the will of my Father which is in Heaven.' Woodsworth insisted that the 'intellectual' approach had become untenable as a consequence of the 'generally accepted conclusions of history and science.' Most interesting, in what was perhaps Woodsworth's fullest exposition of his theology, was his appeal to progressive social science to support his contention that religious beliefs had to be modified to conform to changing social and economic circumstances. Both Charles McCarthy, one of the authors of Robert LaFollette's 'Wisconsin Idea,' and E.A. Ross, a leading American progressive sociologist, had maintained that law must reflect social change or it would ossify and lose its authority. So, too, Woodsworth argued, with 'theological dogma.' 'I am aware that in making this statement,' he remarked, almost as an aside, 'I lay myself open to the charge of being not only a radical in theology, but also a radical in economic thought – which latter is, perhaps, nowadays, fraught with the greater danger.' He did not expand upon the nature of his economic radicalism, but the drift of his theology was evident in the conclusion that 'in judging the suitability of a candidate for the ministry greater emphasis should be placed on a man's character and purpose than on his theological beliefs.'[71]

By 1913 Woodsworth had settled for himself the problem of authority that had troubled him for so long. Authority lay not in institutions, dogmas, or even the Bible; it lay in the individual conscience. 'Character and purpose' were what counted; 'theological belief' was relative. Ethics and not dogma mattered, though Woodsworth appears never to have asked himself Goldwin Smith's question: what authority supported Christian morality if theology and belief were rejected? Instead he immersed himself in 'practical Christianity,' which he hoped would save the church, society, and himself.

In his own activities Woodsworth was becoming more and more the practising sociologist. That was revealed in a series of articles published in the *Christian Guardian* during the summer of 1913 entitled 'A Workman's Budget.' Carefully researched, these articles totalled up costs of food, housing, clothing, medical care, and other necessities and measured these costs against a workingman's income. For many, especially women and those who suffered illness or lacked skills, the picture that emerged from these calculations was a bleak one. Faced with low wages and a labour market glutted by immigration, workers were turning away from the church. One found more satisfactory sermons in the Marxist paper *Cotton's Weekly*. 'What would you do if you were in this man's shoes?' Woodsworth asked his readers.[72] The series concluded with a discussion of 'A Programme of Social Reform,' which insisted that the eradication of slums was a far more pressing Christian need than the abolition of the liquor traffic. Woodsworth praised the Manitoba Conference of the Methodist church for adopting a reform platform that included, together with temperance, the recognition of collective bargaining rights, a minimum wage, tariff reform, the single tax, and even public ownership of certain utilities. 'An environment that permits – nay, that favours – a healthy, happy, human life, without the degradation and demoralization of private charity, that surely is the first principle of brotherhood, the Christian ideal reduced to its irreducible minimum, and that principle and the spirit which finds expression in it points to the Christian Church the luminous pathway to her glorious goal, the Kingdom of God on Earth.'[73] Here was sociology with a message.

Though Woodsworth was certain that he understood the goal of Christianity, he was now far from sure that the organized church was the institution best fitted to work for the achievement of the goal. 'Jesus' work of bringing in the Kingdom is much broader than the programme of the Church' he wrote in 1914. Its institutional structure, its divisions over creeds and dogmas, its ceremonies all meant that the church – and Woodsworth meant the Christian churches generally – was not equipped to engage in the social work which he was convinced was the first order of the day. He had begun to think that an alternative institution would have to be devised, for 'in the Church of the future saving souls will, more and more, come to be understood as saving men, women and children. At least in this world souls are always incorporated in bodies and to save a man you must save him body, soul and spirit. To really save one man you must transform the community in which he lives.'[74] Woodsworth's modernist theology, the view that religion had to be adapted to secular culture, had led him to a full acceptance of the social gospel claim that social salvation did not follow from individual salvation but rather preceded it.[75]

Having decided that the existing church was too limited organizationally and doctrinally to perform effectively in reforming society, Woodsworth cast about for other ways to do his work. He had, of course, tried the Methodist church's social agencies and at the same time contributed to public discussions of social, economic, and educational questions. After 1913, when he left All Peoples' Mission, he assumed leadership in rather more secular organizations – the Canadian Welfare League and the Bureau of Social Research, established by the governments of the three prairie provinces. In these posts he worked with prodigious energy, compassion and intelligence. He conducted social surveys, lectured across the country, wrote articles, and, as a result, gained an enviable reputation as well as some enemies.

But for all of his emphasis on 'practical' work, Woodsworth remained a 'preacher' or, as he increasingly preferred, a 'teacher.' He never lost the ambition to take up teaching as a career, and as his social concerns widened his interests turned to teaching 'Christian Ethics or Sociology.'[76] He wanted to train social workers, to give them a professional standing equal to that of lawyers, doctors, or educators, as was the case in the United States. But they were not to be bloodless professionals: knowledge of social problems had to lead to reform. 'The old individualism in industry, in ethics and in religion is being swept away,' he wrote in the spring of 1914. 'Chaos threatens us. Where are the leaders who will help us reconstruct our social life in accordance with the principles of social justice and welfare?'[77] Obviously, they had to be trained in university schools of social work. His experience, he thought, could best be put to use teaching others – and it would get him out of the 'sanitary and moral atmosphere' of North Winnipeg, which was not what he wanted for his children. If his experience was not enough he was willing to return to school himself, to go to Harvard to study with Francis G. Peabody, whose *Jesus Christ and the Social Question* had impressed him. But, though he was considered for the directorship of the new School of Social Work at the University of Toronto, he failed to find a suitable academic post.[78]

Then, events carried him rather precipitately in another direction. Late in 1916 his appointment as director of the Bureau of Social Research was terminated after he publicly expressed his opposition to the national service registration scheme. Then he resumed pastoral work at Gibson's Landing in British Columbia, only to find himself at odds with local merchants in his congregation over his support of the co-operative movement. But it was the war that more and more preoccupied him. He had become an uncompromising pacifist and the support which the Methodist church, like most other Canadian Protestant churches, gave to the war effort, especially in enlistment campaigns, was unacceptable to him. The time had come to resign from the ministry unconditionally. 'For me,' he wrote, 'the teachings and spirit of Jesus are absolutely irreconcilable with the advocacy of war. Christianity may be an impossible idealism, but so long as I hold it, ever so unworthily, I must refuse, as far as may be, to participate in or to influence others to participate in war.' To this pacifist interpretation of Christianity Woodsworth added an account of the causes of war drawn from 'economics and sociology' as the 'inevitable outcome of the existing social organization with its

undemocratic forms of government and competitive system of industry.'
In closing his letter addressed (ironically, as events would prove) to the
Reverend A.E. Smith, Woodsworth confessed that he had 'a growing
sense of fellowship with the "Master" and the goodly company of those
who through the ages, have endeavoured to "follow the gleam." I still feel
the call to service, and I trust I may still have some share in the work of
bringing in the Kingdom.'[79] A church that had a decade earlier winked
away Woodsworth's theological deviations now accepted the resignation
of the political heretic. For Woodsworth the die was cast. He would find
a new career outside the church, even though his friend Salem Bland
tried to convince him that 'the practical Christians will capture the
Church from the sentimental and dogmatic Christians and bring about
regeneration.'[80]

The 'call to service' that Woodsworth felt was still, as he told his mother,
'to get into Social work as soon as I can.'[81] But the route was to be a
dramatic one – as a longshoreman, a Non-partisan League organizer, a
lecturer, a journalist. These were hard but exhilarating times, played out
against a background of the Russian Revolution and the return of peace.
There was more than a little prescience in a letter he wrote to Charlie
Sissons just after the war ended. 'We are in for stormy times, as I see it,' he
predicted. 'Labor in the West is Revolutionary. The farmers are anti-
monopolist & big interests. The "foreigners" are sore. The French
Canadians nationalistic and aggrieved. Political parties in chaos. Reac-
tionaries in the saddle. Returned men will force the situation.' These
unsettled conditions did not frighten or distress Woodsworth; rather,
they filled him with hope and a new optimism. Amazingly enough, he
thought he was at last on the right road. 'Sometimes I confess I look back
with some longing to the fleshpots of Egypt. But I've tried to think that we
are at least reaching towards the promised land, even though we travel
through the desert and many of us are destined to fall by the way.'[82]

When what Woodsworth believed to be the 'revolutionary' mood of
western workers exploded into a general strike in Winnipeg in the spring
of 1919 he was, by happenstance rather than design, in the midst of it. For
the 'seditious' editorials which he wrote in The Strike Bulletin he was
arrested and briefly jailed, but never tried. The experience strengthened
his sense that his cause was righteous. So strong was his faith in the
triumph of justice that the crushed strike strengthened his chiliastic hope
for the coming of the kingdom. He had found himself in 'The Glorious
Company of Martyrs' and had 'never felt so strongly the call to preach the
good news of the Better Day.'[83]

What gave Woodsworth this heightened sense of expectancy was the spirit of the men and women who during the great strike had gathered at the Labor Church. 'Some of us,' he later recalled, 'felt the spirit of a great religious revival.' Here at last in the Labor Church Woodsworth and others saw emerging the vehicle for which he had searched so long: a vehicle of social reform – part church, part educational forum – based on what his friend Salem Bland called 'the New Christianity.' Like Bland and several nineteenth-century critics of religion and society (Dr Maurice Bucke, for example), Woodsworth now advanced a socio-economic interpretation of religious expression, arguing that religion was a product of social evolution. And, like Flora Denison, Woodsworth had come to believe that man, in effect, created God in his own image and that religious beliefs were an expression of socio-economic aspirations. To express the aspirations of ordinary working people a new church with a new doctrine was emerging. There were more than a few echoes of B.F. Austin's conception of a new scientific religion in Woodsworth's 1920 portrayal of 'The Religion of the Future': '(1) PROGRESSIVE – dynamic not static. It will lay no claim to finality but rather be "going on towards perfection." (2) It will be SCIENTIFIC in its spirit and methods. The universe will be perceived as one and indivisible, each part in relation to the whole. We shall not be afraid of truth, rather welcoming it remembering that the truth only can make us free. (3) It will be PRACTICAL. Our immediate concern is with the present world rather than with some future life. Right relationships with our fellow men are more important than speculative orthodoxy or ceremonial conventionality. (4) It will be essentially SOCIAL in character. No man liveth unto himself. The highest individual development can be realized only in a social organization. The emphasis is on social salvation. This involves fraternity and democracy. (5) It will be UNIVERSAL. When we evolve a religion that is big enough and broad enough and loving, it will make a universal appeal.'[84]

Despite the struggles and setbacks of a long career in the ministry and social action, Woodsworth's secularized theological liberalism left him fully confident that God was on his side, that he could rely 'upon the force which seems to be driving the world onwards and upwards.' When the Labor Church floundered, Woodsworth had to find a more secure way to end his 'precarious existence.' He still preferred teaching – he hoped the UFO–Labour government in Ontario might open the University of Toronto to someone of his qualifications – but he was being pressed towards politics. As a Labour politician he could, perhaps, help workers realize their 'dreams of a new heaven and a new earth.'[85] His own evolution had reached a new plane: it would be not in a church but in political action, not in a statement of religious doctrine but in a political program that he would now find his vocation. His religion and his politics had become one, together aiming at a common goal – the co-operative commonwealth, with 'production for use and not for profit as its economic base.' And what religion was professed by the Independent Labour party member for North Winnipeg elected in 1921? 'The very heart of the teaching of Jesus,' he stated in his profession of liberal faith, 'was the setting up of the Kingdom of God on Earth. The vision splendid has sent forth an increasing group to attempt the task of "Christianizing the Social Order". Some of us whose study of history and economics and social conditions has driven us to the socialist position find it easy to associate the ideal of the Kingdom of Jesus with the co-operative commonwealth of socialism.'[86] Here was the message that he would preach from his desk in the Parliament of Canada for the rest of his life.

For J.S. Woodsworth, religious unorthodoxy had led to social and political criticism. As he rejected the orthodox Christian explanation by which man had long explained his plight in 'this vale of tears,' so he came to believe that the vale of tears itself had to be vanquished. Had he read Marx, he would have agreed that 'criticism of heaven is thus transformed into criticism of earth, criticism of religion into criticism of law, and criticism of theology into criticism of politics.'[87] That was the unmistakable direction of modernist liberal thinking and its social gospel offspring. Jailed for his part in the Winnipeg general strike, one of Woodsworth's close associates, the Reverend William Ivens, summed up the essence of liberal Christianity when he told his friends, Rev. and Mrs A.E. Smith, 'What the world needs today, after its orgy of hate, destruction and blindness is BROTHERHOOD – I mean *real* brotherhood. The kind that includes an effective brotherhood of man. Until such is realized, the Fatherhood of God must be but an unrealized dream. Religion is life & life is religion.'[88]

That was exactly Woodsworth's position: life and religion, the secular and the sacred, would be indistinguishable in the kingdom of God on earth, the co-operative commonwealth. He believed that he had discovered the perfect Christian sociology.

III

When it came to choosing a career, or rather a way of earning a living, Albert Edward Smith faced no dilemmas. The luxury of choice was for middle-class youths who went to college, men like W.L.M. King and J.S. Woodsworth. Smith's background was working-class, and at thirteen he left school to look for work. He had to contribute to the family budget; his father, a British immigrant, too often found consolation in alcohol for his failure as a breadwinner. Smith started out as a machinist's apprentice and then shifted to bookbinding. In his unpublished autobiography he recalled a life of unremitting labour, economic uncertainty, and finally deep depression. In almost Marxian fashion he found an escape in religion. Conversion to Methodism, he remembered, 'opened a new and different world.' He experienced what Woodsworth had missed: an emotional awakening wherein his sins were washed away in a sea of revivalist oratory, tears, and direct experience of God. 'He saw God. He saw Jesus upon the cross. He felt the pain and anguish of the nail wounds ... He saw the Devil and the cutting hissing of his hot breath.'[89]

Conversion pulled him out of his despair and gave him a sense of purpose. He set about improving his education, and church activities assumed a central place in his life. In 1888 he became a lay preacher, conducting evangelistic missions in Hamilton after his day's labours at the bindery were completed. Two years later Dr James Woodsworth (J.S.'s father), who was in charge of finding young men to serve on the growing western Canadian mission field, invited Smith to take a charge in Manitoba. Filled with a 'flaming passion' for Jesus Christ, Smith jumped at this new opportunity to propagate the faith and, doubtless, because it offered some increase in economic security.

After three years of preaching in rural Manitoba, Smith entered the theological course at Wesley College in Winnipeg. He had come west holding fast to the traditional doctrines of Methodism that had been assimilated by his untrained mind. Now he came into contact with professors and students who questioned orthodoxy and expounded advanced positions that were becoming current among modernists. Once he had believed in the verbal inspiration of the Bible; now he was introduced to the intricacies of the higher criticism. At first the shock was profound. A fellow student, J.S. Woodsworth, whose own background was more liberal, helped him over the rough patches. Within a year Smith had successfully absorbed the new teaching and had become something of an advocate of the new learning. The letter of the Bible had to be understood in its historical and critical context. The spirit of God and his plans to bring 'mankind into fellowship with Himself' remained unquestioned.[90]

Following ordination, Smith spent five more years on the mission field. In addition to performing his normal clerical duties, he exercised his social conscience campaigning for prohibition, though without much success. According to his own account, it was not until he was called to McDougall Memorial Church in slum-ridden north Winnipeg that he discovered that 'a mighty struggle was developing in my mind.' He began to observe that 'the masses of the people were outside the church. The most of them did not want to come in.' Their concerns were not with theology or the afterlife, but with survival in the here and now. He turned to the Scriptures again, and discussed his problems with his socially concerned friends at Wesley College. He discovered a new message. 'I saw the Kingdom of God as a social order to be established among men,' he later wrote, 'and the mission of the church was to seek this objective as the purpose of its existence ...[Jesus] was not so much concerned about the salvation of souls of men as he was about the salvation of their social relations.'[91]

Smith's theological liberalism, coupled with his north Winnipeg pastoral experience, led him to what he believed was a much fuller understanding of modern thought. 'There are going forward today two great movements which at present are converging,' he explained. 'The social awakening and the scientific interpretation of the Bible. These movements are not foreign to each other but possess a logical relation and meaning which becomes more evident the more deeply they are contemplated and studied.' Here was the intellectual basis for a social gospel which Smith believed was entirely compatible with his ministry. No doubt his progressive views contributed to the growing recognition that Smith was winning in western Methodist circles. After Winnipeg, he served several congregations in the west before accepting a call to the First Methodist Church in Brandon in 1913. In 1916 and again in 1917 he was chosen chairman of the Manitoba Conference, took a leading part in church union discussions with the Presbyterians, and played an active role in the governance of Wesley College. In the latter capacity Smith participated in the decision to terminate Salem Bland's appointment in 1917. He later greatly regretted this decision and concluded, rather belatedly, that Bland's political views as much as college finances had been the cause of the popular social gospel professor's downfall.[93]

By 1917–18 Smith was caught up in the events that were to sweep him out of the Methodist church and well beyond the boundaries of the Christian social gospel. More than anything else it was the labour unrest at the end of the war that carried him relentlessly forward. Like Bland and Woodsworth, he had concluded that the labour movement was not merely worthy of sympathy, but that it was the chosen instrument for the Christianization of the social order. The general strike in Winnipeg and sympathetic strikes elsewhere, including Brandon, convinced him that the church had to join with the working classes to usher in a new social order. Post-war labour demands represented, in Smith's judgment, 'a mighty revival of religion.'[94] The church's place was with the workers.

Though the board of Smith's church grew more and more impatient with his political views, Smith moved closer to the workers; he became, a supporter wrote, 'a much sought after and well-loved comrade and advisor.'[95] The board found this role unacceptable, and demanded that he cease preaching sermons favouring the strikers. Smith rejected the ultimatum, left the church, and established a 'People's Church,' an action he thought he could take without leaving the Methodist ministry. When the Conference refused to recognize his new, special, status, he left the church in mid-1919.[96]

The People's Church was the Brandon version of the Labor Church. It was more an educational institution devoted to promoting ethical uplift than a church in a traditional sense. Smith was proud to say that 'the People's church has no creed and never intends to have one. The one thing the church needs today is to assert freedom for itself by the abandonment of all dogmatic creeds.'[97] In fact, Smith's church did have a creed: dogmatic insistence that orthodox Christianity, as Smith had once accepted and preached it, was a snare and a delusion. Its articles of faith, like that of more orthodox versions of Christian belief, focused on a particular view of Jesus and his message:

What is Jesus? Who is Jesus? Theology has misrepresented him and the church has misrepresented him. He has been represented as a wandering evangelist travelling about playing upon the emotions of the people by 'healing' and trying to 'save' souls from 'sin' and 'hell'. This is the very thing he did not do, and if he did he was a real failure at the business.

Jesus was a deeply convinced and well informed leader of the Communist order of thinkers and teachers that had been extant for many years in the Hebrew race ... until it was perverted by individualist theologians and politicians.

I am standing with Jesus the Communist, the Religionist, the Social Leader, the Saviour of Society. I have no place for the invention created by false theology, Hymnology and Sentimentalism.[98]

Smith's new faith was in the secular religion of social revolution; it contained no 'supernatural elements' and drew its inspiration for a new social order entirely 'from the experience of mankind.' By the mid-1920s Smith had followed his personal trajectory from Methodist orthodoxy to Marxian orthodoxy. Yet he could not shake off lifelong habits of thought and expression. 'The world is rotten with Christianity – but it has not yet begun to understand the teachings of Christ,' he told one of his new-found comrades in 1925. 'What a pity the name of Jesus has become so involved with the rotten lies of theology and selfishness and greed of bourgeois institutions, and defenders and bulwarks of Capitalist exploitation.'[99]

Marxism evidently satisfied Smith's need for certainty in a way that modernist Methodism was never able to do. Once he learned that there was more to Christianity than the compelling emotion of personal conversion, he moved steadily toward a rejection of religion. When his early beliefs were eroded by the intellectual challenges of the higher criticism and modernist theology he was left with a social message that could best be propagated outside the traditional church. Woodsworth had gone that far with him. But where Woodsworth had been satisfied to live with his conscience as the final arbiter of his action, Smith needed something more. Perhaps unconsciously, or perhaps in a more clear-sighted fashion than many other liberals, Smith realized that the ethics of Christianity were difficult to sustain or justify if theology and biblical authority were rejected. God as he had once known him was dead. In the new scientifically sanctioned social order that Smith believed would emerge from the rubble of capitalism, the principles he had once identified with religious teachings would finally become clothed in reality. But they would be founded upon historical materialism. That, at least, seems to have been what he meant when in 1944 he sent the newly elected moderator of the United Church a copy of *The Communist Manifesto*. 'There are some historical contradictions between this document and Jesus,' Smith explained, 'but there are no spiritual or ethical contradictions.' In his quest for the sociology of regeneration Albert E. Smith had found Karl Marx.[100]

IV

Although their itineraries led them to distinctly different political destinations, King, Woodsworth, and Smith were all children of the nineteenth-century revolution in religious belief. King remained the closest and Smith drifted the furthest from the faith of their fathers, but all three accepted the modernist claim that the mission of Christianity was social regeneration, that the line between the religious and the profane should be erased. But, as their separate prescriptions for a Christian sociology made plain, it remained easier for a camel to pass through the eye of a needle than for a Canadian society to become the kingdom of God on earth.

12

The Sacred Becomes the Secular

Pardonnez! dit Homais. J'admire le christianisme. Il a d'abord affranchi les esclaves, introduit dans le monde une morale ...

Gustave Flaubert *Madame Bovary*

Nineteenth-century social critics concocted many recipes for a perfect Christian sociology. Most included at least one common ingredient – the conviction that 'all true reformers must at heart be religious.'[1] Those words, spoken in 1913 by the agrarian reformer W.C. Good, expressed a new understanding of the relationship between religion and society. If religion had once been called upon to buttress the social order, now its function was to change it; the enemy was no longer 'personal vice' but rather 'social sin.' Here was a view of religion that embraced the conclusions of J.W. Bengough and Phillips Thompson, Dr R.M. Bucke, the Reverend B.F. Austin, Flora Denison and Allen Pringle, Agnes Machar and J.S. Woodsworth. Each of these regenerators accepted a theology which asserted, in a frequently repeated cliché, that 'there is, speaking accurately, no distinction between the *sacred* and the *secular*.'[2]

That melding of the sacred and the profane was the hallmark of the theological liberalism that underpinned the social gospel. It also represented a radical step in the decline of Protestant Christianity as a pervasive influence in English Canadian life, a stage on the road to a secular view of man and society. That, of course, was not the intention of those Christian reformers who called for a 'relevant' religion and who insisted that sociology, not theology, was the crying need of the capitalist world. But whatever the intention, the outcome of this attempt to unite opposites, the sacred and the profane, was predictable enough.[3] As Albert Schweitzer observed, 'there was a danger that modern theology, *for the sake of peace,* would deny the world negation in the sayings of Jesus, with which Protestantism was out of sympathy, and thus unstring the bow and make Protestantism a mere sociological instead of a religious doctrine.'[4] That outcome was the most remarkable consequence (though the least re-marked upon by historians of the social gospel) of the intellectual transformation that took place in English Canada between Confederation and the Great War. As Goldwin Smith suspected and Principal Dawson knew, the path blazed by nineteenth-century religious liberals led not to the kingdom of God on earth but to the secular city.

The challenge to traditional Protestant teachings in the nineteenth century was both intellectual and social. From science and the higher criticism came the demand for a rethinking of theology; the injustices of the emerging industrial capitalist order necessitated a reformulation of Christian social teachings. Each challenge was legitimate, but distinct. Many liberal Protestants confused them, however, contending that if the second challenge – making social action the central focus of Christianity – could be met, then the first could be safely ignored. Attending to the practical tasks of social regeneration became a substitute for the for-midable labour of reformulating theological doctrine. Christian action was given priority over Christian thought, and practice was divorced from theory. 'The best apology for our faith,' the Montreal Conference of the Methodist church resolved in 1892, 'is not the scholarly treatise by the learned professor, but the consistent life which mirrors forth the life of Christ.'[5] In the new age of optimism, traditional teachings about sin, atonement, judgment, and punishment were replaced by a life of Jesus that radiated reason, perfectability, love, and brotherhood. Holman Hunt's sentimental Saviour banished Albrecht Dürer's suffering Christ.

The Reverend Dwight Chown explained the new outlook in a lecture appropriately entitled 'The Relation of Sociology to the Kingdom of Heaven.' The intellectual advances of the nineteenth century, he main-tained, had revealed the sociological content of the Bible, and this new knowledge had replaced the Pauline theology that had preoccupied earlier generations. At the heart of this change was a new vision of Christ. 'Christ himself occupies a very different relation to human thought today as compared to fifty years ago,' Chown argued in a statement of unadulterated theological liberalism. 'Then the theological and philo-sophical interest in the life of Christ and its relation to the redemption of the human soul quite overshadowed its human and social significance.' But the perspective had completely shifted, so that 'while many of the doctrines which centre about Christ have to great multitudes lost their meaning, his personality, his social teachings, have acquired an interest never before felt.' This shift in Protestant thought, Chown continued, made it imperative that clergymen adopt a new role: they had to become 'moral leaders' of society rather than teachers of Christian doctrine. In a startling inversion of the traditional Protestant conception of the chief end of man, Chown advanced a commandment far more sociological than theological. 'The first duty of a Christian,' he informed young Methodists in 1905, 'is to be a citizen, or a man amongst men. We are under no obligation to get into heaven, that is a matter entirely of our own option; but we are under an obligation to quit sin and to bring heaven down to this earth.' For Chown, citizenship in the city of man meant imitating Christ. Christianity had become a civics lesson.[6]

By translating Christianity into a message of social reform and good citizenship, liberal Christians believed that their religion could be revitalized and brought into touch with the needs of the times. That, in turn, would save the church from obsolescence. The strategy was an understandable one but, at least in the long run, it was riddled with difficulties. Most obviously, the 'historical Jesus' invented by theological liberals and adapted to the needs of the social gospel was, like all historical subjects, open to a variety of conflicting interpretations. Every man became his own historian – and theologian. J. Spencer Ellis, the editor of *Secular Thought*, went directly to the central weakness of the claim that the 'real' Christ was a great moral teacher and social reformer when he wrote sneeringly that 'the truth is that the teachings of Christ are so given in parables and homilies and extravagant apothegms that need interpretation that they are open to the greatest divergence of meaning, and in no sense do they afford a true basis for an ethical system. Each man who takes Jesus for his guide is thus able to make Christ to suit his own ideal. We have thus the "muscular Christian," the meek and mild Jesuit, the charity-begging sisters, the comfortably based rector or parish priest, the howling or singing revivalist, the grocer, the stock-jobber, all of whom imagine they are "imitating Christ" when they go once a week to the gospel shop. "Christ," in short, is a chameleon-coated invention which changes colour to suit the spectacles of those who see him.' Here the atheist formulated precisely the same criticism that orthodox Protestant theologians directed at the 'Jesus of history.'[7]

There was a further and perhaps even fatal weakness in the strategy that substituted sociology for theology. Theology, the science of religion, had historically provided clergymen and the church with a recognized place in society. Theology to the clergy was what medical science was to the physician, knowledge of the law to the lawyer, and disciplined learning to the teacher. 'Abandoning theology,' Ann Douglas has written, echoing Goldwin Smith, 'the minister lost his expertise in the realm of what the Psalmist called "God's thoughts"; he was inevitably forced to seek the lowest common denominator in the minds of his listeners: some loosely defined preoccupation with spiritual, social and personal matters.'[8] Men like J.S. Woodsworth realized that loss of faith in the teachings that were the clergyman's professional body of knowledge meant that another kind of expertise had to be found. To him, as to others, sociology and professional social work seemed an obvious alternative. When that failed, then politics (which, together with journalism, remained the last career open to the non-expert) offered the solution. The fictional Ryerson Embury had already shown the way. Mackenzie King, A.E. Smith, J.S. Woodsworth, and others followed. As social workers or politicians they could exercise Chown's 'moral leadership' and preach sociology, though the truths of that science proved no less contentious than those of theology.

The difficulty was that Christian sociology failed to prove as relevant as its proponents had predicted. The essential problem was that Christian sociology, ethics without theology, ultimately rested upon the certainties of religious belief. Theology had, in fact, provided the sanction for Christian ethical teachings. Theory could not be divided from practice. Once the sanction was denied, the theory rejected, than a new sanction was required. That was Goldwin Smith's contention in his pessimistic musings on the prospects of a moral interregnum. But again as Smith foresaw, that new sanction, such as it was, appealed to the 'laws of science,' rather than to the 'laws of God,' laws interpreted by secular rather than religious sociologists. Mackenzie King clearly recognized this problem, and in *Industry and Humanity* had attempted to demonstrate the identity of the 'laws of God' and the 'laws of social science.' The result was hardly encouraging. Woodsworth's outlook and assumptions became increasingly secular,[9] while A.E. Smith followed the logic to its conclusion. When the fog of intellectual confusion lifted, the Christian social reformer had turned into the secular social worker. Principal Dawson, had he lived, would not have been surprised to find that the metamorphosis that began with Darwin had ended with secular social science. Neither would Karl Marx, for whom the rejection of religion, by which he meant theology, could only lead to the 'doctrine that *man is the highest being for man.*'[10] That union of the sacred and the secular, so ardently wished for by Christian social reformers anxious to regenerate the social order, unexpectedly acted as the accommodating midwife to the birth of a secular view of society.

The drift of the times was exemplified, somewhat extravagantly, in the career of S.D. Chown's niece, Alice. Born into a staunchly Methodist family, she devoted most of her first forty years to caring for an invalid mother. Once freed of family responsibilities, she took up a bewildering series of reform causes. (Sara Jeannette Duncan might have had Alice Chown in mind when she wrote in 1893 that 'life amounts to very little in this age if one cannot institute a reform of some sort.') Alice Chown was almost a parody of this age of social regeneration: feminist and Freudian, she worshipped Edward Carpenter, idealized labour, admired the Garden City movement, criticized traditional marriage and sexual conventions, and advocated pacifism and agrarian communitarianism. She revealed herself with astonishing frankness – and naïveté – in her neglected autobiography, *The Stairway*. Yet for all of her unconventionality, she spoke as a late Victorian social reformer when she described what separated her from her mother's world. 'Mother would have made her appeal to an ideal authority whom she called God. I made my appeal to an ideal in every man whom I do not call "the light that lighteth every man that cometh into the world." Her faith was in a Supreme Being who existed perfect, complete; mine in a life force, present in every man, which must grow and develop.'[11] For Chown, looking backward, that change was more matter-of-fact, more conclusive, than for most.

Nevertheless, by the 1920s, when Chown wrote, the late Victorian social reformer's quest for the New Jerusalem was moving steadily toward its unscripted denouement. Mackenzie King's thespian talents ensured that the last act would be long and sometimes melodramatic. But the years between the wars gradually revealed the outlines of the next attraction taking shape behind the curtain of residual Protestant rhetoric. Now regularly resorting to spiritualism, that most Victorian of religious consolations, King continued to fret about the intellectual confusion around him. After a discussion with O.D. Skelton in 1936, the last of the eminent Victorians recorded his own commitment to the old order while recognizing the shape of the new: 'With Skelton, as with many others, the so-called scientific mind which during the last century has been a materialistic mind, has had its influence in obscuring the fine truths which find their expression only in the spiritual interpretation of history. Stanley de Brath is right in speaking of the "soul of history" as part of the working out of God though time, as against the materialistic conception of history being determined by the blind material force which Karl Marx's philosophy has done so much to promote. Spiritual versus materialistic interpretation of phenomena and of history is, in essence, what is fundamental about the world struggle of today.'[12]

Notes

CHAPTER 1   Introduction

1 'Uncle Thomas' 'The Regenerators' *The Canadian Magazine* 1 (March 1893) 64–7; S.T. Wood *A Primer of Political Economy* (Toronto 1901) and *How We Pay Each Other* (Toronto 1916); S.T. Wood *Rambles of a Canadian Naturalist* (Toronto 1916). In a memorial that several Toronto journalists published on Wood's death in 1917, M.O. Hammond and E.J. Hathaway caught the spirit of Wood's generation of reformers well when they wrote: 'An ardent admirer of Whitman and Thoreau, he shared their aversion to conventions. Formality, even in dress, had no appeal for him, and his broad-brimmed hat was as beloved as it was out of style. Often, when finishing the day's work, he stayed at his desk and munched bananas and nuts as he completed an article, while others sat in a café or by their own table. Years ago he frequented a Colborne Street eating house, the resort of kindred spirits where in bohemian surroundings they spoke their minds on the faults of society.' *A Tribute to S.T. Wood* (privately published 1917)
2 W.A. Visser't Hooft *The Background to the Social Gospel in America* (Haarlem 1928); Albert Schweitzer *The Quest for the Historical Jesus* (New York 1968); William R. Hutchison *The Modernist Impulse in American Protestantism* (Oxford 1982)
3 Owen Chadwick *The Secularization of the European Mind in the Nineteenth Century* (Cambridge 1975) 17; see also Owen Chadwick *The Victorian Church* part 2 (London 1970) 40–150.
4 Thomas Haskell *The Emergence of Professional Social Science: The American Social Science Association and the Nineteenth-Century Crisis of Authority* (Urbana 1977)
5 Alisdair MacIntyre *Secularization and Moral Change* (London 1967)

6 Jeffrey Cox *The English Churches in Secular Society: Lambeth, 1870–1930* (Oxford 1982) 265–76
7 'Uncle Thomas' 'The Regenerators' 64, 65

CHAPTER 2 The Roots of Modernism

1 Karl Marx 'Towards the Critique of Hegel's Philosophy of Law: Introduction (1844)' in *The Essential Karl Marx: The Non-economic Writings* edited by Saul K. Padover (New York 1978) 286–7
2 Owen Chadwick *The Secularization of the European Mind in the Nineteenth Century* (Cambridge 1975) 48–87
3 Stanley Ryerson 'Mark Szalatnay,' in *Dictionary of Canadian Biography* vol. 10 (Toronto 1972) 670–1
4 The *Victorian Crisis of Faith* edited by Anthony Symondson (London 1970); Paul Carter *The Spiritual Crisis of the Gilded Age* (DeKalb 1971)
5 John Watson 'Science and Religion' *Canadian Monthly and National Review* (September 1876) 384–5
6 William Leitch *Introductory Address at the Opening of Queen's College* 8 November 1860, cited in A.B. McKillop *A Disciplined Intelligence: Critical Inquiry and Canadian Thought in the Victorian Era* (Montreal 1979) 8
7 John Watson 'Science and Religion: A Reply to Professor Tyndall on "Materialism and Its Opponents"' *Canadian Monthly and National Review* (May 1876) 384
8 Robert J. Taylor 'The Darwinian Revolution: The Responses of Four Canadian Scholars' PHD thesis, McMaster University 1976); P. Roome 'The Darwinian Debate in Canada, 1860–1880' in *Science, Technology, and Culture in Historical Perspective* edited by L.A. Knaffla, M.S. Staum, and T.H.E. Travers (Calgary 1976) 183–206; Carl Berger *Science, God and Nature in Victorian Canada* (Toronto 1983)
9 Sir William Dawson *Fifty Years of Work in Canada: Scientific and Educational* (London and Edinburgh 1901); Stanley B. Frost *McGill University, 1801–1895* (Montreal 1980) chaps. 8, 10, and 11; Charles F. O'Brien *Sir William Dawson: A Life in Science and Religion* (Philadelphia 1971). To place Dawson in context it is necessary to consult James R. Moore *Post-Darwinian Controversies* (London 1979).
10 C.C. Gillispie *Genesis and Geology* (New York 1959) 96
11 J.W. Dawson 'The Present Aspect of Inquiries as to the Introduction of Genera and Species in Geological Time' *Canadian Monthly and National Review* (August 1872) 154

12 David L. Hull *Darwin and His Critics: The Reception of Darwin's Theory of Evolution by the Scientific Community* (Cambridge, Mass. 1973) 451

13 E.J.C. 'Review of "On the Origin of Species by Natural Selection"' *The Canadian Journal* new series 38 (July 1860) 367–87

14 J.W. Dawson *Archaia; or, Studies of the Cosmogony and Natural History of the Hebrew Scriptures* (Montreal 1860); J.W. Dawson 'Points of Contact between Science and Revelation' *Canadian Methodist Monthly* (March 1883) 232

15 Berger *Science, God, and Nature* 72

16 J.W. Dawson *The Story of Earth and Man* (Toronto 1873) 318

17 Sir William Dawson *Modern Ideas of Evolution* (1890; reprint New York 1977) 54, 11.

18 J.W. Dawson 'Points of Contact between Science and Revelation' part 2 *Canadian Methodist Monthly* 16 (April 1883) 380. On the relation of science and society see Robert Young 'Malthus and the Evolutionists: The Common Context of Biological and Social Theory' *Past and Present* 43 (May 1969) 109–41, and 'The Historiographical Ideological Contexts of the Nineteenth-Century Debate on Man's Place in Nature' in *Changing Perspectives on the History of Science* edited by M. Kulas Teich and Robert Young (London 1973) 344–8; Keith Thomas *Man and the Natural World* (New York 1983) 70–1; Raymond Williams *Problems of Materialism and Culture* (London 1980) 70–1.

19 Taylor, 'The Darwinian Revolution' passim

20 Goldwin Smith 'The Ascent of Man' in *Lectures and Addresses* (Toronto 1881) 89; Loren Eiseley *Darwin's Century* (New York 1961) 257

21 *Grip* 13 March 1880

22 Malcolm Jay Kottler 'Alfred Russel Wallace: The Origin of Man and Spiritualism' *Isis* 65 (June 1974) 145–92; Stephen Jay Gould 'Natural Selection and the Human Brain: Darwin vs Wallace' in *The Panda's Thumb* (New York 1980) 47–58

23 A. Ellegard *Darwin and the General Reader 1859–72* (Göteborg 1958) 296 et seq. On Wilson see Bruce Trigger 'Sir Daniel Wilson: Canada's First Anthropologist' *Anthropologica* 7 (1966) 3–37 and Bennett McCardle 'The Life and Anthropological Works of Daniel Wilson (1816–1892)' (MA thesis, University of Toronto 1980)

24 Daniel Wilson *Caliban: The Missing Link* (London 1873) 93–4, 133, 104

25 Morse Peckham 'Darwinism and Darwinisticism' in *The Triumph of Romanticism* (Columbia, SC 1970) 184–8

26 John Watson 'Darwinism and Morality' *Canadian Monthly and National Review* 11 (October 1876) 319; J.A. Watson 'The Evolution of Morality' ibid. (May 1877) 491–501; John Watson 'The Ethical Aspect of Darwinism'

ibid. (June 1877) 638–9; Perry Miller *American Thought: Civil War to World War I* (New York 1963) xiv; Maurice Mandelbaum *History, Man, and Reason: A Study in Nineteenth-Century Thought* (Baltimore 1971) chap. 1.

27 *The Christian Guardian* 28 May 1878, 261

28 Ibid. 10 May 1882, 148, and 22 October 1879, 340

29 Ibid. 16 March 1887, 168, and 20 January 1892, 401

30 Henry Drummond *Natural Law in the Spiritual World* (New York 1888); James McArthur 'Professor Henry Drummond, FRSE, FGS, LID' *Methodist Magazine* 38 (October 1893) 352–5; John Dillenberger *Protestant Thought and Natural Science: A Historical Interpretation* (New York 1960) 243–8; Richard Hofstadter *Social Darwinism in American Thought* (Boston 1955) 96–7; John Laing 'Drummond's "Ascent of Man" and Christianity' *Knox College Monthly and Presbyterian Magazine* 17 (April 1895) 537–51. For a revealing attempt to combine Darwinism and theism, see Gerald Killan *David Boyle: From Artisan to Archeologist* (Toronto 1983) 58–61.

31 *The Christian Guardian* 4 June 1884, 184

32 Ibid. 22 February 1888, 121, and 3 October 1877, 316

33 William R. Hutchison *The Modernist Impulse in American Protestantism* (Oxford 1982) 2

34 John Watson 'Christianity and Modern Life' *Knox College Monthly and Presbyterian Magazine* 14 (July 1891) 164

35 Public Archives of Canada (PAC) W.L.M. King Papers *Diary* 1, 1 July 1894, and 111, 12 November 1898. On evolution and the idea of progress see Robert Young 'The Impact of Darwin on Conventional Thought' in Symondson *Victorian Crisis of Faith* 27–31. That Darwinism did not necessarily lead to liberal Christianity is shown in Moore *Post-Darwinian Controversies* 349.

36 William McLaren, DD 'The New Theology and Its Sources' *The Canadian Presbyterian* 15 (13 October 1886) 662; McLaren was criticizing the Andover theologians who only two years earlier had founded the *Andover Review*, the vanguard of liberal theology in the United States. See Daniel Day William *The Andover Liberals* (1941; reprint New York 1970).

37 Sir William Dawson *Modern Ideas* 21

38 John Dillenberger and Claude Welch *Protestant Christianity* (New York 1954) 195; McLaren 'New Theology' 663

39 J.W. Bengough 'The Higher Criticism' in *Motley: Verses Grave and Gay* (Toronto 1895) 163–5; H.G. Wood *Belief and Unbelief Since 1850* (Cambridge 1955) 63–81

40 D.C. Masters *Protestant Church Colleges in Canada* (Toronto 1966) 46

41 Leslie Armour and Elizabeth Trott *The Faces of Reason: An Essay on Philosophy and Culture in English Canada, 1850–1950* (Waterloo 1981) 85–105

42 J.F. McCurdy *The Life and Works of D.J. Macdonnell* (Toronto 1879); Joseph C. McClelland 'The Macdonnell Hersey Trial' *Canadian Journal of Theology* 4 (October 1958) 273–84; Rev. D.J. Macdonnell *Death Abolished: A Sermon Preached at St Andrew's Church, Toronto, in connection with the Death of Professor George Paxton Young* (Toronto 1890) and Robert S. Weir *Review of Rev. D.J. Macdonnell's Sermon Entitled Death Abolished* (n.p.p., n.d.)

43 G.M. Grant *Sermon Preached before the Synod of Nova Scotia and Prince Edward Island, 26 June 1866* (Halifax 1866); PAC G.M. Grant Papers, S. Macdonald to Grant, 7 May 1879

44 G.M. Grant *Reformers of the 19th Century: A Lecture Delivered before the Young Men's Christian Association of Halifax, January 29, 1867* (Halifax 1867). Though he praised Coleridge and Wordsworth, the highest encomium was saved for Carlyle: 'no prophet has spoken with so an authoritative voice since Luther's time, if then' (at 28).

45 W.L. Grant and Frederick Hamilton *George Monro Grant* (Toronto 1905) 212–15

46 Grant Papers, undated review of George H. Towers *Studies in Comparative Theology*

47 G.M. Grant *The Religions of the World* (London and Edinburgh 1895) 51. On the role of comparative religion in the development of theological liberalism, see Carter *The Spiritual Crisis of the Gilded Age* 199–222.

48 Grant Papers, Grant to J.A. McClymont, 5 January 1893

49 Ibid. Rev. P. Melville to Grant, 2 December 1879

50 Ibid. Grant to Mrs McClymont, 25 December 1901; see also Hilda Neatby *Queen's University 1841–1917* (Montreal 1978).

51 John Moir *Enduring Witness* (n.p.p., n.d.) 174–5; *Presbyterian College Journal* 11 (February 1892) 318; ibid. 21 (January 1902) 207

52 Goldwin French 'The People Called Methodists in Canada' in *The Churches and the Canadian Experience* edited by John Webster Grant (Toronto 1963) 78; Tom Sinclair-Faulkner 'Theory Divided from Practice: The Introduction of Higher Criticism into Canadian Protestant Seminaries' in Canadian Society of Church History *Papers* (1980) 33–75

53 George C. Workman 'Messianic Prophecy' *The Canadian Methodist Quarterly* 2 (October 1890) 407–78, and 'Messianic Prophecy – A Sequel' ibid. 3 (October 1891) 407–55

54 George C. Workman *The Old Testament Vindicated as Christianity's Foundation Stone* (Toronto 1897) 39, 85

55 *The Christian Guardian* 31 December 1891, 824; E.H. Dewart 'A Brief Examination of Professor Workman's Teaching and Methods' *Canadian Methodist Quarterly* 3 (January 1891) 74–86; E.H. Dewart *Living Epistles* (Toronto 1878) 97; E.H. Dewart, *Jesus the Messiah in Prophecy and Fulfillment* (Toronto 1891) vi; William *Andover Liberals* 105–6

56 A.R. Carman 'What Are the Church's Working Doctrines?' *Canadian Methodist Magazine* 28 (July-December 1888) 540–88

57 Rev. J.S. Ross *A Review of George Jackson's Lectures on the Early Narratives of Genesis* (Toronto 1909) 20

58 United Church Archives, Burwash Papers, Margaret to Nathanael, 14 August 1910; PAC Rowell Papers, Chester Massey to Rowell, 2 August 1910; 'The General Superintendent's Address to the General Conference, 1910' *Christian Guardian* 22 August 1910. On the controversy see George A. Boyle 'Higher Criticism and the Struggle for Academic Freedom in Canadian Methodism' (B TH thesis, Victoria University 1965), which sets the tone for the standard liberal interpretation found in Margaret Prang *N.W. Rowell* (Toronto 1975) 70–87 and Michael Bliss *A Canadian Millionaire* (Toronto 1978) 200–2. Studies that demonstrate a better understanding of the theological issues include Lawrence Burkholder 'Canadian Methodism and Higher Criticism' United Church Archives (1976); Tom Sinclair-Faulkner 'Theory Divided from Practice'; Paul Neilson 'The Struggle in the Methodist Church over Higher Criticism and Modern Thought 1889–1910' (research paper, York University 1974); and Michael Gauvreau 'The Taming of History: Reflections on the Canadian Methodist Encounter with Biblical Criticism' *Canadian Historical Review* 65 (September 1984) 315–46.

59 W.S. Rainsford *The Story of a Varied Life: An Autobiography* (New York 1922) 179, 187–95, 376

60 *The Toronto Mail* 18 March 1881

61 McKillop *A Disciplined Intelligence* cited at 216

62 John Watson 'Christianity and Modern Life' *Knox College Monthly and Presbyterian Magazine* 14 (July 1891) 163

63 PAC W.C. Good Papers, Good to Ethel, 18 March 1901. One of the principal influences on Good's religious thinking was Professor J.F. McCurdy, a leading exponent of the 'higher criticism' at the University of Toronto and a member of the Canadian Society for Psychical Research. See ibid., Good to mother, 31 March 1901. On McCurdy and the development of the 'higher criticism' generally, see J.S. Moir *A History of Biblical Studies in Canada: A Sense of Proportion* (Chico, Calif. 1982).

CHAPTER 3 The Anxieties of a Moral Interregnum

1 *The Week* 8 April 1886, 298
2 Goldwin Smith *Lectures and Essays* (Toronto 1881) 104, 116–17
3 Walter Houghton *The Victorian Frame of Mind, 1830–70* (New Haven 1957) 93–109; Gertrude Himmelfarb *Victorian Minds* (New York 1970) 300–13
4 Queen's University Archives, Gregory Papers *Diary* 9 September 1896
5 Matthew Arnold *God and the Bible* (New York 1898) xi
6 Goldwin Smith *Rational Religion and the Rationalistic Objections of the Brampton Lectures of 1858* (Oxford 1861) 11; Goldwin Smith *A Plea for the Abolition of Religious Tests* (Oxford 1864) 28
7 Goldwin Smith *Guesses at the Riddle of Existence* (Toronto 1897) 52, 94
8 Ibid. 101
9 Ibid. 222; Smith to Lord Mount Stephen, 1 February 1902 in *Goldwin Smith's Correspondence* edited by Arnold Haultain (Toronto n.d.) 379; Charles Darwin *On the Origin of Species* reprint Harmondsworth 1968) 458
10 Smith *Guesses* 244, 187, 173–5
11 See Goldwin Smith *In Quest of Light* (London 1906) and *No Refuge but Truth* (Toronto 1908).
12 *Secular Thought* 30 (February 1904) 105; ibid. (June 1907) 201–18; ibid. 36 (June 1910) 191–4
13 Smith *Guesses* 199; W.S. Rainsford *The Story of a Varied Life: An Autobiography* (New York 1922) 188
14 Goldwin Smith 'The Prospect of a Moral Interregnum' *Canadian Monthly and National Review* (December 1879) 651
15 Smith to Tyndall, 21 November 1878, in Haultain *Correspondence* 69
16 Smith 'Prospect' 654, 657, 659
17 Smith to Matthew Arnold, 17 August 1885 in Haultain *Correspondence* 175
18 Smith 'Prospect' 657, 656; Goldwin Smith 'The Immortality of the Soul' *Canadian Monthly and National Review* (May 1876) 410
19 Smith 'Immortality' 408
20 Smith *Guesses* 200; on *prophetae* see Norman Cohn *The Pursuit of the Millennium* (New York 1970) 281–6
21 Smith *Guesses* 4
22 Goldwin Smith *Lectures on Modern History Delivered in Oxford 1859–61* 32–3
23 Goldwin Smith 'On the Supposed Consequences of the Doctrine of Historical Progress' *Canadian Methodist Monthly* 29 (February 1889) 139
24 Goldwin Smith *The Founder of Christendom* (Toronto 1903) 20
25 'A Bystander' *The Week* 6 November 1884, 703

26 Ian Drummond *Political Economy at the University of Toronto: A History of the Department, 1888–1982* (Toronto 1983) cited at 26; Sidney Fine *Laissez-Faire and the General Welfare State* (Ann Arbor 1967) 198–251; A.W. Coats 'The Historicist Reaction in English Political Economy' *Economica* 21, 154, 143–53

28 Goldwin Smith 'The Lesson of the French Revolution' *The Atlantic Monthly* (April 1907) 492; *The Bystander* (November 1880) 608–9 and (March 1881) 151–2

29 Fritz Stern *The Politics of Cultural Despair: A Study in the Rise of German Ideology* (New York 1965)

30 *The Week* 31 January 1884, 132, and 17 July 1884, 407; Wayne Roberts 'Goldwin's Myth' *Canadian Literature* 83 (winter 1979) 50–72

31 W.D. LeSueur 'The Future of Morality' *Canadian Monthly and National Review* (January 1880) 81

32 W.D. LeSueur 'Morality and Religion' *Canadian Monthly and National Review* (February 1880) 170, 168, republished in *A Critical Spirit: The Thought of William Dawson LeSueur* edited by Brian McKillop (Toronto 1977) 112–19; Goldwin Smith 'The Proposed Substitutes for Religion' in *Lectures and Essays* 112

33 Allan Smith 'The Thought of George Monro Grant' *Canadian Literature* 83 (winter 1979) 90–117

34 G.M. Grant 'Canada and the Canadian Question' *The Week* 1 May 1891, 348–50, and 15 May 1891, 380–2; G.M. Grant 'The Religious Condition of Canada' *Queen's Quarterly* 1 (April 1894) 321

35 G.M. Grant 'Goldwin Smith's Political and Social Essays' *The Week* 23 February 1894, 296

36 Smith *Lectures and Essays* 117; LeSueur 'Morality and Religion' 170; G.M. Grant 'Response on Behalf of Canada to Address of Welcome, at the World's Parliament of Religions' *Queen's Quarterly* 1 (October 1893) 161

37 Alisdair MacIntyre *Secularization and Moral Change* (London 1967) 55

38 Smith to Tyndall 21 November 1879, in Haultain *Correspondence* 70. In his recent book, *The Politics of God's Funeral: The Spiritual Crisis of Western Civilization* (New York 1983), the American Marxist writer Michael Harrington advances the same view that Goldwin Smith and many, more eminent, Victorians urged over a century ago, namely, that the death of God has destroyed the basis of morality. His proposed cure for this 'spiritual crisis,' whose symptoms ('Materialism,' 'sexual license,' etc.) sound very Smithian, is 'socialism.' An earlier generation might have called for the building of the 'Kingdom of God on Earth,' which was, in a way, what Marx expected would eventually emerge once religion was banished. The decline of religion is

evidently in danger of joining the rise of the middle class as an all-purpose explanation of historical change.

CHAPTER 4   Positivism, Secular Thought, and the Religion of Humanity

1 Rev. Hugh Pedley, BA 'Theological Students and the Times' *Canadian Monthly and National Review* 18 (July 1880) 90

2 W.D. LeSueur *A Defence of Modern Thought* (Toronto 1884) 39

3 W.D. LeSueur *William Lyon Mackenzie: A Reinterpretation* edited by A.B. McKillop (Toronto 1979) vii–xxxi

4 *A Critical Spirit: The Thought of William Dawson LeSueur* edited by A.B. McKillop (Toronto 1977) 51; A.B. McKillop *A Disciplined Intelligence: Critical Inquiry and Canadian Thought in the Victorian Era* (Montreal 1979) 136–70

5 McKillop *A Critical Spirit* 107

6 W.D. LeSueur 'Morality and Religion' *Canadian Monthly and National Review* (February 1880) 166; 'Mr. Spencer and His Critics' ibid. (April 1880) 413–22; and 'Morality and Religion – A Word with My Critics' ibid. (June 1880) 642–55

7 Herbert Spencer 'Professor Goldwin Smith as Critic' *Popular Science Monthly* 21 (May 1882) 20

8 W.D. LeSueur 'Mr. Goldwin Smith on the "Data of Ethics"' ibid. 22 (December 1882) 156

9 W.D. LeSueur 'Evolution and the Destiny of Man' ibid. 26 (February 1885) 446; 'Evolution Bounded by Theology' ibid. (June 1886) 145–53; 'Ex-President Porter on Evolution' ibid. 29 (September 1881) 594

10 'Fidelis' 'Prayer for Daily Bread' *Canadian Monthly and National Review* (May 1875) 94–5; W.D. LeSueur 'Prayer and Modern Thought' ibid. (August 1875) 145–55; 'Creation or Evolution?' *Popular Science Monthly* 31 (May 1879) 29–39; 'Kidd on Evolution' ibid. 47 (May 1895) 47; 'Idealism in Life' in McKillop *A Critical Spirit* 45, 50

11 Frank M. Turner *Between Science and Religion* (New Haven 1974)

12 W.D. LeSueur 'Materialism and Positivism' *Popular Science Monthly* 20 (March 1882) 616, and 'Science and Materialism' *Canadian Monthly and National Review* (January 1877) 24–5

13 Rev. J.T. Lewis *A Second Lecture on Agnosticism by the Lord Bishop of Ontario* (Ottawa 1884); W.D. LeSueur *A Defence* 39

14 W.D. LeSueur *Evolution and the Positive Aspects of Modern Thought* (Ottawa 1884) 37

15 H.R. Mackintosh *Types of Modern Theology* (London 1947). Writing of Albrecht Ritschl, a central figure in the development of theological liberalism, Mackintosh says, 'Religion tends to become only a new aspect of moral activity. The Kingdom of God, stripped of the eschatological transcendence that belongs to it in the Gospels, is now hardly more than (as with Kant) a realm of moral ends, a purely present and mundane commonwealth' (151–2). See also William R. Hutchison *The Modernist Impulse in American Protestantism* (Oxford 1982) 3–4. Though no complete study of this subject has been done in Canada, there is an excellent discussion in Benjamin G. Smillie 'The Social Gospel in Canada: A Theological Critique' in *The Social Gospel in Canada* edited by Richard Allen (Ottawa 1975) 317–42.

16 LeSueur 'Science and Materialism' 23

17 'Laon' 'Modern Culture and Christianity' *Canadian Monthly and National Review* (December 1875). For the whole debate see 'Laon' 'Messrs. Moody and Sankey and Revivalism' ibid. (June 1875) 510–13; G.M. Grant 'Laon on Messrs. Moody and Sankey and Revivalism' ibid. (September 1875) 250–5; 'Laon' 'Proofs and Disproofs' ibid. (October 1875); and G.M. Grant 'Christianity and Modern Thought' ibid. (November 1875) 437–41

18 'Laon' 'Messrs. Moody and Sankey' 513

19 *Toronto Evening Mail* 5 March 1881

20 Paul A. Carter *The Spiritual Crisis of the Gilded Age* (Dekalb 1971) 114–24

21 Walter L. Arnstein *The Bradlaugh Case: A Study in Late Victorian Opinion and Politics* (London 1965) 8–24

22 Allen Pringle 'Signs of the Times' *The National* 10 December 1875, 4

23 *Secular Thought* 35 (March 1909) 96

24 Rev. J.T. Lewis *Agnosticism: A Lecture Delivered in St George's Hall, on the Occasion of the Meeting of the Synod of the Diocese, July 12, 1883, by the Lord Bishop of Ontario* (Ottawa 1884), and *A Second Lecture* (n.p.p., n.d.)

25 Allen Pringle *Ingersoll in Canada* (Toronto 1880) 25

26 *The Christian Guardian* 12 December 1877, 396

27 'Modern Science and its Relation to Christianity' *Canadian Methodist Review* 1 (April 1875) 359

28 United Church Archives, Burwash Papers, 'Sixty Years of Canadian Methodism' cited in Robert J. Taylor 'The Darwinian Revolution: The Responses of Four Canadian Scholars' (PHD thesis, McMaster University 1976) 255

29 'Bildad' 'The Pulpit and Revivalism' *Canadian Monthly and National Review* (May 1877) 481

30 Pedley 'Theological Students and the Times' 91. On Pedley's later career see A. Ross McCormack *Reformers, Rebels and Revolutionaries: The Western Canadian*

Radical Movement 1899–1919 (Toronto 1977) 78, and Hugh Pedley *Looking Forward* (Toronto 1913)

31 W.S. Herrington *A History of the County of Lennox and Addington* (Toronto 1913)
32 This, and other family information, was generously supplied to me by Jennie A. Pringle, 26 May 1982 and 8 June 1982. Other biographical details may be found in *The Napanee Beaver* 24 July 1896
33 *Dictionary of American Biography* vol. 10 (New York 1936) 111–12
34 Allen Pringle 'Inauguration of Free Thought Lectures in Canada in 1874' *Secular Thought* 34 (February 1908) 33–6 and 34 (March 1908) 65–8; reprinted from *The Index* 16 April 1885
35 *Pringle v the Corporation of the Town of Napanee* [1878] Upper Canada Queen's Bench Reports 306. The judge ruled that free speech was not abridged, since Underwood could make his speech elsewhere without fear of prosecution. 'These discussions which lead to the overturning of the Christian religion are, strictly speaking, illegal, but it is felt that it is better not to make martyrs of men who, however ignorant or misguided they may be, are honestly in search of truth' (at 306).
36 Lennox and Addington County Museum, Stevenson Papers, Allen Pringle to John Stevenson, 21 July 1878
37 *The National* 22 July 1875
38 *Napanee Express* 15 July 1875
39 *The National* 8, 15, 22, and 29 July 1875
40 Allen Pringle 'Science and Religion' *The National* 19 November 1874
41 Allen Pringle 'Darwinism' *The Napanee Express* 9 November 1877
42 *The National* 29 July 1875
43 Ibid. 15 July 1875
44 Ibid. 7 October 1875
45 Edward Royle *Radicals, Secularists, and Republicans: Popular Freethought in Britain, 1866–1915* (Manchester 1981) 97–9; 'Charles Watts' *Secular Thought* 32 (March 1906) 154; Rosanna Ledbetter *A History of the Malthusian League* (Ohio State University Press 1976) 29–32; Warren Sylvester Smith *The London Heretics* (London 1967) 45–52
46 Unfortunately, no complete run of *Secular Thought* has been located. The Toronto Public Library has several volumes from 1904 to 1911; the New York Public Library has a run from 1901 to 1911, although it too is incomplete.
47 *The Labor Advocate* 17 April 1891; Gregory S. Kealey *Toronto Workers Respond to Industrial Capitalism 1867–1892* (Toronto 1980) 400–1; Royle *Radicals, Secularists, and Republicans* 195
48 *Secular Thought* 30 (6 February 1904) 106–8; 36 (August 1910) 223–6; 31 (30 September 1905) 460–3

49 Ibid. 35 (December 1909) 440. By 1910–11 free thought appears to have been on the point of collapse as an organized movement in both Toronto and Montreal. In December 1910 the Toronto Secular Society reported that 'In default of any better arrangement, it was agreed by a few members to meet weekly for the purposes of discussing scientific and philosophical questions and for social intercourse.' *Secular Thought* 36 (December 1910) 377. At about the same time the Montreal group was preoccupied with finding a place to donate its library. 'The reason for this action,' it reported, 'was that at present the books were not used by anybody' (at 377). Still, the group was vigorous enough in 1911 to vote fifty German reichmarks to the Dr Ernst Haeckel Phyletic Museum in Jena, and to note that the president of Portugal had presided over a recent free-thought convention. 'The Man occupies the same position in Portugal as Mr. Asquith in England, or Sir Wilfrid Laurier in Canada, or Mr. Taft in the United States. It is certainly a sign full of hope for the progress of the world that the head of a state should identify himself openly with Freethought.' *Secular Thought* 37 (February 1911) 67. In 1910 Sir Wilfrid, once a suspected free thinker, had attended the Eucharistic Congress in Montreal.

50 S.P. Putnam *Four Hundred Years of Free Thought* (New York 1894) 563–5 and 582–6

51 *Secular Thought* 36 (August 1910) 225. The international connection included reading free thought literature. Sometimes the Post Office prohibited the entry of such literature. One journal, *The Truth Seekers*, was banned during the Macdonald regime. Ironically, it was W.D. LeSueur's task to inform Toronto secularists that the Laurier administration would not lift the prohibition: *Secular Thought* 30 (February 1904) 105.

52 Sidney Warren *American Free Thought, 1860–1914* (New York 1966) 81–9; *Dictionary of American Biography* vol. 5 (New York 1936) 464–70; see also *Complete Lectures of Col. R.G. Ingersoll* (Chicago 1926).

53 *Toronto Evening Telegram* 16 April 1880

54 Ibid. 17 April 1880

55 *Grip* 17 April 1880; *The Christian Guardian* 14 April 1880; *The Bystander* (April 1880) 222–4 and (May 1880) 276

56 Pringle *Ingersoll* 10, 53

57 *Toronto Mail* 18 March 1881

58 *The Christian Guardian* 16 March 1881 and Allen Pringle *'Design' in Nature: Replies to the Christian Guardian and the Christian Advocate* (Toronto 1881) 13

59 Allen Pringle *The 'Mail's' Theology: Being a Reply to the Saturday Sermons of the Toronto 'Mail,' including a Vindication of Charles Bradlaugh against the 'Mail's' Aspersions* (Toronto 1882) 38–9. On the book-banning, see *The Globe* 10, 11, and 13 October 1881.

60 Pringle *The 'Mail's' Theology* 40

61 Ibid. 47–8

62 *The Week* 18 December 1884, 40

63 *The Globe* 15 and 16 December 1884

64 *The Week* 25 December 1884, 52, and 1 October 1885, 692. Pringle, it may be observed, was in no hurry to pull down the religious system. 'With the masses,' he wrote in 1894, 'orthodoxy is, I admit, a powerful policeman. He stands over them with an excellent "hangman's whip" which is "the fear o'hell" for multitudes which unfortunately still need it. That policeman I would not take off duty yet for a while if I could.' Allen Pringle *True Religion vs Creeds and Dogmas* (Toronto 1894) 61

65 Most of the information for Adams's biography is found in Robert Chambliss Adams *Travels Through Faith to Reason* (New York 1884) and *The Truth Seekers* (New York 1902), a reference provided by Brian McKillop.

66 Adams *Travels* 35, 50, 51, 52

67 Ibid. 60, 68, 94, 126, 111–12, 99–100

68 Ibid. 74–5

69 Robert C. Adams *Pioneer Pith: The Gist of Lectures on Rationalism* (New York 1889) 7

70 Adams *Travels* 165, 154–5

71 Ibid. 219, 185, 230

72 Adams *Pioneer Pith* 194

73 *The Northern Echo* 26 May 1880, cited in Arnstein *The Bradlaugh Case* 13

74 H.J. Morgan *The Canadian Men and Women of Our Time* (Toronto 1912) 4–5

75 G. Mercer Adam 'Darwin and His Works' *The Week* 1 December 1887

76 Allen Pringle *Bibles and Religion Out vs In the Public Schools* (Toronto 1881) 15–16

77 Rev. J.A. Macdonald 'Looking Backward' *Knox College Monthly and Presbyterian Magazine* 10 (August 1889) 212. At about the same time, a Queen's alumnus wrote Principal Grant about the need for a more practical religion in a world revolutionized by science. 'The value of the Christian ministry in the coming time will be seen more in its knowledge of *this* world than in that of the *next*.' PAC G.M. Grant Papers, W.G. Brown to Grant, 3 September 1892.

78 Richard Allen 'Salem Bland and the Social Gospel' (MA thesis, University of Saskatchewan 1961) cited at 52

79 'Fidelis' 'Impressions from the Parliament of Religion' *The Week* 20 October 1893, 1114, and 27 October 1893, 1138

80 Pringle *True Religion* 15; 'Laon' 'The Reverend Phillip Brooks on Popular Scepticism' *Canadian Monthly and National Review* (July 1879) 31

81 Pringle *True Religion* 17

82 *Secular Thought* 20 (17 October 1896) 162; *Napanee Beaver* 31 July and 14 August 1896

CHAPTER 5 Spiritualism, Science of the Earthly Paradise

1 Goldwin Smith *Guesses at the Riddle of Existence* (Toronto 1897) 97–134
2 Goldwin Smith 'The Immortality of the Soul' *Canadian Monthly and National Review* 9 (May 1876) 410
3 University of Western Ontario, Weldon Library, Bucke Papers, speech at St Mary's Town Hall, 30 November 1898; see also R.M. Bucke 'Mental Evolution in Man' *Journal of Hygiene and Herald of Health* (December 1897) 309–18. Rev. R. Stainton Moses was a leading member of the London Spiritualist Alliance. See Arthur Conan Doyle *The History of Spiritualism* vol. 2 (1926; reprint New York 1975) 61, 64, 71. Robert C. Adams, a Montreal agnostic and free-thought leader, held a similar view; see his *Travels through Faith to Reason* (New York 1884) 167.
4 R.P. McKay 'Spiritualism' *Knox College Monthly and Presbyterian Magazine* 9 (February 1889) 173–82 and J.H. Brown 'The Hope of Immortality' *The Week* 20 March 1891, 251
5 Richard Allen 'Salem Bland: The Young Preacher' *The Bulletin* 26 (1977) 251
6 United Church Archives, Salem Bland Papers, 9 'My Experience of Spiritualism.' Jay Hudson was a prominent American spiritualist. Bland later read the work of the Fabian socialist and spiritualist Frank Podmore, *Modern Spiritualism* (London 1902).
7 Herbert G. Jackson Jr *The Spirit Rappers* (New York 1972) 23; Carl Ballstadt, Michael Peterman, and Elizabeth Hopkins '"A Glorious Madness": Susanna Moodie and the Spiritualist Movement' *Journal of Canadian Studies* 17 (Winter 1982–3) 88–101; R. Laurence Moore *In Search of White Crows: Spiritualism, Parapsychology, and American Culture* (New York 1977); Geoffrey K. Nelson *Spiritualism and Society* (London 1969); Robert Sylvain 'Quand les tables dansaient et parlaient: les débuts du spiritisme au dix-neuvième siècle' *Mémoires de la Société Royale du Canada* 1 (juin 1963) 221–35
8 *The National* 16 July 1875
9 Moore *White Crows* 87. Chase wrote two autobiographies: *The Lifeline of the Lone One* (1858) and *Forty Years on the Spiritualist Rostrum* (1883)
10 *The Globe* 28 November 1873
11 Howard Kerr *Mediums and Spirit Rappers and Roaring Radicals: Spiritualism in American Literature, 1850–1900* (Chicago 1972) 108–16, and Richard W. Leopold *Robert Dale Owen: A Biography* (Cambridge, Mass. 1940) 321–39, 379–416

12 T. Phillips Thompson 'Spiritualism' *The Mail* 2 December 1873
13 J.H. Brown 'The Hope of Immortality' 251
14 Frank Turner *Between Science and Religion: The Reaction to Scientific Naturalism in Late Victorian England* (New Haven 1974) chap. 4; and Malcolm J. Kottler 'Alfred Russel Wallace: The Origins of Man and Spiritualism' *Isis* 65 (June 1974) 145–92
15 McGill University Archives, Dawson Papers, box 17, Daniel Wilson to J.W. Dawson, 9 February 1888, cited in Carl Berger *Science, God, and Nature in Victorian Canada* (Toronto 1983) 68–9
16 See, for example, George Wolfe Shinn, DD 'What is Spiritualism?' *Methodist Magazine and Review* 49 (3 March 1899) 247–51
17 Rev. B.F. Austin *What Converted Me to Spiritualism: One Hundred Testimonies* (Toronto 1901) 66. In 1852, Nathaniel Hawthorne noted how the spiritualist 'exhibitor affects the simplicity and openness of scientific experiment,' contrasted with earlier, more miracle-like performances: Hawthorne *The Blithedale Romance* (reprint New York 1981) 1; see also R. Laurence Moore 'Spiritualism and Science: Reflections on the First Decade of the Spirit Rappings' *American Quarterly* 24 (October 1972) 474–500.
18 Austin *What Converted Me* 155. On Myers see Alan Gauld *The Founders of Psychical Research* (London 1968) 89–136.
19 Moore *White Crows* 67. Nearly all the Canadians included in Austin's *What Converted Me* attended Lily Dale or some other U.S. spiritualist camp meeting.
20 Moore *White Crows* 40–69 and Nelson *Spiritualism* 147–50
21 Austin *What Converted Me* 156; *The National* 26 August 1875
22 B.F. Austin *The Methodist Episcopal Church Pulpit: A Volume of Sermons by Members of the Niagara, Ontario, and Bay of Quinte Conferences of the Methodist Episcopal Church in Canada* vol. 1 (Toronto 1879) and B.F. Austin *Popular Sins: A Series of Sermons against the Sins of the Times* (Toronto 1880)
23 B.F. Austin *The Gospel of the Poor vs Pew Rents* (Toronto 1884) 15, vii
24 B.F. Austin *The Jesuits* (London 1890); James Miller *Equal Rights* (Montreal 1979) 97
25 *The Proper Sphere; Woman's Place in Canadian Society* edited by Ramsay Cook and Wendy Mitchison (Toronto 1976) 119–65; and Elizabeth Smith *A Woman with a Purpose* (Toronto 1980), especially the introduction by Veronica Strong-Boag at vii–xxxviii
26 *Woman: Her Character, Culture and Calling* edited by B.F. Austin (Brantford 1890) 33, 338
27 Ibid. 44. On the relationship between liberal theology and women see Ann Douglas's brilliant book, *The Feminization of American Culture* (New York 1977), especially chap. 4, and Barbara Welter 'The Feminization of American

Religion, 1800–1860' in *Clio's Consciousness Raised* edited by Mary Hartman and Lois W. Banner (New York 1974) 137–57.

28 Austin *Woman* 202

29 My own favourite is: 'Jesus lived constantly in the open air. He made long, tiresome journeys on foot. He was able to endure both physical and mental hardship under which most men would have quickly broken down. Jesus' remarkable courage is best accounted for by the belief that he possessed an exceptional physique.' *CEST Manual for Tuxis Boys* (Toronto 1918) 44–5. I owe this reference to Leila Mitchell-McKee.

30 B.F. Austin *The Prohibition Leaders of America* (St Thomas 1895)

31 UCA Austin Papers 'Home Book' undated clipping

32 Rev. E. Lee Howard 'Benjamin F. Austin – In Memoriam' *Reason* 29 (February 1933) 7. *Reason* was a spiritualist publication edited by Austin in California. Howard gave no source for his information other than a séance at which 'the spirit of Dr. Austin ... gave a general evidential communication.' *The New Outlook*, an organ of the United Church, devoted three sentences to Austin's death; it mentioned neither his heresy trial nor his spiritualist activities: *The New Outlook* 8 March 1933, 222.

33 University of Toronto, Thomas Fisher Rare Books Library, Flora MacDonald Denison Papers, Flora to Wid, 16 October 1918

34 B.F. Austin *Glimpses of the Unseen: A Study of Dreams, Premonitions, Prayer and Remarkable Answers, Hypnotism, Spiritualism, Telepathy, Apparitions, Peculiar Mental and Spiritual Experiences, Unexplained Psychic Phenomena* (Toronto and Brantford 1898) 5

35 Austin *Glimpses* 97

36 Maurice Bucke *Cosmic Consciousness* (1901; reprint New York 1969)

37 Austin *Glimpses* 110

38 'The Heresy Sermon' *Manitoba Morning Free Press* 27 May 1899

39 United Church Archives, Methodist Church, box 1, file 4, *In re A.H. Goring* v *B.F. Austin* 15 May 1899

40 *The Heresy Trial of the Rev. B.F. Austin, MA, DD* (Toronto 1899). The Sermon Publishing Company published a monthly magazine, *The Sermon*, devoted to Bible spiritualism and psychic research and carried sermons by B.F. Austin. I have not found any copies.

41 *The Heresy Trial* 55

42 Ibid. 58, 59, 60

43 Brian R. Ross 'Ralph Cecil Horner: A Methodist Sectarian Deposed, 1887–95' *The Bulletin* 26 (1977) 94–103

44 B.F. Austin *The Mission of Spiritualism and Original Poems* (Toronto 1902) 19

45 *The Heresy Trial* 20. See also Flora MacDonald *Mary Melville*, where Austin

writes that 'the marvelous features of the story now before us find abundant illustration and confirmation in the Bible and in the attested experiences of patient and careful scientific investigations of our own age' (n.p.).

46 Austin *The Mission* 19

47 Phillippe Ariès *The Hour of Death* (New York 1981) 471

48 William R. Hutchison *The Modernist Impulse in American Protestantism* (Oxford 1982) 2

49 Austin *The Mission* 14, 18

50 See chaper 11

51 James Shaver Woodsworth *The First Story of the Labor Church and Some Things for Which it Stands* (Winnipeg 1920) 15; Alfred Russell Wallace had advocated a similar 'church' in the 1870s.

52 Austin *The Mission* 25. Austin later gave up all hope of a reconciliation between spiritualism and Christianity. He concluded that spiritualism would replace the 'old weather-beaten, water-logged, over-loaded ships with a tremendous load of dead and deplorable dogmas.' B.F. Austin 'Orthodox Churches and Spiritualism' *Reason* 29 (April 1933) 33. This issue of Austin's magazine, published in Los Angeles, listed forty spiritualist groups in that city.

53 Wilma George *Biologist Philosopher: A Study of the Life and Writings of Alfred Russel Wallace* (London 1964) 237–50; Paul R. Cartwright and Michael J. Broadhead *Elliott Coues, Naturalist and Frontier Historian* (Urbana 1981); see also S.E.D. Shortt 'Physicians and Psychics: The Anglo-American Response to Spiritualism, 1870–1890' *Journal of the History of Medicine and Allied Science* 29 (July 1984).

54 Logie Barrow 'Socialism in Eternity: The Ideology of Plebeian Spiritualists, 1853–1913' *History Workshop Journal* (Spring 1980) 50–2

55 Samuel Bernstein *The First International in America* (New York 1965) 112–14, 152–3. On Marx and phrenology, see Angus McLaren 'Phrenology: Medium and Message' *Journal of Modern History* 46 (March 1974) 87.

56 9 April 1880

57 Cyril Greenland 'Mary Edwards Merrill, 1858–1880, "The Psychic"' (Hamilton 1974)

58 *Belleville Intelligencer* 19 April 1880

59 MacDonald *Mary Melville* 6–7

60 Denison Papers, Flora MacDonald Denison 'Robert Ingersoll' MS dated 5 January 1906

61 Flora MacDonald 'The Vision of Mary' in Austin *What Converted Me* 95–6

62 Denison Papers 'The Association for Psychic Research of Canada, Programme for 1921.' The program lists a lecture by Flora MacDonald Denison on 'The Genius of Walt Whitman.' See also Flora MacDonald Denison to

Mildred, 19 February 1919, in which she describes a séance held to 'get in touch with Old Walt.' The séance was held at the home of Dr A.D. Watson, author of *The Twentieth Plane* (Toronto 1918). See S.E. McMullen 'Walt Whitman's Influence in Canada' *Dalhousie Review* (Autumn 1969) 361–8. 'To extend our knowledge of various mental and psychological phenomena, the Society for Psychical Research has been incorporated in Toronto. President, Dr. J.S. King; Vice-Pres., T.F. Corey; Sec., H.G. Paull; Treas., J.H. Trott; Directors, Col. R.B. Hamilton, Dr. W.E. Hamill, S.A. Knox, Prof. J.F. McCurdy, Dr. J.S. Bach. It is the purpose of the Society that all investigations shall be systematically and skillfully conducted and results faithfully recorded; and such reports, whether the work of individual members, branch societies or committees of the parent body or branches, shall be placed with the board of directors of the parent society to be dealt with. The new society following the parent bodies in England and the States, will investigate dreams, apparitions, clairvoyance, discarnate spirits, the influence of the mind on mind, and other like subjects.' *Secular Thought* 34 (August 1908) 259. King, Hamilton, Paull, and McCurdy were all prominent enough to be included in H.J. Morgan's *Canadian Men and Women of Our Time* (Toronto 1912) 613, 495, 890, 759. Paull is the most interesting (though Dr King listed his position with the Society for Psychic Research); he was a prominent architect, a contributor to Austin's *Reason*, and a director of the Methodist Social Union and the Victor Mission Board; he wrote on biblical topics, and especially on Christianity and spiritualism.

63 Ariès *The Hour of Death* 409–17; Douglas *Feminization* 200–27; David E. Stannard *The Puritan Way of Death: A Study of Religion, Culture and Social Change* (New York 1977)

64 D.G. Charlton *Secular Religion in France, 1815–70* (London 1963) 19–22; H.R. Murphy 'The Ethical Revolt against Christian Orthodoxy in Early Victorian England' *American Historical Review* 60 (July 1955) 800–17; Susan Budd *Varieties of Unbelief: Atheists and Agnostics in English Society, 1850–1960* (London 1977) 104–23

65 Neil Semple 'The Nurture and Admonition of the Lord: Nineteenth-Century Canadian Methodism's Response to Childhood' *Histoire sociale/Social History* 14 (May 1981) 159–64; Neil Sutherland *Children in English Canadian Society* (Toronto 1976) 3–36: Phillip Greven *The Protestant Temperament* (New York 1977)

66 MacDonald *Mary Melville* 9

67 Ibid. 149

68 Ibid. 79, 49–50

69 Ibid. 128, 214, 81, 213, 258

70 Ibid. 132, 135, 167–8, 118, 186, 149
71 Deborah Gorham 'Flora MacDonald Denison: Canadian Feminist' in '*A Not Unreasonable Claim*' edited by Linda Kealey (Toronto 1979) 47–70
72 Flora MacDonald Denison 'Under the Pines' *Toronto World* 17 April 1910
73 Samuel Hynes *The Edwardian Turn of Mind* (Princeton 1968) 147
74 MacDonald *Mary Melville* 151; this was the position of the nineteenth-century German materialist, Ludwig Feuerbach. See Claude Welch *Protestant Thought in the Nineteenth Century, 1799–1810* vol. 1 (New Haven 1972) 175.
75 Browning 'Mr. Sludge, "The Medium"' 554. This reference was, of course, provided by Eleanor Cook.

CHAPTER 6 Richard Maurice Bucke: Religious Heresiarch and Utopian

1 Justin Kaplan *Walt Whitman* (New York 1980) 53–4
2 University of Western Ontario, R.M. Bucke Collection *Diary of Dr Charles A Sippi* 22 April 1893
3 R.M. Bucke 'Ingersoll' *The Conservator* 10 (September 1899)
4 For some intriguing parallels, see Eugene Taylor *William James on Exceptional Mental States* (New York 1983).
5 The best source for biographical information remains James H. Coyne 'Richard Maurice Bucke – A Sketch' *Proceedings and Transactions of the Royal Society of Canada* section 2 (1906) 159–96.
6 Bucke Collection, Bucke to H.B. Forman, 5 June 1882
7 Loren Eiseley *Darwin's Century* (New York 1961) 137
8 Michael Ruse *The Darwinian Revolution* (Chicago 1979) 99–116; see also Milton Millhauser *Just Before Darwin: Robert Chambers and His Vestiges* (Middletown, Ct. 1959) 86–115.
9 Bucke Collection 'Books That Have Influenced Me' undated clipping
10 Ibid. Bucke to Forman, 16 May 1869
11 R.M. Bucke *Cosmic Consciousness* (1901; reprint New York 1969) 9
12 Stephen Jay Gould 'Will Man Become Obsolete?' *New York Review of Books* 15 April 1982, 26. On Bucke's reading see *Richard Maurice Bucke: A Catalogue Based upon the Collections of the University of Western Ontario Libraries* edited by Mary Ann Jameson (London 1978) 68–95.
13. Bucke *Cosmic Consciousness* 8
14 Nearly fifty years later Bucke recalled these youthful experiences as the beginning of his 'illumination': Bucke to Traubel 18 July 1891 in *Richard Maurice Bucke: Medical Mystic* edited by Artem Lozynsky (Detroit 1977) 154.
15 R.M. Bucke 'Twenty-five Years Ago' *Overland Monthly* 1 (June 1883) 553–60

16 J.W. Burgess 'Richard Maurice Bucke, MD' *American Medico-Psychological Association Proceedings* 9 (1902) 306; James Horne 'R.M. Bucke: Pioneer Psychiatrist and Mystic' *Ontario History* 59 (September 1967) 201–2 notes some inconclusive evidence of unusual mental states before 1872.

17 R. M. Bucke 'The Correlation of the Vital and Physical Forces' *British Medical Association Journal* 3 (May 1862) 161–7 and ibid. (June 1862) 193–200; see also S.E.D. Shortt 'R.M. Bucke: Vital Force, Evolution and Somatic Psychiatry, 1862–92' in *Proceedings of the 27th International Congress of the History of Medicine* 1 (Barcelona 1981) 149–53.

18 Bucke 'Vital and Physical Forces' 161

19 Bucke 'Books That Have Influenced Me'; Bucke *Cosmic Consciousness* 9. On Buckle see T.W. Heyck *The Transformation of Intellectual Life in the Nineteenth Century* (London 1983) 133–6.

20 Bucke Collection *Bucke Diaries* 28 July 1863; S.E.D. Shortt 'The Influence of French Biomedical Theories on Nineteenth-Century Canadian Neuropsychiatry: Bichat and Comte in the Work of R.M. Bucke' *Proceedings of the 28th International Congress of the History of Medicine* 1 (Paris 1983) 309–12

21 R.M. Bucke 'Sanity' *American Journal of Insanity* (July 1888) citing Ernest Renan *Études de l'histoire religieuse* 8. On Renan's importance in nineteenth-century religious thought, see Albert Schweitzer *The Quest for the Historical Jesus* (New York 1966) 180–92.

22 Bucke Collection, Bucke to Forman, 7 December 1886

23 Ibid. Bucke to Forman, 2 October 1870, and same to same, 30 November 1873

24 Ibid. 14 December 1874

25 William James *The Varieties of Religious Experience* (New York 1961) 313

26 Bucke *Cosmic Consciousness* 9–10

27 Bucke Collection, Bucke to Forman, 11 December 1871

28 Bucke to Whitman, 11 November 1890, and same to same, 8 February 1891 in *The Letters of Dr Richard Maurice Bucke to Walt Whitman* edited by Artem Lozynsky (Detroit 1977) 187, 202–3

29 Bucke 'Sanity' 101; R.M. Bucke 'Mental Evolution of Man' *Journal of Hygiene and Herald of Health* (December 1897) 309–18; Bucke *Cosmic Consciousness* 59

30 Ontario Sessional Papers (1883) 87

31 Bucke Collection, Sippi Diary 22 March 1896

32 On 'moral managers' see Vieda Skultans *English Madness: Ideas on Insanity 1580–1890* (London 1979) 62ff; Andrew T. Scull *Museums of Madness* (London 1979) 48–75; and Michel Foucault *Madness and Civilization* (New York 1973) 241–70. These books, and others, are part of a lively scholarly controversy over the historical origins of the asylum and the relationship between

'reform' and 'social control.' The issues are joined in an exchange between
Michel Foucault and Lawrence Stone in *The New York Review of Books* 31
March 1983, 42–4, and a fine critical discussion of the controversy is pre-
sented in F.M.L. Thompson 'Social Control in Victorian Britain' *Economic
History Review* 34 (May 1981) 189–208.

33 Coyne 'Richard Maurice Bucke' cited at 175–6
34 R.M. Bucke 'Two Hundred Operative Cases – Insane Women' in *American
Medico-Psychological Association Proceedings* 7 (1900) 99–105; Wendy
Mitchison 'Gynecological Operations on the Insane' *Archivaria* 10 (Summer
1980) 130–44; 'R.M. Bucke: A Victorian Asylum Superintendent' *Ontario
History* 73 (December 1981) 239–53; Elaine Showalter 'Victorian Women
and Insanity' in *Madhouses, Mad Doctors, and Madmen* edited by Andrew Scull
(Philadelphia 1981) 327–30.
35 Ontario *Sessional Papers* (1884) 68–9
36 Bucke Collection, R.M. Bucke 'The Value of the Study of the Study of
Medicine: Introductory Lecture to Medical Faculty, McGill College,
1891–92' MS 18, 22, 30, 44
37 Ibid. Bucke to Forman, 24 October 1877 and same to same, 6 June 1880. See
also R.M. Bucke 'Memories of Walt Whitman' *Walt Whitman Fellowship Papers
1897* 36, where he speaks of his 'state of exaltation' when it was 'impossible
for me ... to believe that Walt Whitman was a real man.'
38 Bucke Collection, Seaborne MS 9, R.M. Bucke 'Walt Whitman and His Work'
(1879)
39 R.M. Bucke *Man's Moral Nature* (New York 1879) 200, 139–40
40 Ibid. 183; Bucke Collection, R.M. Bucke 'The Question of a Future Life'
(1882) MS
41 Bucke *Man's Moral Nature* 200, 199. There is some similarity between
Bucke's ideas as presented in *Man's Moral Nature* and John Fiske's *Outlines of
Cosmic Philosophy*, published in 1874. Though there is no direct evidence that
Bucke read this work, he was familiar with some of Fiske's books. See Jameson *Richard Maurice Bucke* 76. A useful summary of Fiske's ideas is found in
Cynthia E. Russett *Darwin in America* (San Francisco 1976) 49–55.
42 Bucke to Jessie, 19 June 1881, in Lozynsky *Medical Mystic* 78; Edward Carpenter *Some Friends of Walt Whitman: A Study in Sex Psychology* (London 1924)
14
43 Bucke to Traubel, 14 March 1892 in Lozynski *Medical Mystic* 179–80
44 R.M. Bucke *Walt Whitman* (Philadelphia 1883) 183. Whitman continues to
attract extravagant commentary: see Harold Bloom 'The Real Me' *New York
Review of Books* 26 April 1984, 3–7.
45 Bucke to Whitman, 17 December 1888; Bucke to Traubel, 18 July 1881; and

Bucke to Wallace and Johnston, 10 April 1892, in Lozynski *Medical Mystic* 112, 154, 184

46 R.M. Bucke 'Cosmic Consciousness' *American Medico-Psychological Association Proceedings* 1 (1894) 316–37

47 Bucke *Cosmic Consciousness* 225

48 Henry S. Levinson *The Religious Investigations of William James* (Chapel Hill 1981) 71–94

49 Bucke *Cosmic Consciousness* 161

50 Ibid. 3

51 James Robert Horne 'Cosmic Consciousness – Then and Now: The Evolutionary Mysticism of Richard Maurice Bucke' (PH D thesis, Columbia University 1964) 62–116; R.C. Zaehner *Concordant Discord* (Clarendon 1970) 40–50

52 Robert S. Ellwood Jr *Alternative Altars: Unconventional and Eastern Spirituality in America* (Chicago 1979) 37ff; Marion Meade *Madame Blavatsky* (New York 1980) 147ff

53 Bucke *Cosmic Consciousness* 383

54 R.M. Bucke 'The Man Walt Whitman' in H. Traubel, R.M. Bucke, and T.B. Harned *In Re Walt Whitman* (Philadelphia 1893) 62

55 Bucke to Walt, 14 April 1891 in Lozynsky *Letters of Dr Richard Maurice Bucke* 219; Bucke Collection, Seaborne MS, Bucke to Elliot, 18 August 1900

56 Bucke Collection *Diary of Dr Charles A. Sippi* 5 March 1895, 22 March 1896, July 1897

57 In 1894 Bucke wrote a friend, 'Yes I read all Carpenter's books and never get enough of them. So I read them over again when the interval is too long to wait from one to the other.' Bucke and Carpenter, both Whitmaniacs, corresponded fairly regularly between 1880 and 1896; see Bucke Collection. On Carpenter see Chushichi Tsuzuki *Edward Carpenter: Prophet of Human Fellowship 1844–1929* (London 1980) and Sheila Rowbotham and Jeffrey Weeks *Socialism and the New Life: The Personal and Sexual Politics of Edward Carpenter and Havelock Ellis* (London 1977).

58 Bucke to Wallace, 25 March 1894 in Lozynsky *Medical Mystic* 185–6; Bucke Collection, 'Notes on Prophecy, Liberalism and Socialism' (n.d.) M.S.

59 Bucke *Cosmic Consciousness* 5

60 R.M. Bucke 'Cosmic Consciousness: A Correspondence' *The Conservator* 12 (January 1903)

61 Bucke 'The Value of Studying Medicine' 47–8

62 Bucke *Cosmic Consciousness* 4–5

63 Henry S. Saunders *The Higher Consciousness: A Little Introduction to R. Maurice Bucke's Cosmic Consciousness* (Toronto 1924); Michèle Lacombe 'Theosophy

and the Canadian Idealist Tradition' *Journal of Canadian Studies* 17 (Summer 1982) 100–18

64 Bucke 'Books That Influenced Me.' He wrote, 'From *Leaves of Grass* very largely, if not entirely, I have derived the sense which I possess of the immanence of God in all things, and the realization of eternal life.'

65 Bucke 'Cosmic Consciousness: A Correspondence'

66 Bucke *Cosmic Consciousness* 6–7

67 Bucke Collection, R.M. Bucke 'The Domestication of Fire' (1882) MS, 11

CHAPTER 7   Toward a Christian Political Economy

1 Goldwin Smith *Lectures on Modern History* (Oxford 1861) 32–3

2 A. Ross McCormack *Reformers, Rebels and Revolutionaries: The Western Canadian Radical Movement 1899–1919* (Toronto 1977) cited at 78

3 *The Palladium of Labor* 8 September 1883 1

4 Ibid. 22 September 1883; 29 September 1883; 6 October 1883

5 Ibid. 27 October 1883

6 Ibid. 9 August 1884

7 Ibid.

8 Henry George *Progress and Poverty* (New York 1882) 7–8

9 Gregory S. Kealey *Working-Class Toronto at the Turn of the Century* (Toronto 1973) and Terry Copp *The Anatomy of Poverty* (Toronto 1974)

10 John L. Thomas 'Utopia for an Urban Age: Henry George, Henry Demarest Lloyd, and Edward Bellamy' *Perspectives in American History* 6 (1972) 135–66 and Thomas Bender *Toward an Urban Vision: Ideas and Institutions in Nineteenth-Century America* (Lexington, Ky. 1975)

11 *Grip* 31 December 1892

12 Charles A. Barker *Henry George* (Oxford and New York 1955) 518

13 *The Kingston British Whig* 13 February 1891

14 Elwood P. Lawrence *Henry George in the British Isles* (East Lansing, Mich. 1957) 54–7

15 PAC Phillips Thompson Papers, Henry George to Thompson, 7 May 1884

16 *The Palladium of Labor* 9 August 1884

17 See Crauford Goodwin *Canadian Economic Thought* (Durham, NC 1961) 32–8 and F.W. Watt 'The National Policy, the Workingman, and Proletarian Ideas in Victorian Canada' *Canadian Historical Review* 60 (March 1959) 1–26

18 Lawrence *Henry George* 89; John Saville 'Henry George and the British Labour Movement' *Science and Society* 24 (1960) 321–33 is corrective to Lawrence's study; and see Norman and Jeanne McKenzie *The Fabians* (New York 1977) 39.

19 The discussion of George, and especially of the single tax, continued in Canada long after the 1890s, as even a cursory reading of *The Grain Growers' Guide* will indicate. Moreover, taxation policies that bore at least some similarity to George's proposal were enacted in various parts of the country. See, for example, Archibald Stalker 'Taxation of Land Values in Western Canada' (MA thesis, McGill University 1913) and F.C. Wade, 'Experiments with the Single Tax in Western Canada' paper presented to the Eighth Annual Conference on Taxation under the auspices of the National Tax Association, Denver, 11 September 1914. W.C. Good's *Production and Taxation* (Toronto 1919) also owed a great deal to George. But by the twentieth century George's general analysis of capitalism was rarely discussed, having been either accepted, rejected, or superseded. People like D.W. Buchanan and F.J. Dixon in Winnipeg tried to keep the faith, but even they seem rarely to have appealed to George's general analysis. See Allen Mills 'Single Tax, Socialism and the Independent Labour Party of Manitoba: The Political Ideas of F.J. Dixon and S.J. Farmer' *Labour/Le Travail* 5 (Spring 1980) 33–56.

20 Henry George Jr *The Life of Henry George* (New York 1900) 351–2

21 *The Globe* 19 September 1885

22 *The Kingston British Whig* 6 March 1891

23 PAC W.L.M. King Papers *Diary* 12 December 1895

24 Morley Wicket 'The Study of Political Economy at Canadian Universities' *Annual Report of the Bureau of Industries for the Province of Ontario, 1897* (Toronto 1899) 106

25 *The Bystander* (July 1880) 384–7; Goldwin Smith *False Hopes; or, Fallacies Socialistic and Semi-socialistic, Briefly Answered* (New York 1883) 5, 21; *The Week* 31 January 1884; *The Bystander* (December 1889) 97–9; Arnold Haultain *Goldwin Smith: His Life and Opinions* (Toronto n.d.) 183–4

26 George *Progress and Poverty* 506–26; *The Palladium of Labor* 9 August 1884

27 A.B. McKillop *A Disciplined Intelligence: Critical Inquiry and Canadian Thought in the Victorian Era* (Montreal 1979) chap. 5

28 W.D. LeSueur '*Progress and Poverty* and the Doctrine of Evolution' *Canadian Monthly and National Review* (May 1881) 287–96; W.D. LeSueur 'The Future of Morality' ibid. (January 1880) 81–93

29 George *The Life of Henry George* 340–1.

30 John L. Thomas *Alternative America: Henry George, Edward Bellamy, Henry Demarest Lloyd, and the Adversary Tradition* (Cambridge, Mass. 1893) 183–4 and the illustration following page 204, which includes D.J. O'Donoghue in Henry George's 'Producerist Circle'; Gregory S. Kealey and Bryan D. Palmer *Dreaming of What Might Be: The Knights of Labor in Ontario, 1880–1900* (Cambridge 1982) 304–11

31 *Proceedings of the Canadian Labor Congress, December 26, 27, 28, 1883* (Toronto 1884) 25

32 *Proceedings of the Trades and Labour Congress of Canada, 1893* (Toronto 1894) 13; see also the *Proceedings* for 1887, 1889, and 1890, and PAC. Toronto Trades and Labour Council *Minutes* 21 April 1893.

33 *The Palladium of Labor* 27 October 1883; *The Labor Union* 17 February 1883; *The Social Reformer* 1 (November 1889)

34 Stanley Paul Kutcher 'John Wilson Bengough: Artist of Righteousness' (MA thesis, McMaster University 1975)

35 *The Labor Advocate* (January 1891); see also John David Bell 'The Social and Political Thought of the Labor Advocate' (MA thesis, Queen's University 1975).

36 *The Christian Guardian* 13 February 1884 and 13 February 1889

37 *Grip* 16 November 1889

38 *The Christian Guardian* 29 January 1889

39 G.M. Grant 'Progress and Poverty' *The Presbyterian Review* 9 (April 1888) 185, 198. For an account of Grant's social ideas see Carl Berger *The Sense of Power* (Toronto 1970) 183–6.

40 *Grip* 7 February 1891; S.T. Wood and J.L. Dawkins to Principal G.M. Grant, 2 February 1891; *The Labor Advocate* 20 February 1891; *The Kingston British Whig* 13 February 1891

41 Henry F. May *Protestant Churches and Industrial America* (New York 1967) 239–41

42 *The Labor Advocate* 23 January 1891

43 'L.I.D.' 'Christian Socialism' *The Week* 30 January 1891, 137

44 Albert R. Carman 'The Gospel of Justice' *The Canadian Methodist Quarterly* (July 1891) 287–300

45 Richard T. Laufield *Why I Joined the New Crusade: A Plea for the Passing of Taxes on Land Values Only* (Toronto 1888) 19; S.S. Craig 'The Church and the Money Question' *Knox College Monthly and Presbyterian Magazine* 19 (January 1896) 377; S.T. Wood and J.L. Dawkins to Principal Grant, 2 February 1891; *The Labor Advocate* 29 February 1891; Agnes Maule Machar *Roland Graeme: Knight* (Toronto 1892); Albert R. Carman *The Preparation of Ryerson Embury* (Toronto 1900); Mary Vipond 'Blessed are the Peacemakers: The Labor Question in Canadian Social Gospel Fiction' *Journal of Canadian Studies* 10 (August 1975) 32–44

46 George *Progress and Poverty* 501–2

47 Ibid. 496; see also Fred Nickalson 'Henry George: Social Gospeller' *The American Quarterly* 22 (1970) 649–54.

48 Carman *Ryerson Embury* 153

49 George *Progress and Poverty* 559–60. George Bernard Shaw virtually plagia-

rized this passage, putting it into more succinct prose, for the closing sentence of his contribution to *Fabian Essays*. He wrote: 'It is to economic science – once the Dismal, now the Hopeful – that we are indebted for the discovery that though the evil is enormously worse than we knew, yet it is not eternal – not even very long lived, if only we bestir ourselves to make an end of it': *The Fabian Essays* edited by George Bernard Shaw (1889; reprint London 1950) 27.

50 *The Labor Advocate* 7 March 1891

51 *The Palladium of Labor* 14 June 1884.

52 W.A. Douglas 'The Science of Political Economy' *Methodist Magazine and Review* 47 (June 1898) 564

CHAPTER 8 'A Republic of God, a Christian Republic'

1 Bob Lawson-Peebles 'Henry George the Prophet' *Journal of American Studies* 10 (April 1976) cited at 43

2 Biographical information is provided by W.W. Withrow 'An Artist of Righteousness: J.W. Bengough, Canadian Caricaturist and Humorous Poet' *Methodist Magazine and Review* 46 (September 1897) 204–5; J.W. Bengough *Chalk Talks* (Toronto 1922) 3–39; and Hector Charlesworth 'A Pioneer Canadian Cartoonist' in *The Canadian Scene* (Toronto 1927) 125–31.

3 *Grip* 5 May 1883

4 Cited in *Canadian Men and Women of the Times* edited by H.J. Morgan (Toronto 1912) 91.

5 J.W. Bengough *Motley: Verses Grave and Gay* (Toronto 1895) and *In Many Keys* (Toronto 1902)

6 *Grip* 10 January 1891, 25 May 1878, 4 December 1875, 29 May 1880, and 16 July 1887

7 Ibid. 7 January 1888, 7 February 1874

8 Bengough *Chalk Talks* 13

9 *Grip* 6 July 1878; A.B. Paine *Th. Nast – His Period and His Pictures* (1904; reprint Gloucester, Mass. 1967) 248. See also Morton Keller *The Art and Politics of Thomas Nast* (New York 1968). Bengough, unlike Nast, was an admirer of Horace Greeley. As a footnote to a poem entitled 'On the Death of Horace Greeley,' Bengough remarked that the American liberal's death had been 'hastened if not caused by the venom of his adversaries, more especially the caricaturists of the opposition journals': Bengough *Motley* 102.

10 On Bengough's view of the war, see his poem, 'The Charge at Batoche,' *Grip* 11 July 1885. During the rebellion Bengough published *The Illustrated War News*, in which he combined artistry and bombast. During the First World

War he wrote a great deal of patriotic verse: McMaster University Library, J.W. Bengough Papers, box 4 'Disbound Poems.'

11 PAC Laurier Papers, Bengough to Laurier, 4 May 1911 and Laurier to Bengough, 6 May 1911. Bengough wrote, in part, that 'precendents have been set in the honoring of cartoonists who are regarded as having "done the state some service." In the United States Mr. Thomas Nast of *Harper's Weekly*, was appointed to a South American consulate, and more recently in Great Britain Mr. Thomas Temith of *Punch* and Mr. F.C. Gould of the Westminster *Gazette*, were given knighthoods.' That Bengough grew close to the Liberal party after Laurier's 1896 victory can be seen in his poem 'Sir Wilfrid at Toronto' *The Westminster* 16 October 1897, 393. In 1919 he wrote a poem for the new Liberal leader, Mackenzie King, entitled 'The Spirit of William Lyon Mackenzie to His Grandson' PAC W.L.M. King Papers, J1, vol. 43, p. 34705.

12. Charles Dickens *Barnaby Rudge* (reprint London 1973) 99; Humphrey House *The Dickens World* (London 1960)

13 'Introductory' J.W. Bengough *A Caricature History of Canadian Politics* (Toronto 1886) 8

14 Bengough *Motley* 163–6

15 *Grip* 31 January 1885

16 Ibid. 24 January 1885, 14 February 1885

17 Ibid. March 11 1893, 3 December 1879, November 5 1892, 11 August 1883

18 Bengough *Motley* 19–22; J.W. Bengough 'Made Whole' *The Methodist Magazine* 37 (May 1893) 510–11; *Grip* 23 February 1878 and 9 January 1875

19 *Grip* 5 January 1878

20 Ibid. 9 July 1887, 10 August 1889; Bengough *Motley* 151–60; Christopher Armstrong and H.V. Nelles *The Revenge of the Methodist Bicycle Company* (Toronto 1977); *Grip* 10 August 1889

21 J.W. Bengough *The Gin Mill Primer: A Book of Easy Reading Lessons for Children of All Ages Especially for Boys Who Have Votes* (Toronto 1888) 7

22 *Grip* 4 May 1874, 6 March 1889, 13 October 1883, 24 September 1892

23 *Flapdoodle: A Political Encyclopedia and Manual for Public Men* edited by an ex-minister, illustrated by J.W. Bengough (Toronto 1881) 14, 18

24 *Grip* 15 August 1885, 24 March 1888, 30 March 1889, 29 March 1890

25 Ibid. 21 September 1891; J.W. Bengough *The Decline and Fall of Keewatin; or, the Free Trade Redskins: A Satire* (Toronto 1876); *Grip* 31 January 1885

26 *Grip* 19 July 1884, 12 September 1891

27 Ibid. 21 January 1888, 12 February 1887

28 Ibid. 27 October 1894, 3 November 1883

29 J.W. Bengough *The Whole Hog Book; Being George's Thoro'Going Work 'Protec-*

tion of Free Trade?' Rendered into Words of One Syllable and Illustrated with Pictures; or, A Dry Story Made Juicy (Boston 1908); *Grip* 25 November 1882; J.W. Bengough 'Address from the Single Tax Association to the Ministers of the Christian Churches' *The Social Reformer* (June 1892); Bengough *Chalk Talks* 118

30 *Grip* 19 May 1888; Laurier Papers, Bengough to Laurier, 14 January 1906; *Grip* 23 July 1887

31 Bengough *Chalk Talks* 124–5; Bengough *Motley* 31

32 PAC W.L.M. King Papers, J.W. Bengough to King, 21 March 1919 and reply 24 March 1919. Although Bengough promoted the single-tax idea all of his lfie, including during his term as a Toronto alderman (1907–9), he became a Liberal party supporter – first working for the *Globe* after 1895, then contributing to the *Canadian Liberal Monthly* edited by Mackenzie King after 1911, and then doing cartoons for the party during the 1921 election. King thus employed both J.W. Bengough and Phillips Thompson.

33 *Grip* 3 October 1885

34 Bengough Papers XIV undated clippings; J.W. Bengough *In Many Keys* 219–20

35 *Grip* 3 January 1891; *The Labor Advocate* 27 March 1891

36 *Grip* 22 September 1888

CHAPTER 9 'The New City of Friends': Evolution, Theosophy, and Socialism

1 *The Labor Advocate* 27 March 1891 and September 1891

2 *The Palladium of Labor* 26 April 1884; *Saturday Night* 2 August 1890

3 *Grip* 11 December 1880

4 T. Phillips Thompson *The Future Government of Canada: Being Arguments in Favor of a British American Independent Republic* (St Catharines 1864) 22–3

5 Phillips Thompson to the Editor *The World* 1 June 1885; *The Week* 4 June 1884, 418; PAC Sir Wilfrid Laurier Papers, Phillips Thompson to J. Israel Tarte, 14 November 1889; Phillips Thompson to the Editor *Secular Thought* 25 February 1905, 122; Phillips Thompson 'The Orange Revolt' *The Week* 2 August 1889, 555

6 *The Mail* 2 August 1873, 6 December 1873

7 *The National* 22 January 1874

8 Ibid. 22 January 1874, 16 July 1875, 4 March 1874, 19 June 1879; Bryan Palmer *A Culture in Conflict* (Montreal 1979) 100–9; Douglas McCalla 'Isaac Buchanan' *Dictionary of Canadian Biography* vol. 11 (Toronto 1982) 125–31

9 *Grip* 15 September 1873 and 5 August 1875; *The National* 6 August 1874

10 *The National* 8 July 1874, 22 April 1874, 24 July 1875

11 Ibid. 3 June 1875

12 'Phillips Thompson' *The American Punch* (July 1879) 80; Henry James *The Bostonians* (1886; reprint Harmondsworth 1966) 7

13 PAC W.D. LeSueur Papers, Herbert Spencer to W.D. LeSueur, 2 April 1880; Richard Hofstadter *Social Darwinism in American Thought* (Boston 1955) 31–50; J.W. Burrow *Evolution and Society: A Study in Victorian Social Theory* (Cambridge 1966) 179–227; *The National* 17 October 1878

14 *Grip* 18 December 1880; *The Globe* 10 January 1882

15 *The Globe* 4 January 1882

16 *Grip* 11 December 1880; Russell Hann 'Brainworkers and the Knights of Labor: E.E. Sheppard, Phillips Thompson, and the *Toronto News*, 1883–1887' in *Essays in Canadian Working-Class History* edited by Gregory S. Kealey and Peter Warrian (Toronto 1976) 35–57

17 *The Palladium of Labor* 9 August 1884, 17 June 1884, 3 January 1885; Phillips Thompson 'The Single Tax Movement in England' *The Week* 1 February 1889, 135

18 Gerald N. Grob *Workers and Utopia: A Study of Ideological Conflict in the American Labor Movement 1865–1900* (Chicago 1969); Gregory S. Kealey and Bryan D. Palmer *Dreaming of What Might Be: The Knights of Labor in Ontario, 1880–1900* (Cambridge 1982); Herbert Gutman *Work, Culture, and Society in Industrializing America* (New York 1976) 97–8

19 University of Toronto Archives, Woodsworth Memorial Collection, James McArthur Connor 'The Labor and Socialist Movements in Canada' MS; Gene Howard Homel 'The Fading Beams of the Nineteenth Century: Radicalism and Early Socialism in Canada's 1890s' *Labour/Le Travail* 5 (Spring 1980) 7–32; Joanne Emily Thompson, 'The Influence of Emily Howard Stowe on the Woman Suffrage Movement in Canada,' *Ontario History* 54 (December 1962) 254–66; Provincial Archives of Ontario (PAO), Phillips Thompson Papers, T.P. Thompson 'Thoughts and Suggestions on Social Problems and Things in General' (1880) MS; *The Labor Advocate* 5 December 1890; T. Phillips Thompson *The Politics of Labor* (1887; reprint Toronto 1975) 73; *The Labor Advocate* 14 August 1891

20 *Grip* 22 April 1893, 11 May 1889; *The Labor Advocate* 1 April 1891; Arthur Nethercote *The First Five Lives of Annie Besant* (Chicago 1960)

21 Arthur E. Morgan *Edward Bellamy* (New York 1944) 260–75; Howard H. Quant *The Forging of American Socialism* (New York 1964) 72–102. There is, as yet, no thorough study of Bellamy's influence in Canada, though some information can be found in W.R. Fraser 'Canadian Reactions' in *Edward Bellamy Abroad* edited by Sylvia E. Bowman (New York 1962), but it is inade-

quate on the pre-1900 period. Bellamy's papers in the Houghton Library, Harvard University, yielded only a letter from Ulric Barthe (27 September 1897) proposing to translate *Looking Backward*. Bellamy was invited to visit Canada at least once, but declined (*The Labor Advocate* 13 February 1891). In addition to many references in *Grip* and *The Labor Advocate*, Bellamy was discussed in Rev. J.A. Macdonald 'Looking Backward' *Knox College Monthly and Presbyterian Magazine* 10 (August 1889) 209–12; 'Edward Bellamy, Religion, and the Church in the Year 2000' *The Westminster* 3 (August 1897) 71–5; J.A. Cooper 'Bellamy and Howells' *The Canadian Magazine* 9 (April 1897) 344–6; W.A. Douglas, 'Bellamy Blunders' *The Canadian Magazine* 10 (January 1898) 268–70. Stephen Leacock, in *The Unsolved Riddle of Social Justice* (Toronto 1920), and O.D. Skelton, in *Socialism: A Critical Analysis* (Boston 1911), both criticized Bellamyite socialism. Bellamy appears to have influenced both J.S. Woodsworth and William Aberhart and was 'recommended as required reading as late as 1953' for members of the CCF. See Walter Young *The Anatomy of a Party: The National CCF* (Toronto 1969) 54; Allen Mills 'The Later Thought of J.S. Woodsworth: An Essay in Revision' *Journal of Canadian Studies* 17 (Autumn 1982) 77; David R. Elliott 'William Aberhart: Right or Left?' in *The Dirty Thirties in Canada* edited by D. Francis and H. Ganzevoort (Vancouver 1980) 17–19.

22 J.D. Edgar 'Theosophy' *The Week* 6 October 1893, 1064; see also 'A New Cult?' *The Christian Guardian* 30 December 1890; Bruce Campbell *Ancient Wisdom Revived* (Berkeley 1980) 29; Michèle Lacombe 'Theosophy and the Canadian Idealist Tradition' *Journal of Canadian Studies* 17 (Summer 1982) 100–18

23 *The Labor Advocate* 13 February 1891

24 T. Phillips Thompson 'Socialism and Secularism' *Social Justice* (December 1902)

25 Phillips Thompson 'Socialism and Theosophy' *Western Socialist* 24 April 1903; W.A. Visser't Hooft *The Background to the Social Gospel in America* (Haarlem 1928) 51

26 *The Labor Reform Songster* edited by T. Phillips Thompson (Philadelphia 1892) 8

27 PAC Phillips Thompson Papers, Henry George to Phillips Thompson, 6 August 1886; PAO Phillips Thompson Papers, 'Thoughts and Suggestions ...'; *The Essential Karl Marx: The Non-economic Writings* edited by Saul K. Padover (New York 1978) 33. Of *Progress and Poverty* Marx wrote in 1891, 'I consider it as a last attempt to save the capitalistic regime.' Thompson *The Politics of Labor* 127, 40, 51

28 Thompson *The Politics of Labor* 83

29 Ibid. 85; Edward Bellamy *Looking Backward* (1888; reprint New York 1951) 198–9; *The Labor Advocate* 27 March 1891

30 Thompson *The Politics of Labor* 95, 112; *The Labor Advocate* 21 August 1891. see also John David Bell 'The Social and Political Thought of the Labor Advocate (MA thesis, Queen's University 1955).

31 Thompson *The Politics of Labor* 158, 193

32 Stephen Yeo 'A New Life: The Religion of Socialism in Britain' *History Workshop Journal* 4 (1977) 5–56; Stanley Pearson *Marxism and the Origins of British Socialism* (Ithaca 1973) 3–58; John L. Thomas 'Utopia for an Urban Age: Henry George, Henry Demarest Lloyd, and Edward Bellamy' *Perspectives in American History* 6 (1972) 135–66; Chusichi Tsuzuki *Edward Carpenter 1844–1929: Prophet of Human Fellowship*, (Cambridge 1980); Thompson *The Politics of Labor* 4

33 'True to the Labor Advocate' *The Labor Advocate* 30 January 1891; another theosophical socialist is examined by J. Donald Wilson '"Never Believe What You Have Never Doubted": Matti Kurikka's Dream for a New World Utopia' Turku (Finland) Historical Archives Jahrbuch (1980) 216–40

CHAPTER 10 'Was Christ, After All, a Social Reformer?'

1 Albert R. Carman *The Preparation of Ryerson Embury* (Toronto 1900) 159

2 Ibid

3 *At the Mermaid Inn: Wilfred Campbell, Archibald Lampman, and Duncan Campbell Scott in the Globe, 1892–93* (Toronto 1979) 6

4 William R. Hutchison *The Modernist Impulse in American Protestantism* (Oxford 1982) 2; W.A. Visser't Hooft *The Background to the Social Gospel in America* (Haarlem 1928) 16

5 PAC G.M. Grant Papers, W.G. Brown to G.M. Grant, 3 September 1892

6 Gerhart B. Ladner *The Idea of Reform: Its Impact on Christian Thought and Action in the Age of the Fathers* (New York 1967)

7 J. Clark Murray *A Handbook of Christian Ethics* (Edinburgh 1908) 297, 17

8 *The Week* 17 March 1887, 253

9 John Charles Dent *The Canadian Portrait Gallery* vol. 4 (Toronto 1881) 173

10 Ruth Elizabeth Spence *Prohibition in Canada* (Toronto 1919) 142, 143

11 Ibid. 145

12 Wendy Mitchison 'The WCTU: "For God, Home and Native Land": A Study in Nineteenth-Century Feminism' in *A Not Unreasonable Claim* edited by Linda Kealey (Toronto 1979) 151–68; Nive Voisine *Louis-François Laflèche* (Ste Hyacinthe 1980) 152–64

13 Alexander Sutherland *The Kingdom of God and the Problems of To-Day* (Toronto 1898) 17, 93, 215, 180–1, 131, 183–4

14 Ibid. 109, 140, 195–6, 212

15 Malcolm Graeme Decarie 'The Prohibition Movement in Ontario, 1894–1916' (PH D thesis, Queen's University 1982)

16 Leslie Armour and Elizabeth Trott *The Faces of Reason: An Essay on Philosophy and Culture in English Canada, 1850–1950* (Waterloo 1981) 105–75

17 Margaret Gillett *We Walked Very Warily: A History of Women at McGill* (Montreal 1981) 113–50

18 McGill University Archives, John Clark Murray Papers, 'A Lecture Delivered to the Ladies Educational Association of Montreal' 2 October 1872, 5, 3

19 W.D. LeSueur 'The Coming Reform' *The Week* 5 September 1890, 630 and 17 October 1890, 795. On Austin see chapter 5.

20 Sidney Warren *American Freethought 1860–1914* (New York 1966) 73–4

21 John Clark Murray *The Industrial Kingdom of God* (Ottawa 1982) 8

22 Ibid. 11

23 Ibid. 13, and J. Clark Murray 'The Law of Supply and Demand' *The Week* 18 January 1889, 101

24 John Clark Murray 'Philosophy and Industrial Life' *The Monist*, 55 (July 1894) 539; See also *Canada Investigates Industrialism* edited by Gregory S. Kealey (Toronto 1973) 41 and Michael Bliss *A Living Profit* (Toronto 1974) 33–54.

25 Murray *Industrial Kingdom* 27, 30–1 and J. Clark Murray 'The Claims of Industrial Co-Operation' *The Week* 1 November 1888, 779

26 Murray *Industrial Kingdom* 59, 115

27 Ibid. 123

28 Ibid. 128, 123; Murray 'Philosophy and Industrial Life' 544; Visser't Hooft *Background* 51

29 Adam Shortt 'A Personality in Journalism' *The Canadian Magazine* 29 (October 1907) 521; see also Barry Ferguson 'Political Economists and *Queen's Quarterly*, 1893–1939' *Queen's Quarterly* 90 (Autumn 1983) 623–43.

30 W. Farquharson 'Socialism as an Antidote to Poverty' *Knox College Monthly* 3 (January 1885) 73–9; G. Inglis 'Christian Socialism' ibid. 7 (February 1888) 213–19; T. Richie 'The Church and the Labour Question' ibid. 12 (May 1890) 30–42; Adam Shortt 'Doubtful Teaching' ibid. 12 (July 1890) 137–9; J.G. Hume 'Socialism' ibid. 17 (March 1894) 601–14 and 17 (April 1894) 661–741; see also James Gibson Hume *Political Economy and Ethics* (Toronto 1892).

31 J.A. Macdonald 'East London and the University Settlement' *Knox College Monthly and Presbyterian Magazine* 10 (May 1889) 23 and J.A. Macdonald

'Looking Backward' ibid. (August 1887) 209–12. On Macdonald and other Presbyterians who thought like him, see Brian J. Fraser 'The Christianization of Our Civilization: Presbyterian Reformers and their Defence of a Protestant Canada, 1875–1914' (PH D thesis, York University 1982).

32 Richard Allen *The Social Passion: Religion and Social Reform in Canada 1914–1928* (Toronto 1971) 10; A.B. McKillop *A Disciplined Intelligence: Critical Inquiry and Canadian Thought in the Victorian Era* (Montreal 1979) 208–9; Salem Bland 'Queen's Theological Alumni Conferences in the 1890s' *Queen's Review* 4 (1930) 237–41

33 Hilda Neatby *Queen's University 1841–1917* (Montreal 1978) cited at 225; G.M. Grant 'Christianity and Modern Thought' *Canadian Monthly and National Review* 8 (November 1875) 437–41

34 G.M. Grant *The Religions of the World* (London and Edinburgh 1895) 201

35 Ibid. 188–9

36 Grant Papers, 26, unidentified clipping; G.M. Grant 'The Relation of Religion to Secular Life' *Canadian Monthly and National Review* (December 1880) 614–24; John Dillenberger and Claude Welch *Protestant Christianity* (New York 1954) 218

37 'Principal Grant's Address on the Wage System' *The Weekly Witness* 5 October 1892; Grant Papers, unidentified clipping

38 D.G. Creighton *John A. Macdonald: The Young Politician* (Toronto 1952) 91; Gregory S. Kealey and Brian Palmer *Dreaming of What Might Be* (London 1982) 448n

39 'Fidelis' 'The Late G.J. Romanes' *The Week* 6 July 1894, 751; 'Fidelis' 'Grant Allen' ibid. May 1891, 510; 'Fidelis' 'Birds and Bonnets' ibid., 24 March 1887, 265–6; 'Fidelis' 'The Rape of the Islands' ibid. 6 July 1894, 759. Biographical details are found in E. Ethelwyn Wetherald 'Some Canadian Literary Women' ibid. 5 April 1888, 303, and Loman A. Guild 'Canadian Celebrities: Agnes Maule Machar' *Canadian Magazine* 37 (October 1906) 499–501.

40 'Fidelis' 'Prayer for Daily Bread' *Canadian Monthly and National Review* 7 (May 1875) 415–25; W.D. LeSueur 'Prayer and Modern Thought' ibid. 8 (August 1875) 145–55; 'Fidelis' 'Prayer and Modern Doubt' ibid. (September 1875) 224–36; 'Fidelis' 'Charles Kingsley' ibid. 7 (March 1875) 249; 'Fidelis' 'Creeds and Confessions' ibid. 9 (February 1876) 146; 'Fidelis' 'Modern Theology and Modern Thought' ibid. 13 (March 1881) 297–304

41 'Fidelis' 'The Source of Moral Life' *Rose Belford's Canadian Monthly* 4 (April 1880) 345

42 'Fidelis' 'The Temperance Problem' *Canadian Monthly and National Review* 11 (April 1877) 369–78, ibid. 12 (August 1879) 183–9; 'Fidelis' 'Higher Educa-

tion for Women' ibid. (February 1875) 144–57 and 'Women's Work' ibid. 12 (September 1878) 295–311; Agnes Maule Machar 'The Higher Education of Women' *The Week* 27 December 1889, 55 and 'The Enlarged Conception of Women's Sphere' ibid. 10 October 1890, 713

43 'Fidelis' 'Healthy and Unhealthy Conditions of Women's Work' *The Week* 27 March 1896, 421–2, and 'The Unhealthy Condition of Women's Work in Factories' ibid. 8 May 1896, 566–9

44 'Fidelis' 'A Pressing Problem' *Canadian Monthly and National Review* 13 (April 1879) 455–69

45 'Fidelis' 'Voices Crying in the Wilderness' *The Week* 13 February 1891, 169 and 'Our Lady of the Slums' ibid. 13 March 1891, 234

46 Peter J. Frederick *Knights of the Golden Rule: The Intellectual as Christian Social Reformer in the 1890s* (Lexington, Ky. 1976) 151, 143

47 Agnes Maule Machar *Roland Graeme: Knight* (Montreal 1892) 239; see also Ruth Compton Brouwer 'The "Between Age" Christianity of Agnes Machar· *Canadian Historical Review* 65 (September 1984) 347–70.

48 Dillenberger and Welch *Protestant Christianity* 207–24 and Jean B. Quandt 'Religion and Social Thought: The Secularization of Post-Millenialism' *The American Quarterly* 25 (October 1973) 390–409

49 'Fidelis' 'Centripetal Christianity' *The Week*, 2 December 1892, 7 See also John Henry Burrows *The World's Parliament of Religions: An Illustrated and Popular History* (Toronto 1893) 2 vols; 'Fidelis' 'Impressions from the Parliament of Religions' *The Week* 20 October 1893, 1114 and 27 October 1893, 1138.

50 United Church Archives, Carman Papers, 24, sermon 98, 'The Higher Criticism and the Lower Socialism'

51 Albert Carman 'The Gospel of Justice' *The Canadian Methodist Quarterly* 3 (July 1891) 287

52 Henry J. Morgan *The Canadian Men and Women of the Time* (Toronto 1912) 201

53 K.W. McNaught *A Prophet in Politics* (Toronto 1959) 6; William R. Hutchison 'Cultural Strain and Protestant Liberalism' *American Historical Review* 76 (April 1971) 400–1

54 Carman *The Preparation of Ryerson Embury* 241

55 Ibid. 228, 229

56 Ibid. 229

57 Canon J.D. O'Meara 'A Plea for Socialism' *The Week* 9 February 1894, 249

58 Hutchison 'Cultural Strain' 403

59 Visser't Hooft *Background* 181

60 S.S. Craig 'The Church and the Money Question' *Knox College Monthly and Presbyterian Magazine* 19 (January 1896) 381

61 James L. Hughes 'An Experiment in Altruism' *Methodist Magazine and Review* 19 (January 1899) 23. See also Bruce N. Carter 'James L. Hughes and the Gospel of Education: A Study in the Work and Thought of a Nineteenth-Century Educator' (PH D thesis, University of Toronto 1966).

62 Thomas L. Haskell *The Emergence of Professional Social Science: The American Social Science Association and the Mid-nineteenth-Century Crisis of Authority* (Urbana 1977)

63 United Church Archives, S.D. Chown Papers, 11, file 51 'The Relation of Sociology to the Kingdom of Heaven'

CHAPTER 11   The Modernist Pilgrim's Progress

1 Gerald Henry Allaby *New Brunswick Prophets of Radicalism* (MA thesis, University of New Brunswick 1972) cited at 80

2 The Social Service Council of Canada, formed in 1907, brought together representatives of the Anglican, Methodist, Presbyterian, Baptist, and Congregational churches, the Salvation Army, the Evangelical Association of North America, the Canadian Purity Educational Association, the Women's Christian Temperance Union, the Trades and Labour Congress of Canada, and the Dominion Grange. Its 1914 congress in Ottawa perhaps marked the apogee of the social gospel in Canada: see *Social Service Congress, Ottawa 1914, Report of Addresses and Proceedings* (Toronto 1915).

3 PAC W.L.M. King Papers, *Diary* 26 February 1898 (cited hereafter as *Diary*)

4 Ibid. 11 January 1902

5 Ibid. 16 September 1904

6 Ibid. 6 December 1985, 17 February 1901, 31 October 1901, 23 July 1897

7 *At the Mermaid Inn* edited by Barrie Davies (Toronto 1979) 6; *Diary* 10 and 22 January 1906. See Laurel Boone 'Wilfred Campbell Reconsidered' *Canadian Literature* 14 (Autumn 1982) 67–82 and 'Evolution and Idealism: Wilfred Campbell's "The Tragedy of Man" and Its Place in Canadian Intellectual History' *Studies in Canadian Literature* 8, 93–116

8 *Diary* 1 July 1895

9 Ibid. 3 October 1898, 15 January 1899

10 Richard Hofstadter *Social Darwinism in American Thought* (Boston 1955) 96–9; Robert M. Young 'The Impact of Darwin on Conventional Thought' in *The Victorian Crisis of Faith* edited by Anthony Symondson (London 1970) 13–36

11 *Diary* 14 January 1902. King's library contained the 1926 edition of *Cosmic Consciousness.*

12 *Diary* 1 January 1901, 18 December 1904

13 Ibid. 21 March 1900, 18 July 1898. On Elizabeth Stuart Phelps see *Dictionary of*

American Biography (New York 1936) 417–19. Phelps, whose father was a theological professor at Andover, a liberal seminary, was, like King, interested in the social gospel and in psychic phenomena.

14 W.L.M. King *The Secret of Heroism* (Toronto 1904) 142–5 and *Diary* 1 January 1902

15 Goldwin Smith *Guesses at the Riddle of Existence* (Toronto 1898). King's copy and his other books are in the National Library of Canada.

16 *Diary* 2 February 1902; William James *Human Immortality: Two Supposed Objections to the Doctrine* (Boston 1898). King, who met James during his Harvard days, read a good deal of the Harvard pragmatist's writings, especially those dealing with religion. His copy of *Memoirs and Studies* (London 1917), which he received for Christmas in 1918, was very carefully read, especially the essays arguing for the validity of the findings of psychic research. His library contained many books on this topic, some dated at least as early as 1906.

17 *Diary* 17 December 1904

18 H. Blair Neatby *William Lyon Mackenzie King: The Lonely Heights* (Toronto 1963) 207

19 *Diary* 12 February 1895

20 Ian M. Drummond *Political Economy at the University of Toronto: A History of the Department, 1888–1982* (Toronto 1983) 26–31; S.E.D. Shortt *The Search for an Ideal* (Toronto 1976) 119–35

21 *Diary* 17 February 1894

22 Arnold Toynbee *The Industrial Revolution in England* (Humboldt Library of Science 1884) 25, 200 (King's italics)

23 *Diary* 11 July 1894, 15 December 1895

24 C.P. Stacey *A Very Double Life* (Toronto 1976) 41–8. The evidence strikes me as more ambiguous than Professor Stacey's rather literal reading of it suggests.

25 *Diary* 19 October 1895

26 Ibid. 28 July 1895, 12 December 1895

27 Ibid. 21 July 1895, 3 July 1897

28 Ibid. 15 August 1899, 7 March 1897

29 W.L. Mackenzie King 'The Story of Hull House' *The Westminster* 6 November 1897, 356; *Diary* 19 May 1897, 11 June 1897; W.L. Mackenzie King 'The International Typographical Union' *Journal of Political Economy* 5 (September 1897) 458–84; *Diary* 13 August 1897

30 *Diary* 12 July 1897, 9 September 1898. On Norton see Frederic Jaher *Doubters and Dissenters* (Glencoe 1964) 143–5; for Norton's views as expressed to King see *Letters of Charles Eliot Norton* vol. 2, edited by Sara Norton and M.A. DeWolfe Howe (London 1913), 331–3 and 381–3.

31 Joseph Dorfman *The Economic Mind in American Civilization* vol. 3 (New York 1969) 265; *Diary* 29 January 1898, 22 January 1898, 1 June 1898
32 *Diary* 18 March 1899, 29 May 1899. On Cunningham and Ashley see Bernard Semmel *Imperialism and Social Reform* (London 1960) chaps. 10 and 11
33 *Diary* 19 April 1899
34 Edmond Demolins *Anglo-Saxon Superiority: To What Is It Due?* (London 1899) 194, 388. See also Harry Elmer Barnes *An Introduction to the History of Sociology* (Chicago 1958) 458–9. Demolin's misconceptions are demonstrated in Martin J. Weiner *English Culture and the Decline of the Industrial Spirit 1850–1980* (Cambridge 1981).
35 *Diary* 19 April 1899 and 10 January 1900
36 A.V. Tucker 'W.H. Mallock and Late Victorian Conservatism' *University of Toronto Quarterly* 31 (January 1962) cited at 237; see also John W. Mason 'Political Economy and the Response to Socialism in Britain, 1870–1914' *The Historical Journal* 23 (1980) 58185, and D.J. Ford 'W.H. Mallock and Socialism' *Essays in Anti-Labour History* edited by Kenneth D. Brown (London 1974) 317–42.
37 *Diary* 5 July 1899, 8 December 1898. The parallel between King and certain university intellectuals in the United States who were tempted by socialism, but moderated their views, is striking. From socialism they turned to the hope that 'through liberal reform a largely co-operative society, in which distributive justice and Christian brotherhood would reign.' Dorothy Ross 'Socialism and American Liberalism: Academic Social Thought in the 1880s' *Perspectives in American History* 11 (1977–8) 64. Ross attributes this change to a quest for status and respectability – that is, university posts. That, too, could apply to King.
38 *Diary* 2 January 1900, 27 January 1900, 1 February 1900, 22 February 1900
39 Ibid. 10 July 1900, 6 October 1898, 12 January 1895
40 H.S. Ferns and B. Ostry *The Age of Mackenzie King* (London 1955) cited at 244
41 W.H. Smith 'The Church and Industrial Society' in *Canadian Problems* edited by W.R. McIntosh (Toronto 1910) 116–17; Brian L. Fraser '"The Christianization of Our Civilization": Presbyterian Reformers and Their Defence of a Protestant Canada, 1875–1914' (PH D thesis, York University 1982) cited at 151
42 There are several good studies of *Industry and Humanity*, though none stresses sufficiently the religious sources of King's ideas. See Ferns and Ostry *The Age of Mackenzie King* 243–83; Reginald Whittaker 'Liberal Corporatist Ideas of Mackenzie King' *Labour/Le Travail* 2 (1977) 137–69; 'Political Thought and Action in Mackenzie King' *Journal of Canadian Studies* 13 (Winter 1878–9)

40–60; and Paul Craven *'An Impartial Umpire': Industrial Relations and the Canadian State 1900–1911* (Toronto 1980) 31–89

43 *Diary* 24 January 1900, 3 March 1915; W.L. Mackenzie King *Industry and Humanity* (Boston 1918) 125

44 Hofstadter *Social Darwinism* chap. 8

45 *Diary* 2 January 1903

46 Donald F. Meyer *The Positive Thinkers: Religion as Pop Psychology from Mary Baker Eddy to Oral Roberts* (New York 1980). Meyer writes that 'one of the main drives of liberal religion has been to purge religious experience and theology of fear as humanly debilitating' (321).

47 *Industry and Humanity* 153

48 Toynbee *The Industrial Revolution* 25

49 *Diary* 15 October 1898

50 *Industry and Humanity* 293, 298, 399. In his *Organization of England*, first published in 1914, King's former professor W.J. Ashley stated the essence of *Industry and Humanity* when he wrote, 'Society is feeling its way with painful steps towards a corporate organization of industry on the side alike of employees and employed; to be the more harmoniously, let us hope, associated together – with the State alert and intelligent in the background to protect the interest of the community.' Semmel *Imperialism and Social Reform* cited at 215

51 *Industry and Humanity* 489

52 W.L.M. King Papers, notes and memoranda, 17: 'What the Bible Says in Regard to the Settlement of Labor Disputes.' The minister was a Dr McDowell.

53 *Industry and Humanity* 528–9

54 *Diary* 4 February 1901

55 Ibid. 23 November 1918

56 Ibid. 6 October 1898

57 PAC J.S. Woodsworth Papers 'To My Brethren of the Methodist Conference' (1907)

58 Kenneth McNaught *A Prophet in Politics* (Toronto 1959) 6–8

59 W.A. Sparling 'The Church's Call to the Students' in *Canada's Missionary Congress* (Toronto 1909) 272

60 United Church Archives, Burwash Papers, Woodsworth to Burwash, 14 January 1902

61 PAC C.B. Sissons Papers, Woodsworth to Sissons, 16 June 1902 and 21 June 1903

62 Burwash Papers, Woodsworth to Burwash, 5 March 1906

63 Woodsworth Papers 'To My Brethren'

64 J.S. Woodsworth *'Following the Gleam'* (n.p.p, n.d.) 8

65 A.B. McKillop *A Disciplined Intelligence; Critical Inquiry and Canadian Thought in the Victorian Era* (Montreal 1979) 212–16

66 Sissons Papers, Woodsworth to Sissons, 13 June 1907

67 Woodsworth Papers, Woodsworth to Lucy, 13 June 1907

68 Sissons Papers, Woodsworth to Sissons, 13 June 1907; McNaught *A Prophet* 37; James Shaver Woodsworth *My Neighbor* (Toronto 1911) 334

69 Allen F. Davis *Spearheads of Reform: The Social Settlement and the Progressive Movement 1890–1914* (New York 1970) chaps. 9 and 10

70 J.S. Woodsworth 'Heterodoxy or Hypocrisy – A Minister's Dilemma' *Acta Victoriana* 37 (January 1913) 205

71 Woodsworth Papers, Woodsworth to James Mills, 14 February 1913

72 J.S. Woodsworth 'A Workman's Budget' *The Christian Guardian* 2 June 1913, 9

73 J.S. Woodsworth 'A Programme of Social Reform' ibid. 27 August 1913

74 J.S. Woodsworth 'The Functions of the Church' ibid. 2 September 1914, 10–11 and 'Sermons for the Unsatisfied' *Grain Growers' Guide* 30 June 1915

75 William R. Hutchison *The Modernist Impulse in American Protestantism* (Oxford 1982) 165n

76 Sissons Papers, Woodsworth to Sissons, 25 April 1912

77 J.S. Woodsworth 'Social Work as a Profession' *Acta Victoriana* 38 (March 1914) 292

78 Sissons Papers, Woodsworth to Sissons, 25 April 1912 and Woodsworth to Sissons, 20 May 1912; James Michael Pitsula 'The Relief of Poverty in Toronto' (PH D thesis, York University 1974) 269

79 Woodsworth Papers, Woodsworth to Rev. A.E. Smith, 8 June 1918

80 McNaught *A Prophet in Politics* 85; Woodsworth Papers, Bland to Woodsworth, 5 July 1918

81 Woodsworth Papers, Woodsworth to mother, 10 June 1918

82 Sissons Papers, Woodsworth to Sissons, 1 December 1918

83 Ibid. Woodsworth to Sissons, 14 August 1919; J.S. Woodsworth *The First Story of the Labor Church and Some Things for Which it Stands* (Winnipeg 1920) 7

84 Woodsworth *The Labor Church* 8 and 15

85 Woodsworth '*Following the Gleam*' 17; Sissons Papers, Woodsworth to Sissons, 20 July 1921; and J.S. Woodsworth 'Unemployment' *The Canadian Forum* (April 1921)

86 Woodsworth '*Following the Gleam*' 19, 18

87 *The Essential Karl Marx: The Non-economic Writings* edited by Saul K. Padover (New York 1978) 287

88 United Church Archives, A.E. Smith Papers, Ivens to Rev. and Mrs Smith, 31 March 1920

89 Ibid. 'The Passing Shadow'

90 Ibid. A.E. Smith 'What Should be the Minister's Attitude Towards the Question of Present-Day Criticism of the Bible?' MS
91 Ibid. 'The Passing Shadow'; Richard Allen 'The Children of Prophecy: Wesley College Students in the Age of Reform' *Red River Valley Historian* (Summer 1974) 15–20; and Smith Papers, A.E. Smith, 'My Religion' MS
92 Smith Papers, undated lecture notes
93 See McNaught *A Prophet in Politics* 79–81 and Richard Allen *The Social Passion* (Toronto 1971) 54–60
94 Salem Bland *The New Christianity* (reprint Toronto 1973) 38–55; Gregory S. Kealey '1919: The Canadian Labour Revolt' *Labour/Le Travail* 13 (Spring 1984) 11–44; and Smith Papers, notes for a sermon
95 United Church Archives, Beatrice Brigden Papers, Brigden to Moore, 26 July 1919; see also W. Leland Clark *Brandon's Politics and Politicians* (Brandon 1981) 93–100.
96 Smith Papers, Smith to M.C. Flett, 13 July 1919
97 Ibid. undated notes
98 A.E. Smith *The People's Church* (Brandon 1923) n.p.
99 Smith Papers 'My Religion' MS; and Smith to 'Comrade,' 27 January 1925
100 Ibid. Smith to Rev. Jesse Arnup, 8 September 1944. On Smith see A.E. Smith *All My Life* (Toronto 1949) and J. Petryshyn 'From Clergyman to Communist: The Radicalization of Albert Edward Smith' *Journal of Canadian Studies* 13 (winter 1978–9) 61–71

CHAPTER 12　The Sacred Becomes the Secular

1 PAC W.C. Good Papers, 19, 'The Reformer and His Methods' (1913) MS
2 Good Papers, 21 'For the Science Club' (1899) MS; W.C. Good *Farmer Citizen* (Toronto 1958); Roy Thomas *The Ideas of William Charles Good, a Christian and Agrarian Reformer: The Formative Years 1896–1919* (MA thesis, University of Ottawa 1973)
3 Mircea Eliade *The Sacred and the Profane: The Nature of Religion* (New York and London 1959) 10
4 Albert Schweitzer *The Quest for the Historical Jesus* (New York 1968) 402 (emphasis in original)
5 *Minutes of the Annual Conference of the Methodist Church* (Montreal 1892) 95–6. John Thomas provided this reference. The Queen's University philosopher John Watson knew that theology had to be reformulated, but he almost despaired at the prospect of taking up the task: John Watson *The Interpretation of Religious Experience* (Glasgow 1912) 361.
6 United Church Archives, S.D. Chown Papers, 'The Relation of Sociology to

the Kingdom of Heaven' MS; S.D. Chown 'Manhood and Citizenship' *The Canadian Epworth Era* (August 1905) 234. Leila Mitchell-McKee provided this reference.

7 *Secular Thought* 23 November 1902, 546; 'The Jesus of Nazareth who came forward publicly as the Messiah, who preached the ethic of the Kingdom of God, who founded the Kingdom of Heaven upon earth, and died to give its work the final consecration, never had any existence. He is a figure designed by rationalism, endowed with life by liberalism, and clothed by modern theology in historical garb': Schweitzer *The Historical Jesus* 398.

8 Ann Douglas *The Feminization of American Culture* (New York 1977) 168. Elsewhere she writes, 'Over the course of the nineteenth century the Protestant minister became the only professional other than the housewife who ceased overtly to command, let alone monopolize, any special body of knowledge' (164); Goldwin Smith *Guesses at the Riddle of Existence* (Toronto 1898) 200. This passage was very carefully marked in Mackenzie King's copy.

9 Allen Mills 'The Later Thought of J.S. Woodsworth: An Essay in Revision' *Journal of Canadian Studies* 17 (Autumn 1972) 75.

10 *The Essential Karl Marx: The Non-economic Writings* edited by Saul K. Padover (New York 1978) 287; Alisdair MacIntyre *Secularization and Moral Change* (London 1967) 68

11 Sara Jeannette Duncan *A Social Departure* (London 1892) 76; Alice Chown *The Stairway* (Boston 1921) 235. During the Great War Dwight Chown, for all his liberalism, became a perfervid patriot and received a sharp and characteristically phrased rebuke from his pacifist niece: 'I have believed that the spiritual life in the world could overcome the evil. I have kept my faith in the sermon on the mount and you have put your faith in force and have acquiesed in the lies of the censored press.' Chown Papers, Alice to Dwight, 17 December [1919?]

12 PAC W.L.M. King Papers, *Diary* 26 December 1936. Stanley de Brath, who had recently sent King a copy of his book *The Drama of Europe; or, the Soul of History* (London 1931), was a scientist who had turned to spiritualism to counter modern materialism. On Skelton see Barry Ferguson 'The New Political Economy and Canadian Liberal Democratic Thought: Queen's University 1890–1925' (PH D thesis, York University 1982) 24–88.

Index